FLYING AMONG HEROES

FLYING AMONG HEROES

THE STORY OF SQUADRON LEADER T.C.S. COOKE
DFC AFC DFM AE

NORMAN FRANKS AND SIMON MUGGLETON

To all the 55,573 airmen lost in the Second World War

Cover illustrations: *Front, top*: Flight of Wellington bombers such those used by Cooke in his early career (Royal Air Force); *bottom*: Squadron Leader T.C.S. Cooke (Simon Muggleton collection). *Back*: Four of the seven figures representing various air crew to be placed in the Bomber Command Memorial in London: navigator, wireless operator, mid-upper gunner, rear gunner (Sculptures © Philip Jackson; Bomber Command Memorial © Bomber Command Association).

First published 2012

by Spellmount, an imprint of
The History Press
The Mill, Brimscombe Port
Stroud, Gloucestershire, GL5 2QG
www.thehistorypress.co.uk

© Norman Franks and Simon Muggleton, 2012

The right of Norman Franks and Simon Muggleton to be identified
as the Authors of this work has been asserted in accordance with the
Copyrights, Designs and Patents Act 1988.

British Library Cataloguing in Publication Data.
A catalogue record for this book is available from the British Library.

ISBN 978 0 7524 8042 8

Typesetting and origination by The History Press
Manufacturing Managed by Jellyfish Print Solutions Ltd
Printed in Malta by Gutenberg Press.

CONTENTS

FOREWORD

BY WARRANT OFFICER HARRY IRONS DFC RAFVR

At the cessation of hostilities in 1945, and while awaiting demobilisation, the relieved surviving air crews of Bomber Command were aware of the past years, their squadron, the stations, runways, flare paths, but most of all, the comrades they had left behind who had lost their lives.

Most of us had no knowledge of the actual 55,573 lost in the conflict until much later. In the aftermath of the Second World War the press started to disclose other figures that had been kept secret from the public during the war. We were told of the Holocaust and shown graphic pictures, the bleak Russian campaign, the treatment of prisoners of war in the Far East, the forced marches: victory came at a cost.

We awaited the Victory Parade with pride, but we were dismayed at the contents of the prime minister's victory speech. There was no mention made to the nation and the Commonwealth of Bomber Command's contribution to victory. No individual campaign medal for the air crews or ground crew to those fortunate enough to have volunteered and survived. High-level protests made no difference, Bomber Command veterans were just left with the words 'Dresden' ringing in our ears.

How about our comrades who had gone before?

The blue priority telegram or a letter from a sympathetic CO or overworked adjutant was the only thing a grieving family had for the loss of a son, husband or brother. It took many years before the Air Ministry, the Commonwealth War Graves Commission and the Red Cross were able to provide some small amounts of information to the bereaved.

Some 20,000 airmen from the Commonwealth and parts of occupied Europe who flew with the RAF and had no known grave were later to be recorded on the tablets of a memorial at Runnymede, close to Windsor.

Over the past sixty years, several attempts have been made to the various authorities to amend the decision not to grant air crew and ground crews of the RAF a campaign medal; one such application even reached the House of Commons, but to no avail.

Some of the air crews who flew after D-Day (6 June 1944) were granted the France and Germany Star, but it had no association with flying; indeed, it was given to members of all the armed forces and the Merchant Service who took part in that campaign.

Prior to D-Day, air crew received the Air Crew Europe Star if they fulfilled the necessary conditions, but this was not given exclusively to Bomber Command members.

Serving on the committee of the Bomber Command Association, I became aware of a growing demand from the membership to raise funds for a fitting memorial to commemorate those 55,573 young men who freely volunteered to fly against the Nazi onslaught and were sadly killed in action.

The Heritage Foundation, chaired by Mr David Graham along with their president, Mr Robin Gibb CBE of the Bee Gees, shared these same thoughts, and initiated a fundraising project in 2008, backed by the *Daily Telegraph* newspaper. The public reacted overnight, and funds came rolling in over the following years, mostly from bereaved relatives. The queen's sculptor, Philip Jackson CVO, was commissioned to mould seven larger than lifesize figures in bronze representing the various trades of air crew, which were to be placed in the centre of the memorial. This memorial will now finally be unveiled on 28 June 2012 in Green Park, Piccadilly, London.

When Doug Radcliffe MBE, the secretary of the Bomber Command Association, approached me to write this foreword I said, 'Why me?' He replied, 'Read the title Harry, get airborne again.'

After sitting in the rear turret as an air gunner for many hours during the two tours of operations I completed over Germany, France and Italy, being on the top deck of a London bus is high enough for me these days.

However, I took note of the title and received my copy from Doug Radcliffe, who had virtually read it overnight and commented to me what a good read it was. It took me a whole week, for I didn't just read it, I made a complete study of it. With my flying log book by my side, I compared my trips against those of Squadron Leader Tom Cooke and his crew, and wonder how they survived. I am sure many other air crew of the Second World War, students and authors will also do the same.

Over the years following the Second World War, veterans of Bomber Command have tried to move away from the word 'hero' – what on earth does it mean anyway? Surely Tom Cooke and his navigator Reg Lewis would shy away from the dictionary explanation: 'a man of distinguished valour or performance'. Man can do heroic things, but it leaves him short of being a hero.

Reg Lewis was a very good friend of mine; we were near neighbours and worked together over many years with the Bomber Command Association. Reading this book about his wartime pilot, I found out many things that Reg had never mentioned to me about his time in the RAF. I am sure he would have laughed at the mention of the word hero, but to me he was a hero.

Heroes – maybe it's not me, but others. This book really pulls out the difference; it enabled me to compare many of the sixty operations shown in my log book with those experienced by Tom Cooke and his crew. Could it be that when Squadron Leader Cooke was over the Ruhr at the controls of his Stirling, I was sitting in the rear turret of my Lancaster some 5,000ft higher looking at the same target? Glancing through the entries in my log book for 1942 and 1943, they certainly match, and I'm sure other veterans reading this book will do the same. Tom Cooke's recollections of his 'ops' are so clear and vivid, with them being well explained in the text.

Training in the RAF was a time to remember; the book boldly points out that air crew, having received the protective rank of sergeant along with the elusive but very proud brevet worn on the uniform, were often at variance with the long-serving sergeants. We were derisively called 'overnight NCOs', little thought being given that we could also 'disappear' overnight.

Looking back, waiting to get my stripes, it took the powers that be just seven weeks to train me as an air gunner – there was no time to fit in an operational training unit, no adapting to the squadron aircraft or turret, just an evening over Düsseldorf!

Come the autumn of 1943, Bomber Command continued their nightly attacks on chosen targets, while the American 8th Air Force, growing in strength and in spite of losing many of their experienced crews, challenged the Luftwaffe in daylight flying operations.

It was about this time that Squadron Leader Cooke added the Distinguished Flying Cross to his other decorations and set his sights on another challenge that only a few other crews in Bomber Command would engage in. He and his chosen crew opted to fly with 138 Squadron out of RAF Tempsford, working with the Special Operations Executive, dropping secret agents into enemy-occupied territory. Tom and his crew would be carrying these agents instead of bombs, and known only to him by their code names, such as 'Roger'. These agents would link up with the Resistance groups and wreak just as much damage and destruction as any stick of bombs could. So now, Tom Cooke and his crew would find themselves flying over France, Germany, Norway, Poland and Italy dropping supplies to the underground, as well as the agents. Their story is well told here.

In the summer of 2009, I joined Reg Lewis and others of the Bomber Command Committee for a fundraising event at Lord's Cricket Ground. The ground had been an Air Crew Recruiting Centre during the war and was a fitting place to watch England take on Australia.

Whilst that match was in full swing a Lancaster aircraft flew over, stopping play – what a salute to heroes, long gone.

ACKNOWLEDGEMENTS

The authors approached Mr Doug Radcliffe MBE, Secretary of the Bomber Command Association, with a request that a veteran of the association, who had taken part in raids over Europe during the Second World War, write a foreword for this book. Mr Radcliffe, without hesitation, suggested Harry Irons for this task.

Like so many others of his generation he answered the call to arms in 1941 and volunteered to join the Royal Air Force, eventually becoming a sergeant air gunner. During his time, he flew over sixty operations with 9, 77 and 158 Squadrons. He was promoted to warrant officer and awarded the Distinguished Flying Cross in 1945. He currently lives in Essex. The authors are grateful for his sincere thoughts and recollections made in this foreword.

The authors are also grateful to both the Bomber Command Association and the artist Philip Jackson CVO for the use of the images used on the back cover of this book. Philip Jackson was commissioned to sculpture seven larger than lifesize figures representing various air crew, to be placed in the Bomber Command Memorial in London. The four images depicted on the cover are: navigator, wireless operator, mid-upper gunner and rear gunner.

Philip Jackson was born in Inverness, Scotland, in 1944, and lives and works in West Sussex. He was elected a Fellow of the Royal Society of British Sculptors in 1989 and has since then undertaken a variety of public commissions which include HM Queen Elizabeth (the Queen Mother) in the Mall, London; the Falklands War Sculpture in Portsmouth; and the 1966 World Cup Sculpture at Newham. He was made a Companion of the Victorian Order (CVO) in the Birthday Honour's List in 2009.

INTRODUCTION

As this book was written the construction of the Bomber Command Memorial in the north-west corner of London's Green Park, and in close proximity to the Royal Air Force Club, Piccadilly, is under way.

For many years after the end of the Second World War, its most distinguished leader, Marshal of the Royal Air Force Sir Arthur Harris GCB OBE AFC LL.D, who died in April 1984, wanted some tangible recognition for all air-crew members who had flown with his Command during the war. He felt a suitable campaign medal should be struck, for he genuinely felt that his chaps had performed magnificently throughout the five-year campaign against the Axis powers of Germany and Italy.

He knew too that of some 125,000 such men from Britain and the Commonwealth, as well as from European countries overrun by the Germans such as Norway, France, Belgium, Poland and Czechoslovakia, a total of 55,573 had been lost. However, Harris' campaign to have such a medal failed, it being said that having the Air Crew Europe Star or the France and Germany Star was adequate recognition for those who had seen active duty within the ranks of Bomber Command.

During those wartime years Bomber Command had lost an estimated 8,325 bomber aircraft during over 365,000 sorties from its 128 airfields spread across the United Kingdom. In addition, 8,403 men had been wounded, while another 9,338 had been brought down and taken prisoner. The average age of a Bomber Command air crew was said to be just 22, and all of them were volunteers. Nobody who joined the Royal Air Force for wartime duty could be made to fly against the enemy, but, of course, there was never any shortage of volunteers.

Sir Arthur would have been very proud if he had known that in recent years there has been another campaign in existence, that of battling to have a permanent memorial built to commemorate the sacrifices of Bomber Command air crew. Not many years ago a few famous men got together to form a committee to see if such a memorial could be built. They were John Caudwell, Lord Ashcroft KCMG, Richard Desmond and Robin Gibb CBE.

Other than choosing a site for such a memorial, the cost also needed to be addressed. Donations came from many people and places, and public subscriptions were also welcome. By 2011 almost £6 million had been raised and the project was on. The RAF Bomber Command Memorial Fundraising Committee, headed by pop star Jim Dooley of the famous Dooleys and the President of the Heritage Foundation, Robin Gibb of the Bee Gees, worked tirelessly. The committee was supported by the *Daily Telegraph* newspaper and, with the *Daily Express*, that has helped to raise awareness of the project; the response of the general public was, and continues to be, amazing.

Once the project could be seen to be moving in the right direction and a location found, Mr Liam O'Connor, who had previously designed the Armed Forces Memorial in Staffordshire, was asked to put forward a design for the Bomber Command Memorial, which he has done magnificently. The memorial will feature as its centrepiece a 9ft-high bronze sculpture by Philip Jackson, depicting seven men of a heavy bomber crew after returning to their base from an operation.

The lead contractor is Gilbert-Ash NI Ltd, a building and civil engineering contractor based in Northern Ireland. This company is well known for its ability to build difficult and complex projects in a flexible manner. Contracted for the stonework is S. McConnell and Sons, another well-known company here and throughout the world. All this was agreed after careful negotiations between Westminster City Council, the Royal Parks and the Royal Air Force Benevolent Fund. Once completed, the Royal Air Force Benevolent Fund will take ownership and be responsible for future maintenance of the structure.

On 4 May 2011, a foundation stone was laid during a ceremony on the site of the proposed memorial. In attendance was a group of distinguished men, led by the Duke of Gloucester and in the presence of the Marshal of the Royal Air Force, Sir Michael Beetham, himself a wartime Avro Lancaster pilot, and the President of the Bomber Command Association. Guests included Lord Craig, who represented the RAF Benevolent Fund, and of course Robin Gibb, John Caudwell, Lord Ashcroft and Richard Desmond. A service was conducted by the Venerable (Air-Vice Marshal) Ray Pentland, chaplain-in-chief of the RAF, and included a reading by Air Chief Marshal Sir Stephen Dalton, Chief of Air Staff.

Others in attendance were the Right Honourable Andrew Robathan, Minister for Defence Personnel, Councillor Alan Bradley of the Welfare and Veterans Organisation, sculptor Philip Jackson and the architect Liam O'Connor. The service ended with a flypast by the Battle of Britain Memorial flight's Avro Lancaster bomber.

The memorial is due for completion in 2012 and hopefully will be unveiled in June.

***

Just a few years ago I was asked to prepare a list of all those men and women who served in Coastal Command in the Second World War to be recorded within the pages of a permanent Book of Remembrance. It was a daunting task for there were over 4,000 of them, tiny in comparison with Bomber Command's 55,573, but nevertheless a huge task.

Thanks to help received from the Air Historical Branch, then in London, and the Royal Air Force Museum, Hendon, I had access to the huge lists of members of the Royal Air Force who had been killed, by whatever means, during the Second World War. It took me several months to trawl through more than two dozen boxes, filled with flimsy horizontal foolscap pages that, from memory, each recorded more than a dozen casualties, giving name, rank, number, command, squadron or unit, date of loss, where lost and where buried (if known).

It became apparent that every loss of life that befell the RAF, in all Commands and in all theatres, whether killed in action or died of a burst appendix, was there. Once the Coastal Command losses were extracted, compiled and typed up, the computer disc was given to a printer who produced several tomes. The main one would be presented to Westminster Abbey for display, a page being turned each day. In due course it was unveiled by Her Majesty the Queen in the presence of a number of former Coastal Command dignitaries.

I only mention this because I should not like to be given the task of doing something similar for Bomber Command's losses, which, if every other serving man and woman in the Command who died in other ways between 1939 and 1945 were listed, would no doubt reach nearer 60,000 than the 55,000 usually noted as lost on operations. War is an appalling blot on humanity but it is something mankind has lived with since the dawn of time and no doubt will continue in the years to come. However, it does generally bring out the best of the brave, the most courageous, the most dogged, and can forge a man's ability to overcome the many trials and tribulations thrown at him.

The subject of this book was just an ordinary sort of chap, nothing special, born into a normal loving family, yet when faced with the need to help defend his country and his country's way of life, willingly came forward to do his bit. Fortunately he was able to do more than his bit and survived to continue a life of peace, but on more than one occasion he risked his life in the often fatal struggle that is war. He was not found wanting.

Millions of men face these and other dangers in wartime, but it seems to me that the flying man, by which I mean the flying man based in Britain during the Second World War, suffered a very different war to his counterparts in the navy or in the army. Other than when home on leave or on some sort of defence duty in Britain, the sailor is at sea, and the soldier can be in any number of hostile places overseas. They lived with the constant danger of being put in harm's way, whether in a naval action in the middle of an ocean or in a trench somewhere in North Africa, Burma or later on the Continent. In some ways they were for-tunate, for they each knew that they had to survive the constant danger during whatever conflict they were engaged with before going home.

The airman, however, whether in Fighter, Coastal or Bomber Commands flying from Britain, faced danger for perhaps minutes, and often hours, but when they had returned to their airfields – if they returned – their world changed to a very civilian sort of existence. They could sleep between sheets in a bed; they could eat as well as wartime rationing allowed; they could go to the local pub or cinema; meet a girlfriend or occasionally go home on leave to a wife or mother and see their old pals. It must have been a constant shock to the system to be one minute in the hell of searchlights, flak and enemy fighters over a German city, and shortly afterwards downing a pint of bitter in a pub. That night they would crawl into a warm bed and with luck sleep soundly, but they knew that it would not be many hours before they were back in hell once more. Also, of course, the majority of them had still been at school when the war began, each contemplat-ing a life far removed from flying over a hostile country where they were the target. We may possibly look at a veteran airman and think how brave he had been, how heroic, yet only a year or so earlier he had been nothing more than a civilian, wanting civilian things, like a good job, a wife, perhaps children. All that changed in September 1939.

Bomber Command air crew, flying a tour of thirty operations, faced this enigma of life every day. Thirty times over a few months, perhaps more than thirty, they would assemble in the flight hut, their stomachs in a knot but trying to stay calm and casual, but waiting for that night's target to be revealed. Was it Berlin? Was it only over to France? Perhaps only a mine-laying trip? Each repre-sented a degree of danger that each man assessed personally, although it was clear that an easy raid could end in death just as surely as a long, hard one. It was the luck of the draw. There was just that little loosening of that knot in the stomach if the target looked a little easier.

If they survived and got home, they almost dreamt their way through debriefing, hardly noticing the tea and sandwiches waiting for them, then staggered off to find either their room in the mess or the cot in some Nissen hut, and they could then hope for a few hours of oblivion. The next day it would begin all over again, and all they could be thankful for was that the tour was at least one trip less than previously. No doubt they would often ask themselves why they were doing this. However, deep down they all knew why – it was their duty.

After the war Albert Speer, Germany's Minister of Armament, wrote: 'The strategic bombing of Germany was the greatest lost battle for Germany of the whole war. Greater than all their losses in all their retreats from Russia, or in the surrender of their armies at Stalingrad.'

Norman Franks
East Sussex
March 2012

PREFACE

RAF Tempsford, situated along the A1 east of Bedford and south of St Neots, was the home of 138 Special Duties Squadron, and had been since March 1942. Its equipment ranged from Westland Lysanders to Armstrong Whitworth Whitleys, to Handley Page Halifaxes, and the men who flew them or in them carried out a more or less secret, cloak-and-dagger war, transporting Special Operations Executive (SOE) agents or dropping supplies or arms and other equipment to partisan units. They ranged as far north as Norway or south-east to Yugoslavia and Poland, as well as France, Holland and Belgium.

In the early days Lysander pilots flew clandestine operations into the occupied territories of northern Europe, landing in fields or on open ground at night, delivering agents or on occasion collecting other agents, and sometimes escaping prisoners of war, back to England. As it became necessary to deliver arms, explosives, radio equipment and so on to Resistance workers or partisan bands, heavier aircraft were needed, so Whitleys began to be employed once they were no longer being used in the bomber role. These in time were replaced by Halifax bombers, even operating from North Africa when the Halifax crews flew a mission across Europe and over the Mediterranean, and from there returned to England over a similar route, dropping supplies to Resistance groups in southern France.

By February 1944, the squadron's Halifax bombers, under the command of Wing Commander R.D. Speare DFC, were the norm for dropping supplies and parachuting agents into these same occupied territories rather than risk landing in darkened countryside. Richard Speare was an experienced bomber man, having won his DFC with 7 Squadron in 1941, and a Bar while with 460 Squadron RAAF in 1943. Everyone was expecting an invasion of northern Europe to take place sometime during 1944, so as the time grew nearer to the planned D–Day, more and more Resistance fighters were being prepared and supported by Britain's SOE, and 138 Squadron's air crews were being kept busy.

On the night of 7/8 February 1944, four of 138 Squadron's aircraft took off for operations over France. At 2252hrs, Flight Lieutenant Downes took off in Halifax 'D' on Operation Dacre 1/Harry 18, carrying an agent, packages and supplies. The mission was a success and the agent and supplies were safely parachuted down into France. At 2302hrs, Wing Commander Speare took Halifax 'J' off on Operation Harry 17, carrying an agent, supply containers and packages, but it was not successful as no recognition signals were received from the ground, so the mission had to be abandoned. Another crew, on a similar operation coded John 35, led by Flying Officer G.D. Carroll in LL114 NF-F, was lost over France, coming down at Autrans, west of Grenoble. None of the crew survived.

The third Halifax on this night's roster was LW275 *O for Oboe*, which went off at 1945hrs with Squadron Leader T.C.S. Cooke DFC AFC DFM AE at the controls on a Jockey 5 sortie. It was to be a long trip, 700 miles or further, as the agent was going to bale out near Marseille. Cooke's crew consisted of:

Flying Officer R.W. Lewis DFC	Navigator
Flying Officer L.J. Gornall	Flight Engineer
Pilot Officer E. Bell	Bomb Aimer
Flying Officer J.S. Reed	Wireless Operator/Air Gunner (WOp/AG)
Flying Officer A.B. Withecombe	Dispatcher
Flying Officer R.L. Beattie RCAF	Rear Gunner

It was Thomas Cooke's sixty-third operational sortie, and it was later noted that his experienced crew had between them a combined total of 291 missions. For Reg Lewis this was his forty-first operation, having been with Tom Cooke's crew in 214 Squadron, while Len Gornall was on his forty-eighth.

We are lucky with this story, because not only do we have Squadron Leader Cooke's flying log books and squadron operational records to refer to, but we also have a recorded interview by him, conducted by the Imperial War Museum archivists in the 1980s, together with a similar one recorded by his navigator, Reg Lewis DFC.[1] The museum have been gracious enough to allow us to make use of these spoken words which appear here in the text in various chapters. Thomas Cooke was later to relate on his tape:

When we delivered agents we were usually flying at 250 feet, and that was the altitude we flew at this night and it was important not to fly over any defended sites. On this trip, as we were going out, we made a mistake. Something went wrong and we went over a defended area near the French coast and were shot up. All seemed to be well, however, so we carried on to carry out what we had been briefed to do. We got well into France and then the starboard-inner engine suddenly caught fire. It started to glow and this glow began to get bigger and bigger, and in the end I had to order everyone to bale out.

Whether or not the engine had been damaged by the anti-aircraft (AA) fire is not clear. The weather had deteriorated a good deal and after taking off cloud prevented any sign of the ground until they baled out over France. He continued:

I went down to get out of the lower escape hatch but found it was jammed, so I came back to the cockpit and looking out I could see we were in a spiral and decided to try and fly it down. However, the wing then became a mass of flames and the altimeter was spinning round, so I struggled back down to the hatch and managed to beat it open, and baled out.

Len Gornall believed they had suffered a cracked carburettor as all the temperature and pressure gauges were showing normal on his engineer's panel. However, with reduced power they were losing height and they were also beginning to ice up. Eventually it became impossible to maintain height so the order came to get out.

Cooke continued:

I landed somewhere between Dijon, towards Valence or perhaps Lyons – right in open country. The main problem was initially to try and find out exactly where we were. I say we because I had met up with my flight engineer and mid-upper gunner [and dispatcher]. We had some maps, but the sky was cloudy so there was no way we could look at the stars to get our bearings. We found some signposts that at this time had not been taken down, but they didn't mean much to us. Unless you have pinpointed the area they don't mean a thing, and they certainly did not show us the name of any town we could recognise or locate on our maps.

I decided our best bet was to go round and come up underneath the border of Switzerland because we knew the border at a place called Jura was heavily guarded and there was no way we could get across there. So we tried to edge round and come up to Grenoble, then up to the southern part of Geneva. The first thing that struck me when I had started with 138 Squadron, was that France seemed to be full of people who would assist us if shot down. Being a flight commander I was one of the few people that saw a secret map of France with all the dropping zones for our agents, so the impression I had was that France was an absolute maze of people wanting to help us. I don't think the other two were really aware of this, certainly Gornell wasn't, in fact he wasn't really sure of what time of day it was. He wasn't my earlier flight engineer, although I had known him for some time.

So we decided to start knocking on doors, and as I was the only one who spoke any French, it fell to me to say that we were English airmen and could they help us. The usual answer was to have the door slammed in our faces, and on the one or two occasions when I was asked to 'come in' I felt uneasy, in case someone was sent along to the local gendarmerie, so we did not hang around long. Eventually we came into contact with somebody who put us in touch with someone in a village called Beaurepaire and although helpful, they put us in contact with who they thought were the Maquis but who turned out to be FTP (Franco Tireurs Partisans) – who were communists.[2]

They sheltered us but were doing odd little sorties, and being able to speak French I understood what was going on. The first time they went out they crashed into a farmhouse, bullied the occupants and all they did was to pinch cigarettes and bread, etc. After a while I asked them why they didn't go out and raid a few bridges or something, but that wasn't very popular with them.

After a period of time, the agent that we had bundled out of the Halifax before we crashed, Lieutenant Cammaerts – although of course we only knew him then by his code name of 'Roger' – turned up, and spoke to this lot, and then he quickly passed us along to somebody else and we finished up with a Monsieur Merle at Valence, right by Valence airfield. He was a great old guy aged 85. He put us in a room at one end of his house while at the other end he was entertaining Germans because they brought him food which he then shared with us! When we eventually left he asked me to drop him a machine gun, but I said that it would not be a good idea but I would try and drop him some coffee if I could, knowing full well that was never going to happen. All I hoped now was that he were going to evade successfully and get home. But would we?

Thomas Cooke's war had travelled a long way since joining the RAF in 1939. He had done a lot of flying and had flown many dangerous bombing operations. It is ironic that his last squadron had been working in co-operation with the French Resistance organisations and now, here he was starting to be helped by those same people in an attempt to get him and his companions home.

Notes

1 Anyone interested in hearing these tapes should contact the IWM at Lambeth. They are to be located under recording numbers 9794 (Lewis) and 10079 (Cooke).
2 The FTP was part of the French Communist Party (PFC), who took the name from the Franco-Prussian War of 1870, which literally meant 'Free Shooters' or Irregular Corps of Riflemen.

A FLYING LIFE FOR ME

Most biographies begin with a birth, so we will start there too. Thomas Charles Seymour Cooke was born in Southsea, Portsmouth, in the borough of Buckland, Hampshire, on 23 July 1921, the only son of Mr and Mrs Herbert Seymour Cooke, previously of Heston's Post Office, Alconbury, just north of Huntingdon. He attended St John's School and College in Grove Road, Southsea, from 1932 until 1938, and acquired the nickname 'Bunny'. In 1938 he acquired the Oxford University General School Certificate.

Upon leaving full-time education he became a junior clerk in the Portsmouth Rates and Electricity Department. As Thomas Cooke later recalled:

> Before the war I wanted to take a short-service commission in the Royal Air Force and my father wanted me to join him in business. This was about the time of the Munich crisis. We reached a compromise, he said why didn't I join the RAF Volunteer Reserve and at the same time I'd be able to do my flying while working full time with him in the business. So I joined the RAFVR, initially in Southampton and later in Portsmouth Town Centre.

Unfortunately it is not clear what his father's business was, but Cooke clearly stated in his RAF personal details that he worked as a council clerk. His home address was 221 St Augustine's Road, Southsea, and while he mentions Southampton and then Portsmouth, Southampton was no doubt where he went into a recruiting office, for his date of enlistment is given as 25 August 1939, for a period of five years. While he may well have wanted to join the RAFVR after leaving school, he obviously did little in the way of taking to the air, for his service commenced on 25 August as 758091 AC2 U/T (aircraftsman second class, under training), and his call up came the day after Germany invaded Poland, 2 September 1939. He is shown as being 5ft 11in tall, chest measurement 35in, with fair hair, blue eyes and a fair complexion. In other words, he was quite average. By this time he had been elevated to the rank of sergeant (sgt), that is, sergeant pilot U/T.

I have to say I was delighted when the declaration of war came. I'd been interested in aircraft since the age of seven and people like Billy Bishop, von Richthofen, Roy Brown, etc., were extremely well known to me. This, with my interest in flying, I had a burning desire to emulate such men, so when war broke out, like all my fellow reservists down at Portsmouth, we were all very interested. We were of course all fully aware of the political situation and what we were about to lose if Hitler was allowed to go on his merry way, so there was that aspect of it. So although we were all young men, we seemed very mature, viz-a-viz, what we were doing and what we were going to fight for.

★★★

While it seems that Tom Cooke would have been delighted to follow and hopefully emulate his First World War flying heroes, they were all distinguished fighter aces. We have no idea how he felt once he began to realise that the RAF had other plans for him – to become a bomber pilot.

By these early days of the war, elements of Bomber Command were already in France, with Bristol Blenheim Is and Fairey Battles, both light bombers, of the Advanced Air Striking Force (AASF) and the Air Component both supporting the British Expeditionary Force (BEF). Not that they would amount to much as bombing aircraft, but the crews were keen to show their mettle in an air war as part of Bomber Command.

While Tom Cooke was starting to feel his way about the service, he and his fellow trainee airmen could never guess how long the war would take to be won, or how many of their fellow Bomber Command brothers would not live to see victory. Already the first deaths in the Command's air war had occurred. On the first night of the war, 3/4 September 1939, two Wellington bombers from 9 Squadron of RAF Honington and five Blenheims of 107 Squadron, based at RAF Wattisham, failed to return from Wilhelmshaven. The targets for a small force of Blenheims and Wellingtons were German warships at Wilhelmshaven and Brunsbüttel, the British not wanting to bomb German land targets at this early stage. In the event most of the aircraft crews failed to find their targets due to low cloud but some attacked warships at Wilhelmshaven.

It was a salutary lesson for everyone when it was learnt that seven aircraft had been lost. Of the twenty-six air-crew members lost, only two survived as prisoners. All the rest were killed. They would be followed by over 55,000 Bomber Command members before the war would be won.

The two captured airmen were Sgt G.F. Booth and Aircraftman First Class (AC1) L.J. Slattery, observer and air gunner to Sgt A.S. Prince, one of the Blenheim pilots. Larry Slattery became the first Bomber Command airman to be taken prisoner, Booth a close second. Author Norman Franks met Larry Slattery in the mid-1960s, living near to each other in south London. Larry had been invited to the first showing in a Wimbledon cinema of the film *The Great Escape*. Talking to him, Franks became aware of a very humble man who had borne his six years as a prisoner with much stoicism and not a little fatalism. In these early days many light bomber crews were made up of AC1 or even AC2 airmen who volunteered to be air gunners, so he and others began their captivity with the lowest rank of air crew. Those that lasted a few weeks received the insignia of the flying bullet to wear on their sleeves. This was a brass bullet design with wings spreading out from either side. It was later replaced by a winged brevet with the letters 'AG' in the centre. In 1940 all air crew below officer rank were given the rank of sergeant and, as Tom Cooke will relate, this was not always popular with the 'old sweats' who had won their three stripes after many years of service, both in England and abroad.

Larry Slattery would end up in the prison camp at Kopernikus and eventually became a warrant officer. G.F. Booth was with him, also becoming a warrant officer, so at least they had each other for company. They would have been extremely surprised if they had known how many other British and Commonwealth airmen would join them or be placed in other camps before the war ended.

★★★

Like most young men of the day, Tom Cooke had to wait for things to happen and it was exactly one month before he received his first posting to No.31 Training Wing, where he underwent all the necessary instruction about the RAF, its history, how to march, how to salute etc., and what he might expect to happen if he showed the necessary personality to continue in the service. He passed, and on 11 December was shown as being attached to No.3 ITW (Initial Training Wing) at Hastings, Sussex, and eleven days later was sent to No.12 EFTS (Elementary Flying Training School), where at last he would see an aeroplane close up.

No. 12 EFTS was at Prestwick in Scotland and he arrived to be taken under the wing of Flight Lieutenant (F/Lt) I.G. Statham RAFVR, his flight commander ('B' Flight). Ivan Statham handed him over to F/Lt D.E. Turner, who was to be his initial flight instructor. In the meantime, Tom Cooke needed to settle in, and as far as the regular RAF NCOs were concerned, it wasn't going to be too easy for him. His first clash with reality came once he and the others arrived at Prestwick. He knew there was going to be some sort of social upheaval but not to what degree:

> We reservists were all sorted out and sent to our various training schools, mine being Prestwick, which was in those days just a 400-yard square field, and we were billeted out. From there I went to Sealand and it was there we first noticed that the Sergeants' Mess was crowded and we weren't the most popular fellows because these chaps who had been working away for 12 or more years in the Service to become a sergeant, suddenly found they'd been invaded by chaps who had been made sergeants overnight. This had also been felt, although less pointedly, at Prestwick. These sergeants found we were crowding their Mess and making things very uncomfortable for them, so they weren't exactly delighted to see us.
>
> They tried, and in fact did, exclude us from their Mess and we then had to live in empty married quarters at Sealand. They were beginning to make special catering arrangements for us, but this didn't affect me because I left before they brought it in.

Cooke got his first taste of being a pilot on 12 December 1939. F/Lt Turner took him over to the RAF's most popular and well-known *ab initio* training aeroplane, the de Havilland Tiger Moth, a two-seater biplane. Turner showed him round N6614, talked to him about the cockpit layout, the instruments, controls and ailerons, elevators and rudder. Then he got Cooke seated and they took off for a forty-five-minute flight, noted as an 'air experience' flight, again showing him the controls, what they did, and generally flew around the locality in straight and level flight without anything fancy. Turner would have no way of knowing if this youngster in the other cockpit would enjoy the experience – or throw up!

Shortly after this, Turner showed him how to taxi an aeroplane, then again took off, flying straight and level once more but doing some climbing, gliding and even stalling the machine to impress upon his student the dangers of losing forward flying speed and how to recover. Two more trips the next day covered the ground again, but included some medium turns, landings, taking off into wind, glide approaches and so on. Two similar flights took place on the 14th and 15th, each flight lasting around forty to fifty minutes.

Spinning took place on the 18th, Turner obviously less troubled by his new man's airsickness probabilities, and these training sessions continued in the cold December skies until the 22nd. On this day, after an initial forty-five-minute trip, now flying N5444, Turner told the chief flying instructor that Cooke was ready for his first solo. F/Lt R. Hanson took Cooke up for a pre-solo test for half an hour and was obviously happy to let the youngster go solo. Climbing out of the Tiger Moth, he told Cooke to take off, fly one circuit and land without breaking anything. Cooke complied, and his ten-minute flight brought his total flying hours to a nice round ten.

★★★

Whether or not it proved an anti-climax for Cooke or not, the euphoria of the flight would have been enjoyed, although with Christmas and the severe winter weather, he did not take to the air again until 3 January. He now had a new instructor, Sgt Roxborgh, a senior NCO pilot. Roxborgh would now begin to put the embryo pilot through his paces, both with dual-control flying and sending him off on solo flights, going through the whole ambit of learning how to fly and control his aircraft. The school now had some civilian Tiger Moths on strength and Cooke began to enter some civilian registration letters in his flying log book, such as G-ADVY, G-AOUC and G-ADHN. By the end of the month his flying hours had reached almost twenty-four, and he had additional dual flying with Sgt Allison and Pilot Officer (P/O) Roberts. Another new instructor name is recorded in his log book on 3 February, Sgt Watson, but it was mainly Roxborgh until 14 February, when he had another hurdle to jump: an RAF flying test with Squadron Leader (S/L) Graham.

Cooke was now on hour-long cross-country flying, where the use of a map and the 'mark-one-eyeball' were essential. He was still recording lots of individual manoeuvres that needed to be practised constantly, including spinning and recovery, low flying, aerobatics, climbing turns and so on. Roxborgh and Roberts were now putting him through everything he needed to learn so that it became second nature to him. Fifty flying hours came up on 5 March, four days after S/L Graham ran him through a further RAF test. Sgt W.A.S. Elder took him up in March along with Watson. Another test of his capabilities, this time with F/Lt N.J. Capper on the 7th, then F/Lt S. Lowndes had him for another RAF test on 3 April.

On the 8th Elder took him up twice for his first experience of night flying in N6811. More night flying on the 16th included a second flight with F/Lt Watson on a test flight, after which he was sent off for a night solo for twenty minutes, thankfully arriving back and landing safely.

His time at No. 12 EFTS was now coming to an end. His last flight at Prestwick was on the 24th, and it took his flying hours up to exactly eighty-eight. His proficiency as a pilot was adjudged 'average' by F/Lt Capper, who was now the chief flying instructor. He had also had seven hours of instruction on the Link Trainer, a wonderful invention where a pilot could be thrown all manner of problems associated with flying and would not be hurt in the event of a crash. Except of course for his pride when an instructor would make some amusing or fatuous remark on what had just happened, and instruct him to start again.

On 27 April 1940 Tom arrived at RAF Sealand, the home of No. 5 FTS (Flying Training School) for intermediate training. If he harboured any thoughts about emulating some of his childhood heroes such as Mick Mannock, Ernst Udet, Baron von Richthofen or Roy Brown, these now looked a very far way off. No. 5 FTS was equipped with Airspeed Oxford twin-engined trainers, so it was clear that he was being groomed for multi-engined aircraft, not single-seat fighters.

At Sealand he was assigned to 'A' Flight, commanded by F/Lt F.E.W. Birchfield. Cooke's first flight in an Oxford was on 5 May in L4566, and in the main pilot seat sat Flying Officer (F/O) Hackney, who would become his regular instructor during the following weeks. In some respects he was starting all over again, running through all the things he had done on Tiger Moths, but now he had two engines to think about, as well as flying a larger and heavier aeroplane which was not as light on the controls. He made his first solo in this type on 12 May, the first flight following the start of the German Blitzkrieg in France two days earlier. The war was coming nearer to Britain and to Sgt Cooke.

★★★

Although this book is centred around Tom Cooke's war flying medium and then heavy bombers, Bomber Command embraced all types of bombing aircraft. At this time the Command had several squadrons equipped with single-engined Fairey Battles, which carried a crew of three – pilot, observer and gunner. It was these aircraft, along with some Blenheim squadrons, that saw action during the 'Phoney War' – prior to the start of the German Blitzkrieg in May 1940 – and then after this event, right up until the BEF retreated out of France. The German assault began at dawn on the morning of 10 May 1940, to begin a push that was hardly checked over the next ten days, resulting in a dramatic defeat for France and Britain. Before the month was out, the main body of the retreating BEF had reached the English Channel between Calais and Dunkirk, and from the latter the equally dramatic withdrawal took place from the beaches there. The Dunkirk evacuation (Operation Dynamo) was hailed as a miracle but the BEF had still been kicked out of France in record time.

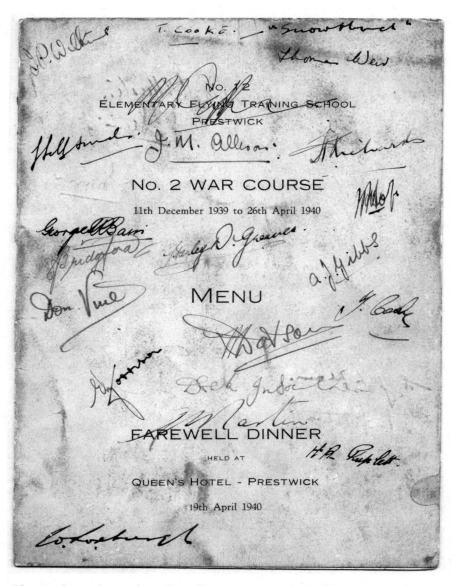

The signed menu by members of No.2 War Course at No.12 Elementary Flying Training School at Prestwick, between 11 December 1939 and 26 April 1940. This was for their farewell dinner that was held at the Queen's Hotel in Prestwick on 19 April 1940.

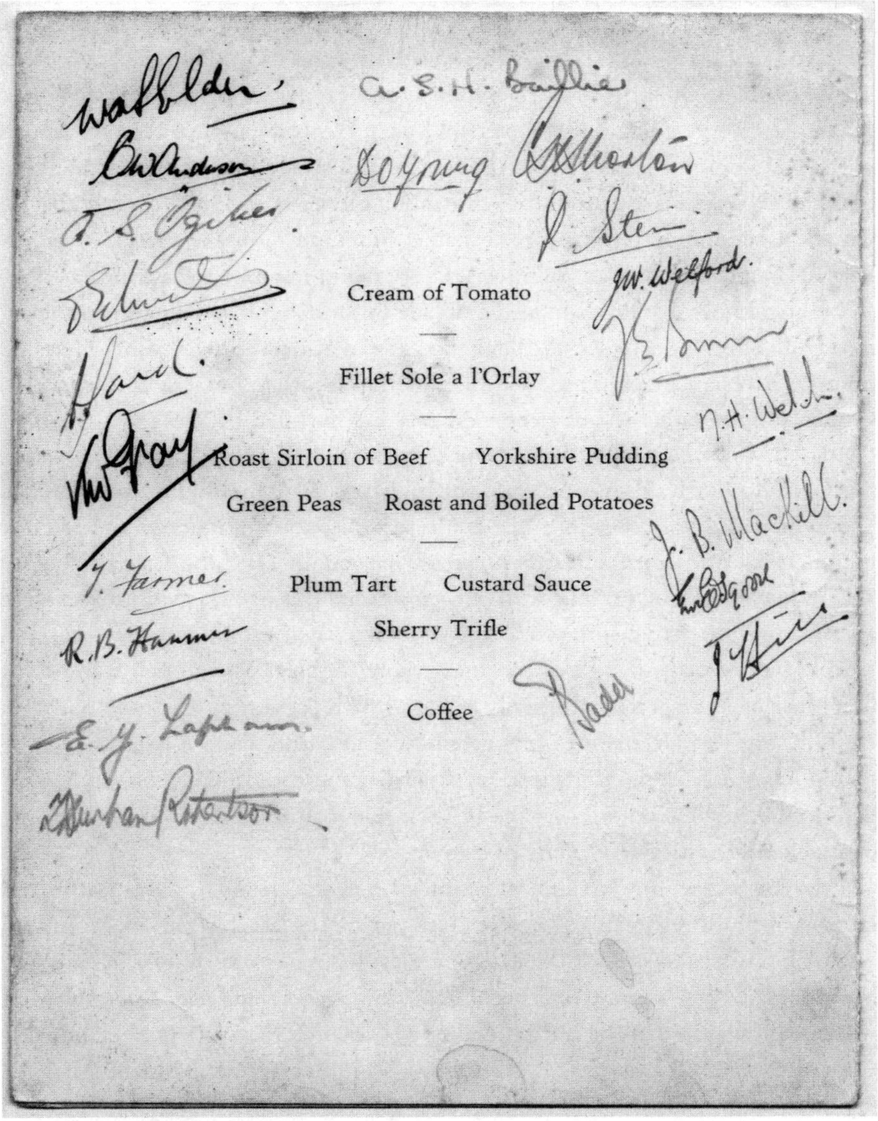

Cream of Tomato

—

Fillet Sole a l'Orlay

—

Roast Sirloin of Beef   Yorkshire Pudding

Green Peas   Roast and Boiled Potatoes

—

Plum Tart   Custard Sauce

Sherry Trifle

—

Coffee

However, on 12 May the Allied generals were painfully aware that some of the bridges across the River Maas and the Albert Canal at Maastricht, Holland, had not been blown up. By this time the Germans had advanced this far and were happy to find their passage across these water features mostly intact. Quite naturally they set up their defences there just in case French or British aircraft should try to destroy the bridges that were still intact. No.12 Squadron RAF, equipped with Battle bombers, were given the task of destroying these important targets, but when the orders arrived the commanding officer knew only too well that he would be sending his crews on a veritable suicide mission. He therefore assembled his men and asked for volunteers. Every man present raised a hand.

We now know that it was indeed a suicide mission and that a disaster was about to engulf 'Shiny Twelve'. Nine Blenheims of 139 Squadron were similarly called upon to make an attack on the German road transport approaching the bridges. One Blenheim failed to get airborne but the others, led by Wing Commander (W/C) L.W. Dickens AFC, headed out to make dive-bombing attacks. However, the German Luftwaffe was up early too and they were met by Me 109 and Me 110 fighters. Seven of the eight Blenheims were shot down, although not all crew members became casualties. Louis Dickens received the DFC for his leadership.

The five Battles of 12 Squadron chosen headed out in two sections and were approaching the target some time after 0900hrs (the sixth had become unserviceable before take-off). They too met enemy fighters as well as a wall of AA fire. Hurricane escorts were heavily engaged with these fighters as the bombers went in low. The Germans on the ground could hardly believe what they were seeing. They had captured the bridges on Friday the 10th, and having set up their defences, were incredulous that the RAF would wait until this Sunday morning to attack. All five bombers were shot down.

This episode, while just one of scores of heroic actions by both Battle and Blenheim bombers during this desperate period, resulted in the award of two Victoria Crosses to one of the Battle crews. F/O Donald 'Judy' Garland and his observer, Sgt Thomas Gray, became posthumous recipients of this award. It was odd, however, that the third member of Garland's crew, the gunner, Leading Aircraftman (LAC) Lawrence Reynolds was seemingly ignored. Indeed, on reading some of the reports of this raid, it often appeared that there was only Garland and Gray in the bomber. Reynolds could have no influence over the events he was part of, but no doubt he was manning his VGO (Vickers Gas-Operated) machine gun against any enemy fighters that were around. The three lie together in Haverlee Cemetery in Belgium. Like other graves of VC winners, Garland and Gray have the VC cross engraved on the CWG headstone, while 20-year-old Reynolds' headstone merely has a religious cross.

Tom Cooke's 100 flying hours was reached on 19 May, but there was still a very long way to go and much more to learn and become proficient on. With the spring weather helping, Cooke was flying at least once almost every day, in fact five times on the 27th, and he was having to do much map reading on flights exceeding an hour. This led to a navigation test on the 31st, under the watchful eye of F/O Worth. Hackney took him up on his first night flight on 5 June, just as the Dunkirk evacuation ended. France had all but fallen in the last three weeks or so, and it didn't look good for retreating armies to the west of Paris either.

As he became more proficient, further night flying came along, generally with Hackney in the cockpit alongside him but occasionally solo. By mid-June Tom was assessed again as 'average' as a pilot on type but with no special faults that future instructors would need to watch for. He was also awarded his flying badge with effect from 20 June – in other words, his coveted 'wings'. It was a proud moment for any pilot. Cooke now progressed to the Advanced Training Squadron at Sealand. Gone was F/O Hackney and along came a variety of sergeant pilots, under the command of F/Lt M.W. Kimpton, who commanded the Flight. On 28 June Kimpton himself took Cooke up for a test flight and 150 hours was reached as July 1940 began. In mid-July there was lots of cross-country navigation, either with or without an instructor, and then came practice bombing. No chance of being on fighters now, even though the Battle of Britain had just started and fighter pilots were desperately needed.

Cooke's last flight at Sealand occurred on 25 July. The squadron assessed him again as 'average', also noting he had done just over five hours in a Link Trainer, plus a further five hours in two long cross-country exercises practising with the Lorenz navigation system. Cooke had also been active with a camera gun on air-firing exercises and had achieved a pass mark on air-to-ground, air-to-air-beam and on low-level bombing, and achieved a good course average, while bombing from 4,000–5,000ft had between only 190 and 240yds of error. Cooke was again assessed as 'average' when signed off from No.5 FTS by S/L G.J. Grindell.[1] His flight commander, F/Lt M.W. Kimpton, also gave him a good send off, adding that Cooke had completed over ten hours of Link Trainer exercises.

Cooke was now ready to proceed to the next stage of his training, moving to No.11 OTU (Operational Training Unit) at RAF Bassingbourn, Hertfordshire (now Cambridgeshire), on 26 July. Further south, the Battle of Britain was well underway.

★★★

Bassingbourn is on the A41 just north of Royston, and had been the home of No.11 OTU since April 1940. It had Vickers Wellington Mk I bombers plus some Avro Ansons for navigational training. For its day, the Wellington was a very well-liked bomber aircraft, designed by Barnes Wallis, who gained further fame in 1943 by inventing the bouncing bomb that 617 Squadron used to attack the Ruhr dams. The Wellington was also an aircraft that would be used throughout the war in every theatre, over land and sea.

Once more it was back to basics, starting with an air-experience flight of circuits and landings, along with F/Lt A.F. Riddlesworth, on 13 August in L4247. Four days later Sergeant Pilot Lupton took him up twice. More flights followed with Riddlesworth, Lupton and Sgt Studd, including some night circuits. Cross-country flying began with long trips, such as base–Stradishall–base, base–Desford–Ternhill–Sealand–Jurby (Isle of Man) and back again, or a similar flight from base, then on to Henlow–Worcester–South Cerney–Andover–Peterborough and back. On one of these sorties on 30 August Cooke reached his 200 flying hours.

These long flights continued into September, by day initially but then at night, with some day practice bombing thrown in. He always seemed to be in the air at least once a day, often twice. High-level bombing, low-level bombing, air-to-ground firing, more cross-country flying, navigational exercises, more air firing over the Wash. Thus not long after, 250 flying hours came up. A week of night cross-country flights came to an end on 15 September, with him and fellow trainee pilot John Cope, with whom he would become close friends, sharing the flying with their crews from Peterborough to Hullavington, Andover and back to base. (During the day of 15 September, the Battle of Britain had reached a climax in the skies over southern England, and this date would be forever commemorated as Battle of Britain Day.) Then it was all over. One final high-level bombing practice on 21 September with a cross-country exercise too, again with John Cope and their two crews, and Cooke's training was finished. As we will read, Cope remained in close contact with Cooke for the early war years, in fact becoming his best friend. He would also be awarded the DFC and DFM with Bomber Command.

Now would follow the moment of truth. A posting to an operational squadron arrived, but with it came a shock. As far as Tom was concerned his final training on Wellingtons should have meant a posting to a Wellington squadron. However, in the way of service life, things that seem obvious often do not work out, and his first squadron was in fact equipped with Armstrong Whitworth Whitley bombers. He was assigned to No.78 Squadron at RAF Dishforth, Yorkshire, and was sent to 'A' Flight, with flight commander S/L Richard K. Wildey, whose DFC would be gazetted in November. The commanding officer was W/C Maurice Wiblin. Tom Cooke recalled:

I didn't like Dishforth very much and I didn't like the aircraft. I'd been trained at OTU at Bassingbourn on Wellingtons and of course, the Whitley was heavy and clumsy after the Wellington, so I didn't like it at all.

It could take an awful lot of punishment and it also would fly in all sorts of extremely bad weather, that sort of thing, so I suppose it did awfully well really. Manoeuvrability was poor, but again that's a personal bias because having just come off Wellingtons. I was unhappy my first squadron didn't have them.

If one talks about comfort, well, all those early aircraft were uncomfortable. The first one I found to be anything like comfortable was much later in the war, and it was the American Liberator [B-24]. Those early bombers had heaters but nine times out of ten they didn't work.

Of course, I ran into the same old business concerning sergeants at Dishforth. The same attitude was going on that I thought was a bit of a sauce, because although we had been made sergeants which the old hands didn't like much, we were going out on raids and we all felt that perhaps we might be entitled to a little more respect, not to say a little more comfort, but it wasn't the case. As the war progressed, this naturally changed, but in the early days there was this atmosphere.

Tom Cooke had made wonderful progress, from AC2 to sergeant pilot, with his 'wings' and now posted to an operational bomber squadron, in just a matter of thirteen months. As the war went on, pilots could expect the training period to be closer to two years at least, and many did their training in the warm, cloudless skies of Canada or Rhodesia. Now, in October 1940, with the Battle of Britain seemingly won, although no one knew if it might begin again in the spring, it was up to Bomber Command to take the war to the enemy.

It is realised today that Bomber Command were far from an efficient force. Air navigation was still in the ascendancy, bombing accuracy could not in any way be guaranteed and the available aids, in contrast to 1943 onwards, were very limited. As yet, there were no four-engined bombers that would fill the skies later on and the operational crews were soldiering on with Wellington, Whitley, Hampden and Blenheim bombers, all twin-engined types. Although some had the range to penetrate deep into Germany, it was generally a long and cold haul to get to German targets and back. It was into this scene that Sgt T.C.S. Cooke now moved. Only time would tell if he had the skill, not to say luck, to survive.

Notes

1 Gordon Grindell, a New Zealander with the RAF, later became Group
Captain DFC AFC and Bar, his DFC being awarded in 1943 for operations
while CO of 487 Squadron RNZAF.

OPERATIONAL – FIRST TOUR

RAF Dishforth was one of the early bomber bases to be built within the aegis of the pre-war RAF expansion schemes. Like many similar bases it had brick buildings and accommodation, and five large C-type hangars situated along the south-east boundary. It had been opened in September 1936. No.78 Squadron, to which Tom Cooke now went, had arrived at Dishforth in February 1937 with Heyfords, but it began to re-equip with Whitleys in July the following year. Not long after the war began, the squadron was really 4 Group's reserve unit, supplementing the Group's pool with trained crews, as well as acting as a Group back-up. However, the unit was then moved to Linton-on-Ouse, but it was back at Dishforth in the spring of 1940 and, along with 51 Squadron, began regular raids upon the enemy.

The Whitley was an all-metal, stressed-skin aircraft with two 920hp Armstrong Siddeley Tiger IX engines, with a wing span of 84ft. Its length from nose to tail gun position was 69ft and it stood 15ft in height at its highest point, weighed 14,275lb unloaded and 21,600lb loaded. It had a maximum speed of 192mph at 7,000ft, cruised at 160mph at 16,000ft, with a range of 1,250 miles, and a service ceiling of 19,000ft. It carried a crew of five: two pilots, navigator/bomb aimer, wireless operator/air gunner and a rear gunner. The rear gunner had four .303 machine guns in his power-operated turret and there was a single .303 gun in the nose turret.

The prototype first flew in 1936, but when Cooke arrived on 78 Squadron, the Mk I type had been replaced by the Mk V, which had a higher speed of some 220mph at 17,000ft, having Rolls-Royce Merlin X engines, and it could cruise at 185mph. Range had increased to 1,650 miles with a bomb load of 3,000lb or 470 miles with 7,000lb, although its service ceiling was a bit less at 17,600ft.

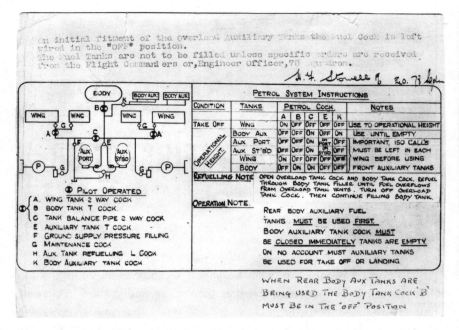

A diagram issued to all pilots and engineers giving the petrol system instructions on how to transfer fuel from one tank to another, and the order fuel tanks should be used. This one was issued by F/O H.F. Stowell of 78 Squadron, Tom Cooke's first operational squadron.

The first Mk I Whitleys entered service at Dishforth with 10 Squadron in March 1937. In August 1940 it had been Whitleys of 51 and 78 Squadrons, plus Hampdens and Wellingtons, that flew the first raid upon the German capital of Berlin, something that so infuriated Hitler that he immediately turned his attention to London. In so doing he eased the Luftwaffe's efforts against Fighter Command's airfields in southern England and thus lost the advantage in the Battle of Britain.

Tom Cooke had his first flight in a Whitley on 1 October 1940. He had been designated as second pilot to Sgt G. Samson, and they flew circuits and landings for ninety minutes. He went solo later that day with an officer in the second seat, and for the next few days, with Samson, he flew air tests and local flying, taking half the time to fly cross-country sorties. Sgt Samson was a pre-war regular, so he too had his reservations about VR sergeants. Cooke was not alone in being subjected to such a conclusion; his immediate friends were all of similar backgrounds and they tended to live in their own little group of VRs.

Later in the war, a newly arrived pilot and crew might, if luck was with them, have a chance of a straightforward trip or two to ease themselves into operations. Often the pilot would go on a raid with an experienced crew to see how it was done. Again if lucky he might be able to get in a second such trip before taking his own crew out. Of course, there were occasions when this new pilot went off and failed to return, much to the stunned bemusement of his crew who, now 'headless', would either have to wait for another 'gash' (spare) pilot to turn up or be split up and join other crews who were a man short. In Cooke's case, it was a matter of being thrown in at the deep end. When the crews reported to the flight briefing room on the afternoon of 7 October, they quickly discovered not only that they were 'on' that night, but that the target was Berlin.

Eight of the squadron's aircraft were assigned to the mission, four being given the primary target of the Reich Presidential Chancellery, the other four going for the Fokker aircraft works in Amsterdam. Samson and Cooke got the Chancellery. The other three members of Samson's crew were P/O G.W. Brown, navigator; Sgt W.G. Cording, WOp/AG; and Sgt J. Barker in the rear turret. Their assigned bomber was P4958 and take-off time was to be 2100hrs. In total, 140 Blenheims, Hampdens, Wellingtons and Whitleys operated that night, although not all were headed for Berlin. Just forty-two Wellingtons and Whitleys were going there and they had twelve individual targets to go for.

Samson flew on the prescribed course and they bombed the Chancellery from 12,000ft. One stick of bombs fell away but results were not observed. The problem was that as Brown guided his pilot through the bomb run, and the actual target was coming up, they were suddenly enveloped in a dazzling white light from a searchlight that blinded everyone moments before the release of the bombs. Enemy opposition was intense, although the weather was kind to them, and they headed for home with the knowledge that at least they had found Berlin, identified the target, and bombed somewhere in the right area. Yet there was another hurdle to get over – fuel. It became apparent that it was going to be touch and go whether they got back, not just to the base but to England. It became so close that Samson had everyone prepare to come down in the North Sea and hopefully get into the aircraft's dinghy. In the event they made it, but had to land at Driffield, some way south-east of Dishforth, and north of Hull. They put down at 0700hrs after a ten-hour flight and flew back to Dishforth later that day. Cooke later recorded:

My very first raid was on Berlin. As far as I recall it was a maximum effort that night and I remember we were briefed to go over the target separately in order to create the impression of a larger force than we were. We also had to de-synchronise our engines, partly in order to put off the echo of the sound detectors we reckoned the Germans were using with their anti-aircraft guns, and also from the point of view of morale – the throbbing noise that was created was supposed to be more upsetting to people on the ground. In addition to that we used to throw empty beer bottles out because they would make a screaming noise as they went down. All part of the psychological ideas put forward to upset the Germans.

Only one RAF aircraft failed to return from the night's attack, and one aircraft from 78 Squadron had to abort due to engine trouble. S/L R.O.O. Taylor of 38 Squadron (Wellingtons), based at RAF Marham, and his all-NCO crew was brought down over Berlin and they were all buried in the Berlin War Cemetery. Another Wellington from 99 Squadron was badly shot up by a night-fighter over the North Sea but managed to struggle back for an emergency landing at Honington. No sooner had it touched down than the bomber caught fire, but all on board escaped the inferno. A Whitley from 58 Squadron, raiding Gelsenkirchen, failed to return after bombing. The crew made it back to the UK but reported problems with one engine and they crashed trying to land at RAF Bircham Newton, Norfolk. P/O R.A. Hadley and his crew all died.

★★★

Four days later, on the 11/12th, the Samson crew were on the roster again; this time the target was the synthetic oil works at Politz, just over the old Polish border, north of Stettin. Only a few miles further north lay the Baltic Sea. There was a large inlet in from Pomeranian Bay, and it flowed past Politz as it headed to Stettin. At this stage of the war there were few raids that concentrated on a single target, and on this night eighty-six aircraft were assigned all manner of targets in Germany, France and Belgium. The only common denominator was that oil and shipbuilding targets were on the schedule. In any event, for Samson and crew it was a tremendous second target after Berlin, for it was a short way east of that city, so another long trip even if less testing.

The squadron put up seven Whitleys, one being flown by the commanding officer, W/C J.N.H. Whitworth DFC.[1] Most of the seven began taking off at 1845hrs, but in the event the target eluded everyone because of terrible visibility; pilots and navigators had to select alternate targets after turning back. The commanding officer went for Borkum, an island base in the East Frisians, and its aerodrome. Samson too had to abandon the attempt on Stettin so flew to an alternate target at Harburg, dropping their bombs from 8,000ft. The bombs had to be dropped through dense cloud after following a dead-reckoning course amidst exploding AA fire.

Again it had been a long trip, especially with time spent trying to locate Stettin and then Harburg. The weather had not helped either and this time they were forced to land at RAF Leeming, near Northalerton, after seven hours and fifty minutes, touching down at 0230hrs. Neither the squadron nor the Command suffered any losses that night.

Four days later, on the 15th, it was another early evening take-off – 1841hrs – and again targets varied from crew to crew. Samson got Leuna in the Ruhr. After orbiting the main target, he concluded that the thick ground mist made it impossible to bomb, headed away and went for the railway across the river/canal junction at Hollenstedt, just to the west of Hamburg, and later the docks at Duisberg in the Ruhr. Hollenstedt was bombed from 10,000ft, the docks from 8,000ft. Bombs were seen to explode in the dock area and some fires were started. There was no opposition.

For the third time in a row they were unable to reach their home base, landing instead at RAF Linton-on-Ouse, north-west of York, at 0341hrs. They had been airborne for nine hours.

★★★

Another long and testing flight came up on the night of 20/21 October, this time to Italy. Some 139 aircraft were on operations that night, with thirty Hampdens going for Berlin. Other aircraft were to range as far as Czechoslovakia, while 78 Squadron mustered nine aircraft. Due to the distance, they flew to West Raynham, an advanced base where their fuel tanks could be topped up. In the end four failed to take off for various reasons. The primary target was the Pirelli Works at Milan, with a secondary target of the blast furnace and steelworks at Aosta.

Samson lifted P4958 off the runway at 1918hrs and headed out over France. After several hours the snow-capped Alps came into view and the Whitley was threaded through and over mountain peaks, locating Aosta, which lay in a valley near the St Bernard Pass. The bomb run was made from 12,000ft, when one stick of bombs was dropped and was seen to explode with blue flames, and a fire was started. Some slight desultory flak came up from what appeared to be neutral Switzerland, more in hope of scaring the bomber away than actually trying to shoot it down. Cooke noted in his log book that they had scored a direct hit on the works.

Once again the return was abnormal. Poor weather over England made it necessary yet again to divert to Linton-on-Ouse, but even this proved problematical and Samson warned everyone that unless he found a break in the cloud, it might well mean a parachute jump. The crew got themselves ready for such an eventuality but luck had not totally abandoned them, Samson finding the break he hoped for and flying quickly through to land safely in clear air.

They touched down at 0530hrs after ten hours and fifteen minutes. Tom's log book now recorded in excess of 300 flying hours.

There followed a spot of leave before operations were on again in early November, and it was Italy once more on the 8th. Again the aircraft assigned flew to an advanced base, this time Honington, with a take-off time of 1800hrs. A large range of targets appeared on the flight rosters: three of 78 Squadron's aircraft were given their primary target as the Pirelli Works in Milan again, with an alternate target set as the marshalling yards and railway station in Turin. Two of the three Whitleys, including Samson and F/Lt D.S. Robertson's crew, bombed the Milan works, while P/O G. Franklin went for the Turin target.

It was a clear moonlit night so there was little difficulty in making out the target once across the Alps. Samson's bombs went down from 10,000ft, Robertson's from 15,000ft. Both crews saw explosions on the target and fires started, Samson reporting seeing these fires still burning from a distance of 50 miles. Light and heavy flak was fired at the bombers, but no hits were scored. Eleven hours and five minutes after take-off, Samson landed back at Honington at 0505hrs, from where they returned to Dishforth the next day.

Cooke made the following observations after the war:

We flew a variety of targets, not only Germany but raids on Italy which were extremely long so we used advanced bases for those in East Anglia to refuel. These were against Milan, Turin and Aosta, and places like that.

The main thing about flying in those days was that most people were aware that we were using 1914–18 war stuff, which also included the bombs. Their trajectories were very, very doubtful and so was the bomb-sight itself almost identical to those used in WW1, and of course, we were flying aircraft that flew rather faster. This did not help us very much in locating targets with our bombs and further more, the Air Ministry was rather going for specific aiming points.

★★★

The main target for the night of 20/21 October had been Berlin by thirty Hampdens, and only one from 44 Squadron was lost over the city. Another got back but had to force-land near Colchester due to running out of fuel. The other target was Pilzen, and this cost Bomber Command three Whitley aircraft, all from 58 Squadron out of Linton-on-Ouse. Two had run out of fuel and ditched off the English coast, the crews being rescued. The other crew had been feeling safe once they were back over England, but they were caught and attacked by a German intruder flown by Hauptmann Karl Hülshoff of I./NJG2. The Whitley came down on fire near Ingleby Greenhow, Yorkshire. P/O E.H. Brown and three of his crew did not survive, the fifth being injured. This appears to be the first RAF bomber to be intercepted and shot down by German night intruder aircraft, although we can't be certain. One might have thought the Germans would have made more use of intruders with so many bombers returning from raids on Germany over the war years. However, III./NJG2 did attack and damage a training aircraft on 24 October over Norfolk. Another intruder shot down a Whitley of 102 Squadron that had just taken off from Linton-on-Ouse. killing three of the crew and injuring two. These intruder sorties certainly gave Bomber Command crews another problem to think about during the war.

★★★

There was now a sudden change for Cooke. He had completed four operational sorties with Samson, but then he was placed in another crew. What exactly happened is not certain, but when sortie number five came along on 13 November he was still second pilot in Whitley P4958, although his pilot was named as Sgt G.W. Holden. Cording was still the WOp/AG, but the navigator was now P/O D. Balmforth and the rear gunner Sgt K.B. Wears.

George Walton Holden was a VR pilot and went on to greater things. He won the DFC for a raid on Brest in July 1941, during a large-scale attack on the port and the German capital ships there, the famed *Scharnhorst*, *Gneisenau* and *Prinz Eugen*. It must have been quite a raid for it produced five awards of the DSO, twenty-six DFCs and twenty DFMs. The RAF lost ten Wellingtons and two Hampdens in that operation. Holden had been a warrant officer at that time and he was later commissioned. By 1942 he was an acting wing commander and was given a Bar to his DFC whilst with 102 Squadron for an attack on Lorient, which he attacked despite losing an engine on the way over and then circling the target for twenty minutes to see what effect the other bombers had on the port.

Seven 78 Squadron aircraft were detailed for the raid on the 13th, the target being an oil refinery at Luena. However, as far as Holden and Cooke were concerned it was not a successful mission. The squadron diary noted that while they diverted to a secondary target at Osnabruck, due to weather they had to jettison their bombs over the target and results were not observed. The port engine became unserviceable due to icing. In his log book, Cooke wrote: 'Returned owing to icing.' So overall, not a good start for the new team.

★★★

On the same night, 10 Squadron at RAF Leeming lost its commanding officer on a raid to Merseburg. W/C Kenneth Francis Ferguson was 29 years of age, the son of Captain (Capt.) C.A. and Lady Edith Ferguson. He and his NCO crew are thought to have been lost over the North Sea on their way home and all have unknown graves. It is understood that W/C Ferguson was the first squadron commander from 4 Group of Bomber Command to lose his life on bomber operations in the Second World War. It soon became frowned upon for squadron COs to fly operations, and was certainly not expected on a regular basis. Many did, of course, but mostly they operated with a scratch crew once or twice a month, sometimes even using a false (junior) name for the record, so that Group HQ would not discover what they were doing. Very occasionally a CO would fly an operation taking one or two of his senior staff with him, and their loss was impossibly difficult to cover up.

★★★

Two days later Cooke and crew were on the roster again, this time with a different rear gunner, Sgt E.C. Gurmin. A total of sixty-seven Hampden, Wellington and Whitley aircraft were scheduled and flew out in two waves, eight hours apart, the target being Grasbrook oil refinery and the shipyards at Hamburg. No.78 Squadron again had seven aircraft available. Five of these bombed the primary and two others went for secondary targets. This time Cooke flew T4236, and take-off time was 1800hrs. The target was reached without undue problems and they bombed the refinery from 12,300ft in one stick, but again results were unobserved, although fires had been started by falling incendiaries. Heavy flak was encountered and they were attacked by a German night-fighter. There is not much mentioned about it in the Operational Records Book, so it must have been little more than an attacking pass with no more seen of it. It is recorded in war reports that this was Bomber Command's most successful raid of the war thus far, the Blohm and Voss shipyards being particularly badly hit.

The next operation was on 17/18 November, still with Gurmin in the back and Balmforth again seated at the navigator's table. Once more seven aircraft were made ready, the target being the oil refinery at Gelsenkirchen. Take-off was at 1830hrs and while the target was located the skipper decided to drop bombs individually rather than in one stick. Selecting targets, the bombs were dropped one at a time from 12,500ft and 3,500ft despite heavy AA fire and searchlights. Haze and lack of distinguishable pinpoints made things difficult but they survived and were back home at 0230hrs, although not at home base but at Kirton Lindsay, from where they flew back on the 18th.

There was no rest for they were back 'on' the night of the 19/20th. Holden and Cooke were in the cockpit, but Sgt A.W. Steven took over the navigation and Wears was back in the rear turret. Take-off came at 1735hrs with the target being another synthetic oil works, this one at Ruhland. Eight aircraft took off but only two attacked the primary, while four bombed alternate targets, one of these being Holden's T4236. Being unable to locate the refinery, they went for a rail line, rail station, sidings and a military camp. Some large fires were started and buildings were hit, with walls seen collapsing. They were back at 0433hrs, landing at RAF Abingdon, after just about eleven hours' flying time. Tom Cooke remembered:

...being sent to an oil refinery called Ruhland which is down by the back of Leipzig, and we were supposed to find this refinery, which was in the middle of the countryside, about six or seven hours' flying time away. Our navigational instruments was the sextant and very little else. Even our compasses didn't have Gyro sights in those days. Our chances of getting there were very remote. We had a target on one occasion that we couldn't find so we flew along a railway line and every so often we dropped a bomb and blew the line up, and then the inevitable happened, we came across a train so we flew up and down and machine-gunned it, and then flew on and came across a turn table and one of those small engine houses, so bombed that as well. We then proceeded back across Germany but all that happened at our next briefing was to get a telling off. In no uncertain manner we were advised that we were not Blenheim crews and if we couldn't get to a target, we were to bring our bombs back.

We felt we had been more of a nuisance to the enemy and did some damage, rather than just flying all the way to some minute target somewhere and then bring our bombs all the way back again – at least we had done something.

This was further brought home to me some time later. One night I came back and had just turned off the flare-path and was watching the next chap come in and as he touched down he blew up. He was bringing his bombs back and one had been jolted loose. That upset me quite a bit, so I always got rid of my bombs, even in the later stages. Once I was taking off in a Stirling and had an engine failure but still continued to get off, then flew directly to the Wash and dropped our bombs there, rather than risk landing back with them still on board. It was certainly an uncomfortable feeling landing with all the bombs still on. What if an undercarriage leg collapsed or a tyre burst, anything could develop. I have in fact crash-landed with sea mines on board but luckily they didn't explode.

In the early days one was more conscious of these things than we were later on in 1943, by which time we were becoming a bit blasé about such things.

One aircraft of 78 Squadron did not return. T4156 'L', piloted by P/O R.E.H. George was brought down and all five crew members became prisoners of war. After the war, George returned home as a flight lieutenant, having spent most of his captivity in the infamous Stalag Luft III, together with his navigator, P/O R.C. Mordaunt. His three NCO air crew were all sent to Kopernikus POW camp, but the rear gunner, who became a warrant officer while a prisoner, was moved to the officer camp at Stalag Luft III to meet up with his former officer crew mates.

Operations were coming thick and fast despite the winter weather, and it was the same crew that went to Bordeaux on 22 November. Six squadron aircraft were part of the force that went to the French port, while Bomber Command also sent aircraft to the Ruhr. The target is listed as an aircraft factory and its aerodrome. Take-off was begun at around 2140–2150hrs, and although squadron records indicate that the bombs were dropped from heights between 5,000ft and 7,000ft, Cooke's log book notes 3,500ft. They landed back at Boscombe Down at 0740hrs after a nine-hour and fifty-minute flight.

The final operation for November was on the 28/29th. There was the same crew but this time they were flying T4203. It was to be another long-range job, with six of the squadron's Whitleys making for Stettin's shipbuilding yards, where three of them would bomb while the other three went for the oil refinery at Politz. One aircraft had to abandon its task because of engine trouble, but Holden reached Politz and bombed from 8,000ft. The bombs were seen to burst in the target area. It was a fine and starry night, which aided the flak and searchlight activity, and one 78 Squadron aircraft, P5026, captained by P/O J.R. Denny, was shot down and again all five crew members were taken prisoner. Denny ended up in Mühlburg camp, on the Elbe, but his navigator and second pilot went to Stalag Luft III. The two NCOs went to Stalag Luft I at Barth, on the bleak Baltic coast, but the rear gunner was later moved to Stalag Luft III when promoted to warrant officer. Most RAF prisoners initially went to Dulag Luft, the Luftwaffe's transit camp, as RAF personnel came under the jurisdiction of the German Luftwaffe. Dulag Luft, some 15km north-west of Frankfurt-am-Main, was used as the reception and interrogation centre for captured Allied airmen from where, once processed, they were sent off to various NCO or officer POW camps.

On 28/29 November there was also a raid on Düsseldorf and one Blenheim IV (T1893) aircraft of 105 Squadron failed to return. F/Lt C.D. Swain and his two crewmen were captured. Cyril Swain, from Shropshire, ended up in Stalag Luft III POW camp, being one of the men who escaped from there in the mass breakout in March 1944. Recaptured, he was one of the fifty murdered by the Gestapo. He was 32 years old and had been a pre-war airman.

Cooke and Holden only achieved two operations in December. The first was on the 8th, another trip to the French port of Bordeaux, and then visiting another port in Germany on the 13/14th – Kiel.

For the Bordeaux trip they had Sgt F.H. Unwin as navigator and they took off at 1700hrs, assigned to bomb the submarine pens. They were back at 0200hrs, having bombed from 8,000ft in good weather with just some slight opposition from AA fire. No results could be seen but most bombs that fell on these and other U-boat pens during the war had very little effect. The U-boats were berthed beneath huge reinforced concrete roofs and the bombs did little more than bounce off them. Sometimes the dock installations might be hit and damaged; otherwise it was little more than bombing and hoping for the best.

Kiel was another favourite target for Bomber Command, being a major German port situated in the north of Germany. Sgt Steven was back and they took off at 1636hrs. Of the seven squadron aircraft detailed, only four managed to bomb the primary target, with one bombing an alternative. Another crew had to jettison their bombs off Flamborough Head due to engine trouble and one aircraft failed to return. P/O M.L. Stedman had to order his crew out when over the Wash (N1485). He and his co-pilot did not survive and nor did his WOp/AG, although the other two were rescued uninjured.

Holden flew across the target at 11,000ft and they dropped the bombs in one long stick; the glow of their explosions – on target – could be seen through a veil of cloud. Heavy flak kept them awake and so did the pilot of a night-flying Me 109E single-seater fighter, who started a chase but abandoned it once they were over Kiel amidst bursting AA fire. They landed back at Abingdon once more, after a mere six hours and thirty-five minutes – something of a doddle.

This had been Tom Cooke's thirteenth operation. It had also taken place on the 13th of the month. The more superstitious airmen were never happy flying number thirteen, or even on the 13th day, but apart from one German fighter pilot trying his utmost to do him harm, Cooke and his crew survived; they would enjoy Christmas and then wait to see what the new year of 1941 would bring. It is also an interesting fact that this thirteenth operation came almost exactly one year after Cooke's first air-experience flight. A lot had happened in one year, and his flying hours had almost reached 400.

★★★

With Cooke off on leave, he missed the raid on Mannheim on the night of 16/17 December 1940. Interestingly it was a raid authorised by the War Cabinet who wanted a general attack upon a German city in retaliation for recent heavy raids on English towns and cities, in particular Coventry and Southampton. For the first time the target was the city and not any particular industrial centre.

An original force of 200 RAF bombers was later cut down to 134: sixty-one Wellingtons, thirty-five Whitleys, twenty-nine Hampdens and nine Blenheims. This number still represented the largest number the Command had sent to a single target. It would be opened by eight experienced Wellington crews who would attempt to start fires in the centre of Mannheim, virtually a forerunner of the later Pathfinder technique. Following bombers would aim at these fires. Unfortunately, the target marking was not accurate and in consequence the later bombing became scattered.

Losses were just two Hampdens and one Blenheim, but two additional Hampdens, two Wellingtons and a Blenheim crashed upon their return to England. One of the Hampdens that failed to return was from 61 Squadron at Hamswell, piloted by Sgt G.E. Cowan, who had just received the Distinguished Flying Medal, which would appear in the *London Gazette* on Christmas Eve. George Cowan had flown more than twenty-six operations. His award was for heroism in a sortie during which their Blenheim was attacked by a Me 110 night-fighter, which wounded his wireless operator. Getting back over England the weather was bad and, as the wireless had been knocked out, they could not call for instructions. With a wounded man on board they could not bale out, so Cowan elected to try for a crash-landing in nil visibility, which he carried out with no injury to himself or his crew, and fairly light damage to his aircraft. Cowan was 24 years old, married and came from Ipswich, Suffolk.

The final loss to Bomber Command during this momentous year occurred on 31 December. A total of twenty-two Blenheims headed into Germany and Holland with a variety of individual targets for each. In the event only six found targets and two Blenheims failed to return. One was lost following an attack upon a German aerodrome at Gilze Reijen, Holland; the other didn't get back from Cologne. The crew of the latter bomber, from 139 Squadron, was S/L R.C. Beaman, with Sgt H. Robson DFM, navigator, and 21-year-old Sgt Douglas Trigwell, from Seaford, Sussex, air gunner. Robert Beaman, a pre-war airman, had been recommended for the DFC whilst flying with 110 Squadron and, in fact, this was gazetted in October 1941. Henry Robson, aged 31, was another married man from Forest Hill, London, and had also flown with 110 Squadron. He had been awarded his DFM after thirty-three operations and was gazetted but, like his pilot, not until October 1941.

Notes

1 Later Air Commodore Whitworth CB DSO DFC and Bar, Czech MC.

AIRCRAFT CAPTAIN

During Cooke's leave, 78 Squadron had lost another crew. On 28/29 December, during a daring raid on Lorient, Sgt A.J. Mott, in P4950, had been hit by ground fire from low level. With the Whitley on fire Mott ordered his men out. Most of his crew had been captured, but Mott had managed to evade and went on the run. So too did his rear gunner, Sgt A.J. McMillan. After a series of adventures, John Mott found himself in Nantes by September, where he met up with McMillan. However, McMillan and the family he was staying with were betrayed and he was finally captured. Mott eventually got into Spain and flew back from Gibraltar in mid-December, almost a year after being shot down.

John Mott later flew Lysanders with 161 Squadron, the unit that flew clandestine operations into northern France taking and collecting SOE agents. As a flight lieutenant he landed in unoccupied France one night in May 1942, but his aircraft became bogged down and he was unable to take off. Once again he began a series of adventures that later led him into northern Italy and eventual freedom. Mott was Mentioned in Dispatches in January 1943 and made a Member of the Order of the British Empire (MBE) a year later.

Tom Cooke's first flight of 1941 came on 1 January, with S/L Wildey taking him up on a night flight of one hour and ten minutes. The reason, as it turned out, was that Cooke was to be given his own crew and made aircraft captain. His new crew consisted of Sgt L. Thorpe as second pilot, Sgt A.W. Steven as navigator (air observer), Sgt E.C. Gurmin as WOp/AG and Sgt E.A. Crunsell as rear gunner. At least this was the first crew that he took out on ops on 3 January, in Whitley T4215. Steven had also been with him under Holden.

In the meantime, 78 Squadron lost T4204 on the night of 1/2 January. Scheduled for an attack on Bremen, Sgt H.A. Davis and crew were defeated by atrocious weather and, although they got back to England, were forced to abandon the Whitley over Yorkshire. One of the crew was killed but the others all survived.

Cooke's first operation as captain, on 3/4 January, was to Bremen. The squadron diary states that six aircraft were detailed for operations but all attacked alternate targets. However, Cooke says in his log book that the target was Bremen and the Form 541 shows their designated target had been the gasworks in that city. They found and bombed this target from 12,000ft in one stick but, as in so many cases, results were unobserved. The weather had been kind, which is more than could be said for the flak and searchlights that they encountered. They did not get back to Dishforth but diverted and landed at RAF Langhan on the north Norfolk coast after six hours and twenty minutes flying time.

One 78 Squadron aircraft was lost this night due to wireless failure and, one must assume, navigational problems too, as the crew had to abandon the Whitley at 0340hrs in the vicinity of South Molton, Devon, some way from home base. Fortunately the crew survived their parachute jumps but P4937 crashed into the ground. Dishforth also lost a Whitley from 51 Squadron, which shared the aerodrome with 78 Squadron. Sgt A.D. Roberts and his crew simply disappeared without trace.

Nine squadron aircraft were on the line for the 9/10th, the target being synthetic oil plants at Gelsenkirchen. One aircraft aborted due to its wireless becoming unserviceable, but the rest reached the target, although only two bombed the primary and five alternate targets. Tom Cooke had his same crew and had taken off at 1737hrs, returning at 0005hrs – for once to his home base. They had gone for an alternate target, a railway junction at Hamborn, delivering their bomb load from 10,000ft in the face of medium flak. One Whitley of 78 Squadron did not get back (T4203), shot down by a German night-fighter flown by Oberleutnant Reinhold Eckardt of II./NJG1 (its 6th Staffel) over Holland. It was his first night victory of an eventual twenty-two, although he was killed on 30 July 1942, shortly after downing his last victory. He had received the Knight's Cross in August 1941. Sgt C.A. Smith and his crew did not survive.

What appeared to be a simple raid on the night of 13/14 January did not turn out well. The RAF's main target this night was the port of Wilhelmshaven, with other aircraft attacking ports at Dunkirk and Boulogne, just across the English Channel. Three of 78 Squadron's bombers were given Dunkirk, taking off at around 1915hrs. However, one aircraft failed to locate the target and jettisoned its bomb load into the sea. The second aircraft bombed Dunkirk from 14,000ft but results could not be seen; Cooke did not find the target either, and similarly dumped the bomb load into the Channel. He was back by 2205hrs, so just four hours and fifty-five minutes in the log book. The only change on this night was that he had Sgt G.R. Armstrong as WOp/AG and a familiar gunner, Sgt Wears, in the rear.

The squadron did not fly any bombing operations in February 1941. Instead, some crews flew down to Ringway, together with others from 51 Squadron, and then all flew out to the island of Malta in the Mediterranean. Here they took part in Operation Colossus (on 10 February), the first Allied airborne operation of the war and one during which British paratroopers attacked and destroyed a large aqueduct at Tragino, in southern Italy. Unhappily, the paratroopers were all captured the next day, their tracks towards the coast being clearly seen in the snow. One of 78 Squadron's Whitleys developed engine trouble and P/O Jack Wotherspoon ordered his crew to bale out while he crash-landed in the mouth of the River Sele. All were captured, Wotherspoon ending up in Stalag Luft III.

★★★

A Wellington of 311 (Czech) Squadron, based at East Wretham, became the sole loss on the night of 6/7 February against Boulogne, out of a force of twenty-five. P/O F. Cigos had to make a forced landing in enemy territory and he and his crew were taken into captivity. The Germans salvaged the bomber (L7842 KX-T) and later test flew it at their experimental and test unit at Rechlin. One of the crew was P/O Arnošt (Ernst) Valenta from Svébohov. He ended up in Stalag Luft III and became part of the 'Great Escape' in March 1944. As part of the escape organisation in the camp, one of his jobs was to use pressure (blackmail) on a German guard to get hold of a camera to use for passport photographs, which he achieved. He was one of the first out of the tunnel on the night of the breakout but he was recaptured and was one of the fifty escapees to be murdered by the Gestapo. He was by then a flight lieutenant and was 31 years of age.

★★★

Tom Cooke had not been part of the operation from Malta and in fact he did not fly again until 5 March. During this period the squadron had continued operating and on the night of 11/12 February had lost Whitley N4190. Sgt J.W. Quincey had been forced to crash-land east of Kilmarnock after returning from Bremen, but all the crew survived. Then on the night of 26/27th the squadron lost its CO, W/C G.T. Toland, in P4996, on a raid to Cologne. On his return the wing commander crashed into a mountain 3 miles east of Craig, Ross and Cromerty, and all aboard were killed. Gerald Thomas Toland was 30 years old and left a wife in Inverness-shire.

Bomber Command lost another commanding officer this night too. W/C William Walter Stainthorpe AFC commanded 83 Squadron at RAF Scampton. He was 30 years old and came from Yorkshire. Like Toland, he and his Hampden crew were returning from Cologne and amazingly he too flew his machine into high ground near Derrington Cross, near Stafford. All four men were killed. The rear gunner, Sgt D.V. Weaving, had survived a bale out earlier in the month. The aircraft in which he was flying hit a balloon cable over Birmingham, returning from a raid on Bremen on 11/12 February. As his pilot ordered everyone out, he set the bomber on its autopilot and it flew on to crash into the Irish Sea.

With the loss of Stainthorpe, 83 Squadron was then commanded by W/C R.A.B. Learoyd VC, a post he held until June 1941. Roderick 'Babe' Learoyd had won his Victoria Cross on 12 August 1940 flying Hampdens with 49 Squadron. His was the first of nineteen VC awards to members of Bomber Command, if one discounts Garland and Gray's awards flying light bombers with the AASF in May 1940.

On the same night, 115 Squadron nearly lost its CO, W/C A.C. Evans-Evans on their return from Bremen, being forced to abandon their Wellington south of Saffron Walden, Essex. W/C Evans-Evans did not survive the war, being killed on operations on 21/22 February 1945. By this date he was a group captain and station commander of RAF Coningsby, so had no need to fly at all. The award of the DFC had been gazetted just a few days earlier. He was flying an 83 Squadron Lancaster on a raid on Gravenhorst, which was shot down by a night-fighter and fell over Holland; all aboard except the rear gunner were killed. At 43 years of age he was one of the oldest senior officers to die in Bomber Command. He had an experienced crew with him too, including S/L W.G. Wishart DSO DFC and Bar. William Geoffrey Wishart, at 22, was one of the youngest squadron leader navigators in the RAF, having earlier flown with 97 Squadron in 1943–44. Two other veterans in this crew had been F/Lt William Cross Fitch DFC and holder of the George Medal, as well as F/O D.A.J.W. Ball DFM who was also a navigator, previously with 207 Squadron.

★★★

On the night of 1/2 March 1941, on another raid on Cologne, 78 Squadron's Sgt Quincey, who had survived that crash-landing in February, failed to return after bombing (N1525 E). All his crew were killed, including two of his crew from the crash-landing. Jim Quincey was 26 years old and came from Hatfield, Hertfordshire.

An event of note occurred on the night of 3/4 March 1941. While the main bombing effort was against Cologne, 7 Squadron from RAF Oakington put up seven of their new Short Stirling bombers for a raid upon Brest. The Short Stirling was the first of Bomber Command's up-and-coming four-engined bomber fleet that would soon dominate the air war. Just one of the new bombers was lost, that being flown by S/L J.M. Griffith-Jones DFC (N3653). John Griffith-Jones had been awarded the DFC for operations flown with 149 Squadron in 1940. In his crew was Sgt W.T. Watkins, an observer/navigator, who had received the DFM at about the same time as Griffith-Jones, having flown twenty-eight operations with 149 Squadron too. It was due to his achievements that he had also been posted to 7 Squadron to help develop the new Stirlings. All eight men aboard the bomber were lost and have no known graves.

★★★

After several more days of air tests and night-flying practice, Tom Cooke was on the operational roster for the 10/11th, for a raid on Boulogne. That night he flew Z6490 with Sgt W.G. Rogers in the co-pilot's seat, and with three sergeant air crew, J.W. Boggis (navigator), R. Smith and M. Chadwick. Sgt L. Thorpe, his previous co-pilot, had now been elevated to crew captain and given his own crew; he was also out that night. French ports were again on the menu, 78 Squadron assigning just three bombers to Boulogne. They went out singly at 1830hrs, 1848hrs and Cooke at 1920hrs. All three bombed the primary target, the harbour and shipping therein, Cooke running in at 10,000ft and seeing their bombs bursting on wharves alongside the quay. Medium flak and searchlights were a nuisance, and Cooke watched another Whitley caught in the searchlights for several minutes, but there were no losses.

There were losses elsewhere, however, including a Halifax bomber. This was the first time the new Handley Page four-engined Halifax bombers were used in the Second World War, and one was shot down on its return over the south coast of England by an RAF night-fighter. Most of the crew were killed, just the pilot and one crewman surviving. Perhaps the RAF night-fighter crew had no idea the RAF were now operating with multi-engined bombers and assumed their target was a Focke-Wulf Kondor. The Halifax pilot had received the DFC flying a tour with 51 Squadron in 1940. Cooke landed at RAF Manston, Kent, as some of his instruments, including his air-speed indicator, had become unserviceable.

There was another lull in operations in mid-March. What flying occurred was mostly air testing of aircraft, some fuel-consumption tests, and gunnery practice, such as when Cooke took up his navigator, Sgt Boggis, and six air gunners, who each took a turn in the rear turret. So it was not until 27/28 March that Cooke was again sitting in the briefing room, seeing the wall map showing that tonight was a trip to Düsseldorf. The crew was the same with the exception of the rear gunner spot, this being taken by Sgt G.A. Fraser.

These pre-flight briefings were always a cause of immense interest and not a little apprehension. Crews were generally informed if there were any plans for operations that night, whereupon the RAF station would be effectively closed down so no one could telephone out to tell a wife or girlfriend to say that 'Ops were on!' This was for general security. As information is received from Group Headquarters, the various groups of airmen would be detailed as to bomb load, fuel required, time of attack and so on, which enabled everyone to begin planning for the night's operation. Pilots would check with their ground crews to see if their aircraft was serviceable and in all probability they would make an air test to ensure all was well.

The aircraft would be checked over by all the various trades, instrument workers, riggers, motor mechanics, armourers and so on. Later in the war radar mechanics too would take their turn. In the meantime, the crew briefing time would have been announced and just prior to the appointed time, the crews would start to congregate outside the briefing room. Once ushered in they sat together on long benches, with the more senior – or early arrivals – grabbing the few armchairs that might be around. All eyes would be on the curtain that was pinned across the map of Europe, each man wondering where the red piece of tape would stretch to tonight. No doubt some idea had been already gleaned from NCO air crew, who would have chatted up the ground crew personnel as to bomb and fuel loads. This would give an indication of a long flight (smaller bomb load, but more fuel) or a short operation (more bombs, less fuel).

Once it had been agreed that everyone was present, the doors would be locked after the senior station and squadron staff had entered. They would move down to the platform in front of the curtain and after everyone had been asked to be seated the squadron commander, or perhaps the intelligence officer, would take down the curtain and reveal the target for that night. An audible sigh or slight gasp would precede some audible whispers that would be silenced by the CO. He would then describe the target, its importance and why they were going there. No squadron commanders flew every raid, so some might conclude his part of the briefing with something like, 'Good luck, chaps – I wish I was going with you', which might elicit a good-natured hoot of derision.

This would be followed by a briefing from the weather expert, informing them what sort of weather they could expect en route to the target, over the target and on their return flight. This too was greeted with even more audible derision, each man knowing how often this 'forecast' had proven wrong and sometimes been downright useless. Then the intelligence officer would give details of where the known AA defences were believed to be situated along or near the planned route, what night-fighter activity they might also expect to meet, and searchlight positions. Radio call signs would be issued, wavelengths for various radio channels, and so it went on.

Finally, the station commander, or even someone from Group who had appeared, would add their words of encouragement to the assembled personnel. The air would be filled with cigarette smoke, a pall of grey smoke hanging in the air. Under this there would be talk about how difficult this target would be, or how easy – 'piece of cake tonight, chaps'. The brave ones would probably keep quiet; the anxious ones would start chattering to one another; the worried would be laughing nervously at the usual banter of stupid jokes. Everyone knew that tonight some of them would not return, but each man lived with that thought. Or the thought that it would be someone else. 'If you get the chop, Jimmy, can I have your egg at breakfast?' It always raised a smile but it was a serious question even if asked to be funny.

After the meeting, pilots and navigators would collect maps from the map store and mark them with the course and tracks they would use. Then everyone collected their parachutes from the store together with the life preservers – Mae Wests. In the crew room valuables would be handed in with any personal belongings (except for lucky mascots, cigarettes and a lighter) before changing into flight gear, checking helmets, flying boots, goggles, gloves and so on. Sandwiches and flasks of coffee would arrive for each man, and everyone would also be given an escape kit, some chocolate and perhaps some sweets. As the time drew near, buses or trucks would begin to screech to a halt outside and soon they would clamber aboard to start the drive around the peri-tracks to their aircraft, crews being dropped off at each individual aircraft's dispersal area. Some exchanges with their ground crews, some stinted conversations, a final 'Everything OK, Chief?' to which the flight sergeant would nod and confirm. Too late now if it wasn't. There was the formality of the skipper signing the Form 700, which meant he was happy to take over responsibility for his aircraft. A quick walk round to check the obvious things, such as ailerons, flaps etc., and the rest of the crew would feel happy. Depending on time there might be a minute or two to have a last smoke and a chance for a final pee. In some squadrons this might be done up against the rear wheel, which was not liked by the ground personnel because of the element of corrosion that could occur on the metal elements.

Then it was time to get on board. The two pilots and navigator would climb in and move to the cockpit area. The wireless operator would follow, to his spot, while the rear gunner would squeeze his way into his turret right at the back. More final checks and a quick check of the oxygen bottles and intercom to ensure all worked satisfactorily. With everything seemingly okay, it was soon time to start engines. The raid was on.

★★★

Eight Whitleys were on the line on 27/28 March, and six bombed the primary target while one returned early due to wireless problems. One did not get back. It was a pretty low-key affair, with just thirty-nine aircraft attacking the city, twenty-two Hampdens, thirteen Whitleys and four Avro Manchesters. The Manchester was another new bomber in the RAF's arsenal, but with just two engines it was underpowered; however, fortunately it was later developed into the mighty four-engined Avro Lancaster. Cooke took off at 1924hrs and on the way out he later reported seeing a white revolving light beacon on the island of Schouwen, on the Dutch coast. The target was not difficult to locate and Cooke made his bomb run from a height of 15,000ft, which resulted in producing a large red-coloured fire. As they headed for home Cooke spotted an aircraft held in searchlights for some ten minutes by six of the flaring lights, but its pilot seemed to switch on his IFF (Identification, Friend or Foe) light and the searchlights lost it. Cooke was back on the ground at 0015hrs, but at Langhan, not Dishforth.

The new squadron CO, W/C B.V. Robinson was operating on this raid and he dropped five flares over the target in order to identify the aiming point positively, seeing two of the flares shot down by light AA fire. However, he bombed successfully. Basil Robinson would receive the DFC in July, and in 1943 he would add a Bar, by which time he was with 35 (Pathfinder) Squadron and had also added the DSO and AFC to his list of decorations.

The squadron's loss this night was P/O K.F. Seager and crew in Z6470 G. He fell to the guns of another pilot from NJG1, Oberfeldwebel Gerhard Herzog, of the 2nd Staffel, his second night victory. Half an hour later Herzog downed a Wellington on a raid on Cologne. Another pilot from NJG1 shot down a Manchester on the same night. Carried in Seager's machine had been a Royal Navy sub lieutenant, A.J. Hold, going along to see what it was like.

Two other aircraft were lost going to Düsseldorf, a Whitley of 10 Squadron whose crew had to bale out on their return to England, but all got down safely, and a Manchester of 207 Squadron. This bomber seemed to have been hit by flak and at some stage by a night-fighter. As the aircraft was going down, the pilot, F/Lt J.A. Siebert DFC, ordered his crew out but, as in so many cases, he remained at the controls until he knew all had done so and thus left little time to get out himself. In the event he hit the ground before his parachute deployed and he was killed, but all his crew were saved even if taken prisoner. John Siebert had won his DFC with 44 Squadron in 1940.

Another loss this night was from a force that raided Cologne. A Wellington of 9 Squadron, flown by F/Lt J.T.L. Shore was attacked by a night-fighter flown by Oberleutnant Walter Fenske from III./NJG1 over Belgium, his first victory. Shore's radio operator got off a message to say they were going to force-land, and all became prisoners. However, Shore managed to escape some weeks later and got home via Sweden. He was awarded the Military Cross, but was killed in a Lincoln crash after the war, as a wing commander. One of his crew, P/O J.L.R. Long, a Bournemouth lad known as 'Cookie', was sent to Stalag Luft III and was one of the fifty escapees murdered by the Gestapo in March 1944.

★★★

Cooke's next mission was his nineteenth and last with 78 Squadron. The target was Brest on 30/31 March. Again the target was the German battleships kept there, the *Scharnhorst*, *Gniesenau* and the *Prinz Eugen*. It was fairly routine and an equally routine result – no hits achieved. The only good thing was that Bomber Command sent 109 aircraft there and 109 returned home. Cooke had Sgt B. Ward with him this night instead of Fraser. They took off at 1915hrs and were back at 0155hrs, having bombed from 15,000ft. The stick straddled the dock area and the flak and searchlights did not prove a major problem.

On this raid 103 Squadron lost its commanding officer, W/C C.E. Littler, upon his return. Trying to make an emergency landing, he had to bank steeply to avoid hitting a house and his Wellington (R1043) hit a tree and crashed near Yeovil, Somerset. Little was the only fatal casualty, although all of his five-man crew were injured.

Another Wellington from the same squadron (W5612) was attacked by a night-fighter as its pilot, S/L Mellor, was landing at Newton shortly after midnight. Mellor managed to make a successful forced landing in a field about a mile from the airfield. All his crew survived and only he was injured with cuts about his legs. In point of fact Mellor was not at the controls, having handed over to his second pilot who was on his first mission. They also hit a telegraph pole and the aircraft had begun to disintegrate.

A Blenheim of 101 Squadron (T2281) also became a casualty. Sgt L.E. Kiddie overshot on landing at St Eval and crashed into a field. He and his observer were killed and his gunner injured.

Early in April 1941, Brest was the target on the 4/5th, on which date 106 Squadron was to lose its commanding officer, 32-year-old W/C Patrick Julian Poleglese, from Cornwall. He did not return in his Hampden (AD738) after being shot down by AA fire over St Renan, by Finistère, and his crew were killed, the only loss of the night.

A few days later, on the night of the 9/10th, 12 Squadron lost its CO, W/C Vyvian Quentery Blackden, aged 34, a married man who left a wife in Horam, Sussex. It had been a busy night for Bomber Command, with bombers going to Berlin, Emden and Vegasack, as well as some mine-laying sorties. Blackden and his Wellington (W5375) went to Emden and was shot down by Oberleutnant Egmont Prinz sur Lippe-Weissenfeld of IV./NJG1 over Holland. It was the German's third night kill and he would go on to amass a score of fifty-one before being killed in a flying accident on 12 March 1944. An Austrian, from Salzburg, he was aged 25 and had received the Knight's Cross with Oak Leaves. Vyvian Blackden was the son of Brigadier General L.S. Blackden CBE (his mother Mary was an MBE), of Marden, Kent, and his two brothers had also died in action. His elder brother, Second Lieutenant Arthur had died in the Great War with the Royal Field Artillery, in September 1916, while his 31-year-old brother Walter had been lost flying with 224 Squadron of Coastal Command in November 1944.

★★★

Sgt Tom Cooke was now to have a change of aircraft and a change of squadron. In April 1941, 104 Squadron was re-formed at RAF Driffield, Yorkshire. Until now this had been a training squadron for 6 Group of Bomber Command and became No. 13 OTU. When it was decided to re-form the unit back into a front-line squadron, experienced crews from other squadrons needed to be posted in, and Cooke was one of them.

RAF Driffield is near the town of Great Driffield and only a few miles inland from the North Sea coast, just down the road from Bridlington. Although he may well have been sad at leaving 78 Squadron, at least he would be flying Vickers Wellington II bombers, the aircraft on which he had received his OTU training back in the summer of 1940. Cooke became a member of 'A' Flight under S/L Philip R. Beare DFC, formally with 102 Squadron, while his new squadron commander was S/L D.G. Tomlinson DFC. Dennis Tomlinson had previously been with 10 Squadron at RAF Leeming, had received his DFC at the end of 1940 and was a pre-war pilot.

Cooke's first flight with his new squadron was on 13 April and for the rest of the month, as well as the first week of May, he and others were engaged in local flying, mostly getting used to their new aeroplane type. Towards the end of April he seemed to have teamed up with a regular co-pilot, Sgt Huggins, while the rest of the crew were P/O Verver, navigator; Sgt Haines and Simokin as First and Second WOp/AGs; and Sgt Stevenson as rear gunner. There were six men in a Wellington crew as opposed to just five in a Whitley. On the last day of April Cooke was given a night-flying test by his flight commander for an hour, then they were deemed ready for action.

Finally the new squadron was pronounced operational and the Cooke crew were scheduled for their first mission with 104 Squadron on 8/9 May 1941. Six Wellingtons left for Germany, four bombing Bremen, one bombing Wilhelmshaven and one returning early with rear turret problems. Cooke took off at 2318hrs in W5435 EP-F, reaching the target without difficulty, and they dropped their bombs from 15,000ft. There was a bright moon, just right for enemy night-fighters, but none were seen although the flak was heavy. A total of 133 aircraft had gone for Bremen and the main target was the A.G. Weser Submarine Works. They scored no direct hits, but the town was knocked about somewhat. One casualty that night was Sgt Lawrence Thorpe and crew of 78 Squadron (T4147 D). Thorpe, who had been Cooke's co-pilot back in January, came from Leytonstone, Essex, and was aged 20. It would have been a sad moment for Tom Cooke.

The next night they were on again, this time heading for Ludwigshaven and its neighbouring town Mannheim. Cooke took off at 2214hrs, along with six other crews, and carried out a straight and level bombing run from 13,000ft, dropping bombs and incendiaries. All were seen to fall in the target area, where fires started. It had been a seven-and-a-half-hour trip.

★★★

The night of 10/11 May saw yet another bomber commander go missing. W/C Herbert Reginald Dale, of 15 Squadron, failed to return from Berlin in Stirling N3654 LS-B. Dale was 33 years old and left a wife in Longparish, Hampshire. The Germans buried him in Bergen's general cemetery. He had become another victim of Oberleutnant Lippe-Weissenfeld of IV./NJG1, his fifth victory. Only Dale received a burial, the rest of his crew have no known graves.

Another Stirling downed by a night-fighter this night came from 7 Squadron. Flt/Lt N. Williams DFC RNZAF was caught by Feldwebel Heinz Säwert of I./NJG3, his fourth victory. Neville Williams had received his DFC in 1940 whilst flying with 75 (New Zealand) Squadron. On a July night of that year he had been on a raid to the Ruhr and on the way back his Wellington had been attacked by three enemy fighters. Despite his aircraft being riddled with gunfire, his rear gunner, Sgt L.A. White, claimed two of the German aircraft shot down and the third driven off. Lewis White received an immediate DFM.

★★★

In between operations Tom Cooke, according to his flying log book, seems to have been one pilot chosen to take up new second pilots and to give them instructions on both day circuits and landings, and on night flying. However, it was back to the main task on 15 May, this time the target being Hannover. The detailed aiming points were the post office and telephone exchange, but how accurate the planners expected their bomber crews to be is unclear. However, 101 bombers were sent over to try, including eight Wellingtons from 104 Squadron. These had mixed fortunes. One failed to reach the primary target and so bombed Cuxhaven instead. Another aircraft, W5479 EP-W, flown by the squadron CO, was struck by lightning after bombing which knocked out the IFF, but they got home. Another Wellington force-landed at Malton upon its return, but there were no crew injuries. Cooke, with his usual crew, took off at 2225hrs, bombed from 14,500ft and saw bursts on the target and fires started.

This night saw Tomlinson's last operation with his squadron, with fate trying hard to be a nuisance with that lightning strike. Perhaps he was chancing his luck for he was no longer officially in command. On the 11th, four days earlier, a new CO had arrived, W/C W.S.P. Simonds. William Simonds was another pre-war pilot, having been made squadron leader in early 1939. He would be awarded the DFC after Tom Cooke left 104 Squadron, for his part in the same operation as Cooke's former pilot, George Holden, got his DFC, a large-scale attack on La Pallice that July.

Three nights later it was Kiel. Ten Wellingtons had been prepared but in the event two failed to get away due to engine troubles. All the others reached the target and bombed with some success, although cloud, haze and reflection from fires prevented accurate observation. Cooke had got off at 2259hrs and bombed from 15,000ft, dropping one 1,000lb, three 500lb bombs and four containers of incendiaries. He and the crew also found difficulty in watching the results because of the reflected light from fires and ground haze.

Tom Cooke now took some leave. He had now completed twenty-three operations. He was back on 7 June but only flew twice before his twenty-fourth operation, which came on 13 June. At least nobody had bent his 'personal' aircraft, *F for Freddie* (W5435), in his absence. The mission was to attack railway installations and yards at Schwerte, to the east of Essen in the Ruhr Valley. Bomber Command had sent eighty-four aircraft to this target the previous night but ground haze made it difficult to locate and only forty-one bombers had bombed. Now, on the 13th, forty-two aircraft would try again, although only six of them would be Wellingtons and these came from 104 Squadron. In the event only four located the target and bombed; Cooke and one other crew failed to find the target due to thick cloud and so bombed nearby Dortmund instead. Cooke made his run-in from 9,000ft and let go three 500lb and one 250lb bombs, plus six containers of incendiaries. Explosions were seen and fires began. They had left at 2308hrs and were home by 0500hrs. Cooke noted in his log book: 'Clouds 7,000 feet, descended to 3,500 feet, target not identified, returned to Dortmund. Widespread fires started. Fire Raiser.' His comment about being a 'fire raiser' was because in recent attacks towns had been bombed with incendiaries following bombing with high-explosive bombs. This was so the bombs could create wreckage amongst buildings and factories which could be set alight more easily with falling incendiaries. There were several references to 'fire raisers' in the newspapers of the day.

***

There was a sortie flown on 9 June 1941 that was a departure from the normal bombing operation. Termed as a reconnaissance, it was in essence a mission to find and sink enemy shipping off the French and Belgian coasts. This was 'bread and butter' for some of the Blenheim squadrons of either Bomber Command or, more usually, Coastal Command. That day eighteen Blenheims, four Wellingtons and two Stirlings were sent out, and some shipping was attacked off Dunkirk, The Hague and Terschelling, although none was sunk. Two of the Blenheims from 18 Squadron were lost, one shot down by a Me 109 fighter, the second last being seen entering a fog bank off the Dutch coast. Two Blenheims were claimed by the Germans, one by Me 109 pilot Leutnant Wolfgang Kosse of V./JG26, the other by Feldwebel Heinz Ahnert of III./JG52, neither flying the Me 110 night-fighter. Kosse was the Staffelführer of the 5th Staffel, and this was his seventh victory. For Ahnert of JG52 this was his second victory.

JG26 was also involved in the action against the Wellingtons, Oberleutnant Walter Schneider shooting down R1758, a Mk Ic flown by the CO of 9 Squadron from RAF Honington, W/C Roy George Claringbould Arnold, aged 30, another married man who left a wife in Daventry, Northamptonshire. The Wellington went into the sea off Zeebrugge with Arnold the only loss, the crew being able to bale out to become prisoners of war. It was Schneider's twelfth victory.

A second 9 Squadron Wellington (T2620), piloted by F/O D.F. Lamb DFC, was brought down by AA fire, all crew members except the rear gunner being killed. Sgt W.A. Eccles ended up in Stalag Luft VI at Heydekrug. Douglas Lamb had received his DFC earlier in the year with 9 Squadron. Schneider was killed in a flying accident on 22 December 1941 having achieved twenty victories.

★★★

Three nights after the Schwerte trip, Cooke was to find it necessary to go in low again, on a mission to bomb Cologne on the 16/17th, and once again he would note 'fire raiser' in his log book. Forty-nine Wellingtons and forty-two Hampdens were sent to Cologne this night. Ten of the former came from 104 Squadron and all reached the target and bombed it. One Wellington was attacked by a night-fighter and was shot up, the second pilot being wounded. The captain had been Sgt Michael de Beauchamp Collenete and for this and other operations he would received the DFM in May 1942. His aircraft had been set on fire during the attack, although his crew managed to put it out. So badly damaged was his aircraft, W5394 EP-X, that he had to make a crash-landing at RAF Oakington. His hydraulics had been hit so, unable to halt his landing run, he overran the aerodrome perimeter.

Cooke and his crew had to descend to 4,000ft before they identified the target, letting go three 500lb and one 250lb bombs, and no less than eighteen containers of incendiaries. A bad oil leak in the front turret made the bomb aiming by P/O Verver difficult, but the crew observed their incendiaries burning close to the aiming point. Having taken off at 2251hrs, they were back at base by 0434hrs for their bacon and egg breakfast after de-briefing.

His former 78 Squadron lost another aircraft on this raid, Whitley Z6492, piloted by P/O D.S.W. Lake. Denys Lake was 21 years old and came from St John's Wood, London.

Another loss on this night was a Wellington of 103 Squadron, attacking Duisburg. Its pilot was S/L D.D.A. Kelly who, it had been noted, had been Mentioned in Dispatches three times. He and his crew all perished. Kelly was the son of Brigadier D.P.J. Kelly OBE MC, from Barnes, south London, while his brother Piers Kelly had been a Battle of Britain pilot flying with Sailor Malan in 74 Squadron. Piers was awarded the DFC in 1943 and he would retire as a group captain.

Two nights later, 18/19 June, it was back to Bremen, and a more reasonable bombing height of 10,000ft. Visibility (due to ground haze) hindered the attack, certainly by the six Wellingtons from 104 Squadron, but Cooke ran in at 10,000ft with one 1,000lb and five 500lb bombs, but they only noted that they fell within the assigned target area. One crew, unable to find the target, decided to drop its bombs on a concentration of searchlights and AA positions at Wesermunde, which no doubt gave them some personal pleasure and satisfaction. For Cooke it was another six hours and fifteen minutes in the log book, and operation number twenty-six in the bag.

Cooke's old 78 Squadron suffered two more losses on this Bremen raid. P/O T.C. Richards in Z6661 fell south-west of Oldenburg, Germany, with all aboard killed. F/Sgt V.H. Marks and his crew in Z6560 were never seen again.

Tom Cooke's final operation with 104 Squadron came on 25 June, and this time his second pilot was Sgt Hodge, while his Second WOp/AG was Sgt Davey. The target was Kiel again and 104 Squadron put up nine Wellingtons, Cooke taking off at 2232hrs. His primary target was the Krupps shipbuilding yards and he carried out an attack from 10,000ft. Flak was heavy and a close explosion sent shards of metal shrapnel into the cockpit, hitting the instrument panel in front of him. Bombs were seen to burst on target and fires broke out on the quayside. They even dropped propaganda leaflets over the port as they flew off.

He landed back at 0435hrs to find his first tour had come to an end. The number of operations a pilot was required to make to complete a tour of bombing operations varied from time to time, and even from pilot to pilot. Once the bombing campaign against Germany settled down to a routine, thirty operations could be said to be the norm, although sometimes a squadron commander might feel that a particular pilot may be showing signs of tiredness or nervousness and decide that one or two operations short of the norm was enough. Not that there is any suggestion that Cooke was showing signs of either. He had been operating since 7 October 1940 and most of his targets had been in Germany, or places such as Brest or Bordeaux, even a couple to Italy, so he had done his fair share. Otherwise, it was also deemed to be enough if a pilot had flown 200 operational hours.

He remained with 104 Squadron until July began, probably taking the time to give Sgt Hodge time to become more familiar with the Wellington prior to him taking post as aircraft captain. His last flight was on 2 July, still flying his *F for Freddie* (W5435) which he would now leave behind. He had flown all eight missions in this Wellington while with 104 Squadron, and it would eventually be written off in a crash-landing at Thewhitts Farm, Boroughbridge, Yorkshire, on 3 September 1941. It crashed on returning from a raid on Frankfurt, while attempting to land in poor visibility, but the crew, despite injuries to them all, survived the experience.

Cooke would now be rested and, on receipt of a posting, was off to No.22 OTU at RAF Wellesbourne, coming under the watchful eye of the 'B' Flight commander, S/L W.H. Shaw. Walter Shaw would later be awarded the DFC and Bar whilst commanding 83 Squadron.

No.22 OTU flew Wellingtons so Cooke did not have to change aircraft type. Having done quite a bit of training while with 104 Squadron, it must have appeared to 'higher authority' that he had something of a knack for instructing. However, merely being a pilot did not necessarily give him the skill that enabled him to pass on experience and know-how to embryo pilots straight out of flight school. Of course, being what was called 'a screened pilot', that is one not flying operational sorties against the enemy, did not mean he was immune from death and danger. Some thought that taking new and inexperienced pilots up during day and night exercises could be just as hazardous as flying over Germany. There may not have been flak, searchlights or enemy night-fighters, but there were scary moments while in the hands of a new pilot still trying to find his feet in the air. Only time would tell if Cooke would survive his 'rest' period.

★★★

During his period with 104 Squadron, the unit had not suffered any serious casualties. However, his old 78 Squadron had not been so lucky and had lost ten Whitleys during this time. Z6483 had crashed on its return from Cologne, the crew baling out over the UK on 3/4 May 1941. T4147 *D*, as mentioned earlier, had failed to get back from Bremen with his former co-pilot Lawrence Thorpe in command, on the 8/9th. Unteroffizier Pross of III./NJG1 had shot down Z6493 *Z* over Holland on the night of 16/17th when returning from Cologne, while on the 28/29th Z6484 had not returned from Kiel.

In June Z6571 crashed returning from Dortmund on the 8/9th and all aboard were killed. A raid on Cologne on the 15/17th had Z6492 *K* lost with its crew, and on the 18/19th Z6560 and Z661 didn't make it back from Bremen and, again, all crew members died. On the 29/30th Z6664 and crew were lost on a Bremen raid, and Z6558 went down raiding Cologne on 2/3 July, shot down by Leutnant Reinhold Knacke of II./NJG1 over Holland, killing everyone on board. It was the German's eighth victory and he shot down a Hampden a few minutes later for his ninth. Knacke would go on to claim forty-four victories before his death in action on 3 February 1943. He received the Knight's Cross with Oak Leaves.

One has to wonder if Cooke would have survived if he had stayed with 78 Squadron. He had been on the 8/9 May raid and Bremen on the 18/19th. Was it luck? The chances of surviving a tour of night operations were always stacked against the crews that nightly went out over enemy territory. Experience and skill might make a difference but, as any former Bomber Command air-crew member will tell you, there were no guarantees. You either made it or you didn't.

4

ON REST – INSTRUCTING

RAF Wellesbourne was in Warwickshire, just to the east of Stratford-upon-Avon, or to be precise, Wellesbourne Mountford. No.22 OTU were supposed to train three crews each fortnight, an output that was quickly doubled. Bombing practice used the range at Prior's Hardwick. Just after Cooke arrived there the base had a satellite opened at nearby Stratford to help relieve the pressure on training. The down side, as far as Cooke was concerned, was that his new home operated older Wellington IC machines rather than his more recent Wellington Mk IIs.

However, with almost 567 flying hours in his log book, S/L Shaw would have welcomed the new man, and he in fact took him up for his first flight on 6 July, on an air test – or was it a pilot test – for thirty minutes in X9701. Almost daily for the next few weeks he was instructing two sergeant pilots, Turner and Robb, and at the end of the month these had changed to Sergeants Vautour and Wityck.

Two things then happened to Tom Cooke. Firstly, in August, he was informed he had been awarded the Distinguished Flying Medal, a recommendation having been made on 21 July by his old squadron; then, on 1 August, he was discharged from his present circumstances on appointment to a temporary commission. From then on he was an officer and a gentleman – a pilot officer RAFVR. He was now eligible to upset long-serving regular RAF NCOs even further!

The recommendation for his award was written up and signed by 104 Squadron's commanding officer, W/C W.S.P. Simonds, and approved by the Air Officer Commanding (AOC) 4 Bomber Group, Air-Vice Marshal C.R. Carr DFC AFC after a discussion with the station commander.[1]

The citation for his DFM appeared in the *London Gazette* on 23 September, and read:

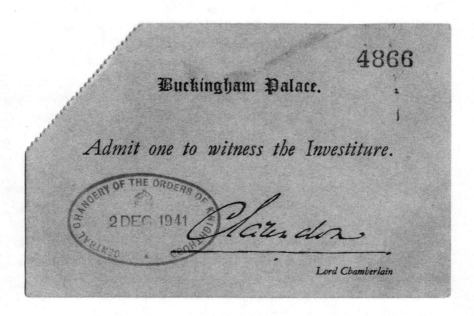

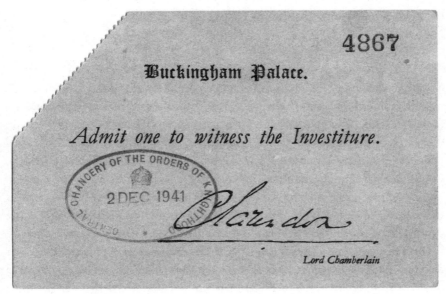

Two passes to his investiture at Buckingham Palace, date stamped 2 December 1941 and signed by the Lord Chamberlain. This is when Tom received the Distinguished Flying Medal from HM King George VI.

Of the 28 sorties carried out by this pilot, 23 were successfully completed. Since Sergeant Cooke joined No. 104 Squadron, he has completed 8 operational trips as Captain of aircraft. On each of these occasions, he has displayed determination, courage and a fine sense of leadership and has pressed home his attacks to the full. Very strongly recommended for the award of the DFM.

Although twenty-eight operations are mentioned in this recommendation, Cooke only records twenty-seven in his flying log book.

★★★

Throughout the summer, autumn and winter of 1941, and early spring 1942, Tom Cooke diligently took on his role of flying instructor. He continued flying with pairs of pilots and individuals, both during the day and also at night. Most trips were of short duration of less than an hour, while others were in excess of two, but he seems to have been constantly in the air, so that his flying hours gradually increased and with it his experience. At the end of 1941 his hours topped the 700 mark and at the end of February 1942 there appears in his log book a famous signature, that of Hughie Edwards VC DFC, who at the time was the chief flying instructor at No.22 OTU.

★★★

Meanwhile, Bomber Command continued pounding the Germans with almost nightly raids upon its factories, military installations and towns. It was an unceasing battle, and virtually the only way Britain had of hitting back at the enemy, whilst trying desperately to damage the infrastructure that helped the Fatherland continue to wage war in Europe and the Middle East, let alone the epic struggle on the Eastern Front with the Soviet Union that had begun on 22 June 1941.

On the day of the invasion of the Soviet Union, Bomber Command lost its first American B-17 Flying Fortress bomber. Although designed and built as a day bomber, B-17s were purchased by Britain to see if they could become a useful asset in operations. While it later became the mainstay of the USAAF's daylight offensive over France and Germany from 1942 until the end of the war, with the US 8th Air Force in England, it was not something the RAF found a real home for, except later with RAF Coastal Command.

On 22 June one of the Fortress Mk Is that had equipped 90 Squadron at RAF West Raynham flew an air test. At the controls was F/O J.C.M. Hawley, assisted by American Lt Bradley of the US Army Air Corps. They had been flying in cumulous cloud at 33,000ft and somehow the aircraft had suffered structural failure. Wreckage was scattered over a wide area north of Catterick, Yorkshire, and apart from one man who baled out the other seven aboard all died. Amongst them was F/Lt J.B.W. Humpherson DFC, a successful fighter pilot who had seen action over France and during the Battle of Britain. Another loss was S/L D.A.H. Robson MB CH.B, who, as these letters show, was a doctor. No doubt he was gleaning information regarding the effects of high–altitude flying on airmen.

★★★

Very little of genuine excitement happened for Tom Cooke over these months, just a perpetual, perhaps even boring routine. However, his private life away from the RAF had developed, for he was courting Miss Constance Joyce Baker. Unfortunately we know little of how they met or how they managed to meet from time to time during his period as an instructor. One other diversion was his invitation to Buckingham Palace on 2 December, where King George VI invested him with his DFM.

In mid–March 1942 he was sent on an instructor's course at the Central Flying School (CFS) at RAF Upavon in Wiltshire. It seems odd that after so many months of being a flight instructor he should be sent on a course that would show him how to instruct. While at Upavon, being officially attached to No.11 Short OTU CFS Course, he flew Airspeed Oxford aeroplanes, and during flying he learned the art of 'patter'. This is where the pilot under instruction talks through what he is doing and going to do, to his instructor, in order to show thoroughly his understanding of what is happening and to give the instructor confidence that his pupil is acting correctly. His main instructor here was F/Lt Hatton, assisted by Flight Lieutenants Foster and Smith and P/O Lyon. Most of the flying was by day, with only three night flights recorded. At the end of the course, on 10 April, he was assessed as 'average' as a flying instructor, and the comment in his log book by the CO of the CFS was: 'Should make very good Instructor.' Considering he had been one for many months this seems a trifle fatuous. This CO was W/C G.F.K. Donaldson AFC, who as a group captain in 1944 would be awarded the DFC while commanding 117 Wing. While on his course, Cooke completed four hours in a Link Trainer, getting used to the updates to the Lorenz system.

★★★

Cooke was posted back to No.22 OTU on 14 April and it was back into the old regime the following day. He remained with 'B' Flight, under F/Lt J.C.

Cairns DFC, who had won his decoration with 10 Squadron in 1940, and then in late May he was off on another course, this time with No.1501 BAT School at RAF Abingdon. BAT stood for Beam Approach Training, formally No.1 Blind Approach Training Flight, flying Oxfords once more. He was on No.1 Course as a first pilot. Basically it was a place where pilots were taught to be talked down during bad weather and also using a beam system of approach. In other words, a pilot was in the hands of someone on the ground talking him down with the aid of radar, where generally the first sight of the runway was moments before touch down. He completed nearly eleven hours of day flying plus a further six hours in a Link Trainer.

★★★

On 17 April 1942, while Tom was instructing new pilots in the art of flying the Wellington, a Victoria Cross was won by a South African pilot in the RAF, F/Lt John Dering Nettleton, aged 24. Shortly before the war started he was on holiday in England and decided to join the RAF, where he was accepted for a short service commission in December 1938. In June 1941 he was posted to 44 Squadron at RAF Waddington to fly Hampdens. By the end of the year he had been Mentioned in Dispatches. By Christmas, his squadron had been chosen to equip with the new Avro Lancaster bomber, and by March 1942 had started to fly them operationally. A second unit, 97 Squadron (Pathfinders), also changed over to Avro Lancasters.

The next month it became clear that something was in the wind, for the crews of both squadrons were flying long cross-country flights in daylight, and then the orders came. They were going to fly a daylight bombing raid upon the Messerschmitt works at Augsburg, in southern Germany. If night-bomber crews had mixed reactions at briefings when they finally saw where the red ribbon stretched to their 'target for tonight', one can imagine the crews of 44 and 97 Squadrons seeing that ribbon stretching away towards Augsburg – and this was going to be in daylight.

At 1512hrs Nettleton and five other Lancasters headed out and later met up with six from 97 Squadron, and as they went out across the English Channel they were flying at 50ft. Shielded at first by a raid by Bostons of 2 Group, plus some 800 fighters that were making an attack some way from the Lancasters' route, they were fortunate not to encounter any airborne opposition. However, they flew too close to a German fighter base and Luftwaffe reaction was swift, engaging 44 Squadron's two 'vic' (V-shaped) formations. Attacked by a fighter from II./JG2, four of the Lancasters went down before the fighters, already short of fuel, had to break off.

Both remaining Lancasters reached the target but in the attack Nettleton's lone companion was shot down. Turning to return after bombing the target, Nettleton could now use the darkening sky to get home, which he did.

In the meantime, 97 Squadron, who had not met the fighters, reached the target and the alerted gunners. Two of the Lancasters were shot down in the act of bombing, a third pulling away with one engine on fire. In all, seven Lancasters failed to return. Nettleton received the VC before the month was out, and a number of DFC and DFM decorations – and a DSO – were also awarded. The raid had cost forty-nine members of air crew out of the eighty-five engaged.

Sadly, Nettleton failed to return from an attack on Turin in July 1943, on a second tour with 44 Squadron. Officially missing, his loss was not formally announced until 23 February 1944, the same date that the announcement was reported that his son had been born on the 19th.

★★★

Cooke returned to Wellesbourne on 30 May, but this time there was something in the wind. He no had no sooner dumped his gear than he was called to briefing – for operations. The commander-in-chief of Bomber Command had decided that he would send 1,000 bombers into Germany that night to raid the major city of Cologne. Today the RAF might call such a strategy by the title of 'shock and awe' and it certainly would shock the German nation and strike awe into their defensive systems.

News had been received as early as 25 May that something was on, and all aircraft were prepared for operations, which meant servicing them and keeping them serviced in readiness. On the 27th orders were received about the so-called 'Thousand Plan' and all personnel were confined to the base from 1330hrs; 'living-out' people were accommodated within the camp. In all, thirty-seven aircraft were on the line at Wellesbourne, but then the operation was postponed. On the 28th orders again came to stand by but yet again it was postponed. The same happened on the 29th, and the next day Tom Cooke arrived back. Just his luck!

Cooke was given a scratch crew. The second pilot was a Canadian, P/O F.T. Johnson; navigator, Sgt J.G. Cameron; and WOp/AGs Sergeants A.J. Owen and W.A. Austin. He was assigned Wellington R1522 – *C for Charlie*.

In order for the Command to have 1,000 aircraft ready to fly, aircraft and crews had to be taken from units other than frontline squadrons, which is why several OTUs were asked to have as many bombers and reasonably experienced or advanced training crew members to be made available. Obviously instructors such as Tom Cooke, with a tour of operations already behind them, became an obvious choice to be asked to 'volunteer'. In this way Harris got his 1,000 bombers, in fact some 1,047 of all shapes and sizes. No.22 OTU's diary records:

> Stood by for 'Thousand' plan. 35 Wellingtons (14 [from] parent station, 11 [from] satellite, 10 [from] Elsham) took part. 15 crews briefed at Parent Station at 18.00 hours and 13 at satellite at 19.30. Very heavy rainfall at time of take off. First aircraft airborne at 22.43 hours and last by 23.47 hours. 2 aircraft returned early, one owing to sickness of the Captain [actually the rear gunner], the other owing to generator failure. 4 aircraft failed to return.

Three of the losses were aircraft from the parent station and there were some experienced men amongst them; all but one of them died, with the other being taken prisoner. F/Sgt C.J. Matthews had two DFM winners in his crew; F/Lt A.C. Hamman, the pilot of another, had received the DFC and Bar. A South African from Cape Town, he had joined the RAF before the war and had been awarded his decorations flying with 115 Squadron and later with 148 Squadron. F/O H.R. Blake DFC had a crewman with a DFM. Blake had been on 150 Squadron in 1941 and his WOp/AG, 23-year-old F/Sgt J.R. Wanbon, had completed a tour of thirty trips with 51 Squadron in 1941, including raids on Berlin, Pilsen, Leipzig and Turin. He had been injured in a bale out coming back from Bremen in February 1941. He left a widow in Norwich. P/O W.A. Fullerton DFM had been on 104 Squadron at the same time as Tom Cooke, while F/Sgt J.K. Napier had won the DFM after thirty trips as a WOp/AG with 51 Squadron in 1941.

All the other crews reported bombing the primary target, and even the crew that had to abort only did so after dropping their bombs on the port of Zeebrugge. Cooke and his crew took off at 2326hrs, bombed the target from 16,000ft with their two 500lb bombs and four incendiary canisters, and explosions were clearly seen. They landed back at 0353hrs. That historic night of 30/31 May cost Bomber Command forty-one aircraft. Fifteen aircraft from OTUs and two from other non-frontline squadrons were lost that night, several pilots of these being decorated airmen.

The city of Cologne was hit hard, with a recorded 2,500 fires being started and over 3,300 building destroyed, with nearly another 10,000 left with various degrees of damage. Fire rather than high explosives had been the major cause of the destruction. German casualties were surprisingly light at around 480, but over 5,000 more received injuries. Many others were bombed out and from a population of around 700,000, anything up to 150,000 fled the city after this raid. Cooke's log book entry doesn't give away much: 'Over 1,000 aircraft on target, very large fires left.'

A Victoria Cross was awarded for an action on this first 1,000-bomber raid. F/O Leslie Thomas Manser had been born in India on 11 May 1922, so he was just 20 years of age on that night. Turned down by the navy and then the army, he was finally accepted into the RAF in August 1940 and trained to be a pilot. His first operational squadron was No.50, flying Hampdens from RAF Swinderby. After only a few operations he spent a period at No.25 OTU and then had a brief stay with 420 (Canadian) Squadron until he finally got back to 50 Squadron, by now flying Avro Manchester bombers.

On the night of 30 May he had been assigned Manchester L7301 *D for Dog*, an apt name for it was not the best of aeroplanes. As he and his crew headed for Germany the engines began to overheat, but knowing it was a 'Maximum Effort', Manser carried on towards Cologne, even if no one would have blamed him for turning back. Despite intense AA fire over the target, Manser kept his aircraft flying straight and level in order for his bomb aimer to put their bombs on target. As he was finally free to make a turn the bomber was hit by flak and one of the bomb doors was blown away, and the rear gunner reported he was wounded. Two of the crew, Sergeants Baveystock and Horsley, went back to make sure their incendiaries had been dropped as Manser struggled with his crippled bomber that had now plunged to low level. Then the port engine burst into flames, the wing also beginning to burn, but later began to go out.

Heading for home, Manser ordered everything that could be to be thrown out to lighten the aircraft, but he soon became aware they were not going to gain enough height to reach England. Still losing height he told his crew to prepare to bale out, as the Manchester rapidly neared stalling speed. At last he had to give the order and everyone except Baveystock went out. It was Leslie Baveystock's duty to fix Manser's chest parachute to his harness, but Manser would have been aware that as soon as he let go the controls the bomber would stall in and crash, so ordered his co-pilot to leave and get out, which he did. By this time they were so low that Baveystock splashed into 5ft of dyke water just moments before the Manchester hit the ground and blew up. Manser did not survive.

Except for one crewman, all the others were helped by local Belgians to evade and all later got into Spain and then Gibraltar, and home. Their report about their gallant pilot led to Manser being awarded a posthumous VC in October. The other five members of the crew were either awarded the DFC or DFM, including of course Les Baveystock (DFM), who went on to win the DSO, DFC and Bar with RAF Coastal Command.

★★★

If Cooke had thought he might deserve a bit of a breather, he was wrong. The next day he was up in R1522 for an air, wireless and Lorenz test, and then that night the news came that a second 1,000-bomber raid was being planned for 1/2 June. This time No.22 OTU had thirty-four aircraft readied: twelve from Wellesbourne, thirteen from the satellite and nine from Elsham. The target this time was Essen. Cooke had the same crew and the same Wellington, his take-off time being 2255hrs. Reaching the target, his observer identified the primary target area and again two 500lb bombs and four incendiary canisters went down from 16,000ft. No results could be seen and then they headed for home. North of The Hague an unidentified enemy aircraft made an ineffective attack on them but all was well and they landed back at base at 0340hrs. It may have been reported as ineffective, but the German night-fighter pilot had been persistent, for Cooke noted in his log book that the fighter had made six quarter attacks over the Dutch coast from both starboard and port sides.

In contrast to Cologne, the OTU suffered no losses on this second raid. Most crews reported that the River Rhine was clearly visible all the way to Hamburg, and dummy fires were found, a useful guide to the town of Essen. The weather had been poor with 5/10th cloud and another thin layer of cloud over the target, but most aircraft bombed with the help of flares dropped by 3 Group bombers. Flak and searchlights did not play a very great part either. Two aircraft reported attacks by fighters without result and one aircraft was followed for some distance by four Me 109s without any combat taking place.

The mention of single-seat Me 109 fighters may be strange to some readers, but the Germans employed them at night where conditions were favourable, certainly in moon periods. They were not radar controlled but once the RAF bomber stream had been located and confirmed, as well as the likely target, Me 109s were sent up to try to spot bombers and attack them. The bombers might be illuminated by searchlights or picked up against a burning city below. These were known as *Wilde Sau* aircraft (Wild Boar) as opposed to *Zahme Sau* (Tame Boar) aircraft controlled by radar from both the ground and within the aircraft. These aircraft were Me 110s, Ju 88s and even Dornier 17s. Later these were joined by Me 210, Me 410 and He 219s.

Despite all the hype, only 956 aircraft went to Germany that night and 3 Group had indeed led the way with flares being dropped by the 'raid leaders'. The cloud and haze did hamper the bombing, which became quite scattered. Damage to the city was far less than that in Cologne, and thirty-one RAF aircraft failed to return. One such loss was S/L D.G. Tomlinson DFC, flying a Whitley of No.10 OTU. He had been Tom Cooke's CO and flight commander when 104 Squadron had been formed a year earlier. He and his crew all died after being shot down by

Hauptmann Alfred Haesler of III./NJG1, although he claimed it was a Halifax. It was his first night victory. Dennis Tomlinson was 26 and a married man. It must have been a shock for his wife, thinking he was less likely to become a casualty being away from a front-line squadron.

Another loss worth mentioning was a 7 Squadron Short Stirling flown by F/Lt N.E. Winch DFC (cited in the *London Gazette* on 16 March 1943, with effect from 14 May 1942). On board was Group Captain (G/Capt.) H.M. Massey DSO MC acting as 'second pilot', but in reality he was from 5 Group HQ out on a 'jolly' shortly before leaving for America. They were shot down and while everyone baled out successfully, Massey suffered a serious injury to a foot which kept him in a German hospital for some time. Once recovered, he was sent to Stalag Luft III where he became the senior British officer. Massey had won the Military Cross in the Royal Flying Corps in the First World War and in early 1917 had been shot down by the German ace Werner Voss, surviving with just burns while his observer had been killed. He had received the DSO for his work in Palestine in 1936. Due to his age (46), the Germans repatriated him in May 1944, which in some ways was strange for he could then report in some detail of how fifty of his fellow prisoners had been killed 'escaping', although suspiciously none had been wounded. In fact, under direct orders from Hitler, they had been executed, or to be precise, murdered. Norman Winch also ended up in Stalag Luft III.

In all, twelve bombers from Training Command were lost that night, eleven from OTUs and one from a conversion unit. While G/Capt. Massey had been the most senior loss on the Essen raid, the CO of 305 (Polish) Squadron, W/C R.J. Hirzebandt OBE DFC PAF had been killed upon his return in a Wellington. Trying to make a one-engine landing at Manor Farm, Billingford, Norfolk, having been damaged over Germany, the bomber crashed and all his crew were killed. One of these was F/O K.Z. Wieliczko, who had been awarded the George Medal for, with the help of a leading aircraftman, going into a burning crashed Wellington at No.18 OTU to save the life of its rear gunner.

★★★

During late 1941 and into 1942, while Tom Cooke had been instructing, several more airmen who would become involved in the 'Great Escape' and be murdered were brought down while operating with Bomber Command.

On 16 October 1941, on a raid on Duisburg, S/L T.G. Kirby-Green, a Wellington pilot with 40 Squadron, was shot down and he was the sole survivor of his crew. Becoming an integral part of Stalag Luft III's escape organisation,

Tom Kirby-Green was head of security, and known as 'Big S'. After recapture he was shot by a roadside.

Two were captured in June 1942, F/Lt J.C. Wernham RCAF of 405 (Canadian) Squadron on the 9th, and F/O Pawel Tobolski, aged 38, of 301 (Polish) Squadron on the 26th. James Wernham's 405 Squadron were part of the attack upon Essen, and that night of 8/9th the squadron lost three of its crews. All but one man from the other two were killed, but Wernham's crew was captured except for its pilot, F/Lt J.A. Maclean RCAF, who successfully evaded. Helped by the French Resistance, Maclean went along the famous Comet line escape route through Belgium, France, Spain and finally to Gibraltar. He was back in England in early September 1942 to receive the DFC. Curiously his DFC citation records that he was shot down one night in September 1942 rather than June, probably to cover his escape and evasion. Jim Wernham escaped from Stalag Luft III but was recaptured on a train and shot a few days later.

Tobolski and his crew were part of yet another 1,000-bomber raid, this time on Bremen, from which a massive forty-eight aircraft of Bomber Command were lost – a new record. The heaviest losses were from OTUs, which had twenty-three losses. Tobolski's pilot was W/C Stanislaw Krzystyniak, and all aboard Wellington IV Z1379 GR-A became prisoners after ditching in the North Sea and being rescued by a German lifeboat. This was 301 Squadron's commanding officer and he too ended up with Tobolski in Stalag Luft III.

Another Polish crew lost on the night Tobolski was shot down was one from 305 (Polish) Squadron, operating out of Lindholme. They failed to make it back and F/Lt E. Rudowski was forced to ditch his Wellington (Z8528 SM-R) off Great Yarmouth. They were picked up after eight hours in a dinghy, but one man did not survive. This was G/Capt. S.J. Skarżyński, Lindholme's station commander, who should not have been flying but went as second pilot. Once the aircraft had come to rest on the water, Stanisław Skarżyński stepped out of the cockpit on the wrong side, was hit by a wave and swept away. The others, clambering into the dinghy from the correct side, heard his calls for help, but a rough sea made it impossible for them to rescue him and he drowned.

In May 1933, Skarżyński, then a captain in the Polish Air Force, had made a spectacular flight across the South Atlantic from St Louis, Senegal, to Maceio, Brazil, in twenty and a half hours, thereby establishing a new international distance record of 3,582km (2,224 miles) for a light aircraft – the RWD 5bis.

Another Polish airman to mention is F/Lt A. Kiewnarski, navigator with 305 Squadron. On the night of 27/28 August 1942, his Wellington IV (Z1245) was shot down by a night-fighter near Eindhoven. His pilot and two others were killed, and another evaded capture, but he was put into the bag and ended up in Stalag Luft III. Antoni Kiewnarski was no youngster, having been born in January 1899. After being recaptured after getting away in the 'Great Escape', he was another airman to be murdered on the orders of Adolf Hitler.

★★★

Suddenly it was back to routine instructing for Tom Cooke. He was constantly in the air instructing pilots on both day and night flying. As one looks through his flying log book and reads all the names of pilots he took up, one has to wonder how many of them managed to survive a tour of operations once they eventually proceeded to operational bomber squadrons. Had Cooke noted their initials rather than just a surname it might be possible to see, but perhaps that would be too morbid to contemplate. In the meantime, his flying hours increased during the early summer and there are no references at all to any sort of problems or flying accidents. During a two-hour and forty-five-minute flight on 22 August 1942, taking Sgt Caldwell up to do some instrument flying, and making a quick landing at RAF Alconbury, his flying hours topped the 1,000 mark. His flight commander at this stage was S/L H.H.J. Miller DFC, another ex-Whitley pilot who had received his decoration flying with 77 Squadron in 1940–41.

Very occasionally Tom managed to get flights on the station's DH Tiger Moth or its DH Moth Minor, when he and another instructor would make visits to friends at other bases. These must have been welcome diversions from the Wellington, getting back to real 'wind in the hair' flying. In the meantime, his forthcoming wedding was in its final stages of preparation. Whether he had been reluctant to consider marriage in the middle of a war is unknown, but obviously if he did have any reservations his fiancée pushed them aside. Then, just days before the momentous event, Cooke found himself on operations once more.

A Maximum Effort must have been called for, as some OTU aircraft were asked to support Bomber Command's main force squadrons on a raid upon Düsseldorf on the night of 10/11 September 1942. This must have played havoc with his unit for they were in the middle of preparations to move from Wellesbourne to RAF Gaydon, a few miles east of Warwickshire. Wellesbourne's runways were going to be repaired. Five Wellingtons were made ready and all took off that evening; all five aircraft returned safely. Unfortunately the Cooke crew of Sgt R.A. Williams RCAF, F/Sgt K.E. Crosby, Sgt R. Cuffey RCAF and F/Sgt P.S. Murphy, who had taken off at 2030hrs, ran into problems. They were carrying four 500lb general-purpose (GP) bombs, but approaching the Dutch coast Cooke just couldn't get the bomber (R1621) to gain height so he was forced to abandon the trip. They turned for home and jettisoned the bombs into the sea. They landed at base at 2343hrs.

While the RAF Gaydon part of No.22 OTU did not suffer losses, their other Flight at the satellite station of RAF Stratford lost two Wellingtons. One was Wellington X9932 flown by Sgt D.L. Pablo and crew, which crashed in Germany. All were Royal Canadian Air Force (RCAF) men, Pablo being an American from Montana. The other was also crewed by Canadians, under Sgt J.D. Williams. Their R1616 fell to a night-fighter over Holland shortly before midnight. In all, thirty-three bombers did not return home, from a force of 479. Aircraft from No.16 OTU at RAF Upper Hayford lost a dispiriting five out of thirteen sent out.

★★★

In addition to those losses, a crew from Cooke's old squadron failed to return. No.78 Squadron had been re-equipped with Halifax II four-engined bombers, but the Düsseldorf raid cost them DT491, P/O C.J. Stevenson and crew all being killed. No.7 Squadron lost two Stirlings that night too, one being captained by F/Lt L.R. Barr DFC and Bar, flying with a scratch crew to help produce the Command's call for a Maximum Effort. Les Barr had won two decorations whilst flying with 15 Squadron in 1942 and had come to 7 Squadron as a flight commander. In his crew was Flight Engineer Sgt M.S. Pepper, who had also been with 15 Squadron from 1941–42 and his DFM had been of the immediate variety. During a raid on Münster in January 1942, his crew had just completed their bomb run and had turned for home when a night-fighter attacked after being caught in searchlights. Maurice Pepper was wounded in one hand and knee, but made his way to the astrodome where, standing on one leg and in considerable pain, he directed his pilot in evasive manoeuvres during what was thought to be fifteen successive attacks. In his pilot's opinion, the aircraft would not have survived without Pepper's performance that night.

One of Barr's crew, the navigator, P/O P.G. Freberg RCAF, had baled out west of Düsseldorf and began to evade to the west through the Ruhr Valley. Eventually he reached the River Maas and, finding a small boat, managed with the aid of a plank of wood to paddle across before it sank. Fortunately he carried an escape map which enabled him to find his way into Belgium and, even more fortunately, he came into contact with someone who put him in touch with the famous Comet escape line. Taken across into Spain, he returned to England from Gibraltar on 25 October. He was awarded the DFC and returned to operations with 7 Squadron. Sadly this gallant Canadian, Philip Freberg, was killed in action on 11 April 1943 during a raid on Frankfurt. His Stirling aircraft (R9275 MG-Y) crashed at Koerich, 14km west-north-west of Luxembourg, and they are believed to be the only Bomber Command crew to lose their lives in the Grand Duchy of

Luxembourg during 1943. Included in this crew was F/Sgt R.H. Genesis DFM, the flight engineer, who had flown some forty operations in Bomber Command.

***

Cooke was not going to be let off that easily following his aborted mission, for another Maximum Effort was called for on the night of 13/14 September. The target this time was Bremen and it would be his fourth visit to this city. He took Wellington R1776 with P/O F.T. Johnson, Sgt D. Heap, P/O J.A. Neville and Sgt Cuffey again. This time nine Wellingtons were scheduled and all took off without problems, but three failed to return. Cooke's bomb aimer let go one 500lb bomb and forty-eight 30lb incendiaries from 12,000ft, although results could not be observed. There are no remarks in the unit's war diary, but in his log book Cooke recorded: 'Operations Bremen. Flak intense and accurate. Aircraft hit 36 times. Fuel pipes severed, emergency procedure adopted.' Obviously the Wellington suffered thirty-six hit by bits of flying shrapnel from exploding AA shells, but nevertheless it was a daunting experience and one they were lucky to survive.

The missing Wellington R1588 was yet another all-Canadian crew, led by P/O F.H. de Nevers, which had taken off from Stratford. Two of the crew were Americans, both WOp/AGs who had, like so many Americans, found it easier and quicker to get into the war by way of joining the Royal Canadian Air Force. Frank de Nevers was 21 and came from Vandura, Saskatchewan. R1658, captained by Sgt J.H. Davies with four Canadian crewmen, and HD991, with Sgt G.S. Bickerton RCAF in command also went missing. John Davies was 22 and came from Pembrokeshire, and he and his crew have no known graves. Bickerton is known to have been shot down by a night-fighter flown by Leutnant Lothar Linke of V./NJG2, the German's ninth victory. In all, thirteen bombers were lost from various OTUs and two from conversion units. Fifteen such crews had failed to return from Düsseldorf on the night of 10/11 September, so these units were taking a beating.

There were two more flights after this raid on the 15th and 16th, the latter with W/C Blanchard aboard, again on a night instruction sortie. Then Cooke was off on a special leave. He and Constance were married at St Jude's church, Portsea, Hampshire, on 19 September 1942.

***

No doubt Tom Cooke was not scheduled for the raid on the night of 16/17 September because of his pending marriage. It was perhaps just as well for it proved another costly operation for Bomber Command and its OTUs. The target was Essen and another Maximum Effort was called for: 369 bombers were dispatched and thirty-nine were lost.

These included another instructor from Cooke's No.22 OTU, F/Lt John Dawson DFC, who had been decorated for his tour with 9 Squadron in 1941. Another experienced member of this crew was Warrant Officer (W/O) P.S.O. Brichta DFM RCAF. He had only recently completed a tour with 419 RCAF Squadron as a navigator. By the time his DFM was promulgated in the *London Gazette* on 22 September, he was dead. Part of his citation covered his actions on the night of 16/17 June 1942 during a raid on – as it happens – Essen. Anti-aircraft fire and an attack by a night-fighter set the underside of the fuselage, the front turret of the Wellington III and his own navigator's table on fire. Despite the danger of falling through the floor of the burning bomber, Philip Brichta began to tackle the blaze by stamping out the flames, disregarding his own safety. Having done this he accurately navigated his pilot back to England and safety. No.419 Squadron lost two Wellingtons on this raid, one being shot down by a German night-fighter we have mentioned before, that of Oberleutnant Prinz Wittgenstein of NJG2, who scored two victories that June night, his eighth and ninth in total.

Losses from other OTUs on the 16/17 September Essen raid totalled eight-een, with one more from No.1654 Conversion Unit. Therefore, almost half the night's losses were from training units, with both tour-expired and screened crew members as well as inexperienced combat crews during their final training for operational duties. Even amongst the main force squadrons there were serious losses. Two flight commanders were lost, S/L C.M. Howell of 106 Squadron, who was the pilot of one of three crews this squadron lost that night. Also there was S/L D.B. Barnard of 142 Squadron, their first Wellington III loss, but at least Barnard and two of his crew managed to evade capture. They had been downed by a night-fighter over the St Omer area. In fact four evaded but one was later captured. The others were all picked up by the Resistance and eventu-ally returned to England in January 1943.

Someone else of note who was shot down that night was Sgt W.S.O. Randle of 150 Squadron. At 16,000ft on the way to the target, his Wellington III (BJ877) was hit in one engine by AA fire, but he continued on and dropped his bombs on Essen. More hits by flak on the way home and then the other engine began to prove a problem, forcing the crew to bale out over Belgium. One crew member was captured, but Bill Randle and the rest of his crew all evaded successfully and returned to England. Randle was picked up by the Resistance and taken along the Comet line to Spain and Gibraltar, and was back in the UK on 25 October. He received the DFM before the year was out, was commissioned, later Mentioned in Dispatches and in 1945 received the Air Force Cross. He retired as a group captain and later became Chairman of the Royal Air Force Escaping Society in 1974.

★★★

Following his honeymoon, Tom Cooke went back to Gaydon, only to be advised of a new posting to RAF Mildenhall, in Suffolk, where he was to join 149 Squadron which was acting as a conversion unit while the main squadron operated from RAF Lakenheath. He flew himself there on the 27th in company with two pilot officers, one of whom would fly the Wellington back. One was his close friend John Cope.

At Mildenhall, Cooke was to convert to the Short Stirling, a four-engined bomber and one of the new breed of multi-engined bombers being made available to Bomber Command, along with the Avro Lancaster and the Handley Page Halifax. The Stirling was an odd beast. It was the first ever four-engined monoplane bomber to enter service with the RAF and the first to fly operationally in the Second World War. Back in 1936, when the Air Ministry had put out Spec. B.12/36 for such an aircraft, this specification placed a limit on wing span because the new design would need to fit into the standard RAF hangar. This forced the designers to build it with a very low-aspect wing ratio. With an all-up weight of 31 tons, the wing loading would have to be kept within reasonable limits. This had the unfortunate effect of limiting the aircraft's service ceiling, which would not be good news for bomber crews over Germany. As the Short Company also built the Sunderland flying boat it was natural for them to design a wing not unlike their waterborne success, although the Stirling would end up with its span at 99ft, whereas the Sunderland was in excess of 112ft.

Although the new design prototype made its maiden flight on 14 May 1939, it crashed and was totally destroyed. It had swung on landing due to one brake seizing up causing the undercarriage to collapse. A second prototype was flown successfully shortly before the outbreak of war. It was not until August 1940 that the first RAF squadron began to equip with the new type, and the first missions were flown in February 1941. The bomber was powered by four 1,650hp Bristol Hercules XVI engines, and it had a range of 2,010 miles when carrying 3,500lb of bombs or 590 miles carrying 14,000lb. The service ceiling, at 17,000ft, was far less than the Lancaster's 24,500ft or the Halifax's 24,000ft.

By this stage of the war the RAF was beginning to get away from its policy of having two pilots per crew. The Whitley and Wellington had soldiered on in this way since the war started, and only the Hampden carried just one, due to its small single-seat cockpit. Now the four-engined bomber crew would generally consist of seven men. These were a pilot, flight engineer, navigator, bomb aimer, wireless operator and two gunners, one for the mid-upper turret, the other in the tail. It must have seemed obvious at the start of the war that with two pilots there was a better chance of an aircraft getting home should the main pilot be incapacitated. However, if the aircraft did fail to return, it meant two fully trained pilots were lost.

It was not lost on the crew members that with just one pilot, they would be lost anyway if he was killed or seriously wounded, so many pilots gave some rudimentary flight training to a crew member who felt he could at least fly the bomber back to England, even if he could not land it. This usually fell to the engineer or even the navigator, if they were willing, and there are a number of instances where another crew member got the bomber back to England; even a few stories of them making a good or at least reasonable landing. Just to get them back over England gave them a chance to bale out over friendly territory should the embryo pilot not feel expert enough to try for a landing.

The one feature that did stand out with the Stirling was when it was viewed from the ground for the first time. It appeared huge, mainly because the nose and cockpit area was some 22ft from the ground. Pilots like Tom Cooke, when he first climbed in and sat himself down in the cockpit, found he had lots of room, in fact his words were: 'It's vast!' He had his first flight in one on 29 September 1942, in N6079, for a forty-minute dual instruction with P/O E.W. Whitney DFC. Earlier in the year Eric Whitney had his bomber severely damaged over the Ruhr by flak and then collided with a German night-fighter. However, he had managed to struggle back to the North Sea, where he carried out a success-ful ditching 8 miles off the Dutch coast. All his crew escaped (except the rear gunner), climbed into their dinghy and were rescued.

On 7 October 1942, No.1657 Heavy Conversion Unit was formed at RAF Stradishall, Suffolk, by merging 7, 101, 149 and 218 Squadron conversion flights. The base was between Haverhill and Bury St Edmunds, Whitney flying Cooke there on the 4th in preparation for the transfer. By the 20th Cooke was flying a Stirling by himself, getting used to the new machine as well us having four rather than two engines to deal with. In early November Whitney began instructing him on night flights, but after just four such sorties he was posted back to an operational squadron, No.15 at RAF Bourn, commanded by W/C D.J.H. Lay DFC, on 8 November 1942. He had just thirty-five flying hours on Stirlings.

W/C Douglas John Horatio Lay was a peacetime airman, having been awarded the DFC in 1938 as a pilot officer 'For gallant and distinguished services rendered in Palestine'. He had been awarded a Bar to his DFC whilst operating with 7 Squadron in 1942 as a flight commander.

Notes

1 Charles Roderick Carr had won his DFC in 1919 flying fighters with the North Russian Expeditionary Force. Born in New Zealand, he had served in the First World War with the army, Royal Naval Air Service and then the RAF. He also served in Russia, was part of Shackleton's Antarctic Expedition 1921–22, served in Egypt and on secondment to the Royal Navy on aircraft carriers. He retired in 1947 as Air Marshal Sir Roderick (Roddy) Carr KBE CB DFC AFC, plus French and Russian decorations. His last command had been as Air Officer Commanding-in-Chief of the RAF in India. For his command of 4 Group (1941–45) he was also Mentioned in Dispatches. He died in 1971.

5

BACK ON OPS – SECOND TOUR

RAF Bourn is situated 7 miles to the west of the university city of Cambridge, adjacent to the A45, and had only been in existence since 13 August 1942. It was able to accommodate about 2,000 personnel of all ranks and had hard-standing for thirty-six bombers. Tom Cooke was placed in 'A' Flight under the command of S/L K.D. Faulkner DFC. After W/C Lay left in December 1942, 15 Squadron was commanded by W/C S.W.B. 'Paddy' Menaul DFC AFC, who had been with the squadron earlier, in 1941. He retired as an Air-Vice Marshal CB CBE.

The reader is reminded that all operational RAF air crew were volunteers, thus nobody was forced to become air crew. Also, if one survived a tour of operations and was then screened, he needed not volunteer again for this dangerous occupation. Therefore, anyone who returned to operational flying for a second time – even a third time – did so without any coercing. They continued to be volunteers.

By this time Cooke had gathered a new crew together, all NCOs: Sergeants R.W. Lewis (navigator), J.S. Reed (First WOp/AG), E. Bell (bomb aimer), J. Harrison (mid-upper gunner), R.L. Beattie (rear gunner) and A. Collins (flight engineer). For the first few days the crew flew air tests, local flying, low-level bombing practice and fighter affiliation flights. The latter was where they would rendezvous with RAF fighters who would make dummy attacks on them. The bomber crew could then practise their tactics, the air gunners telling their captain which way to manoeuvre as each fighter made a pass. On 17 November the weather must have been poor, as Cooke noted in his log book that they were to fly a fighter affiliation sortie over Wittering, adding disdainfully that the 'fighters would not take off'.

Reg Lewis, Cooke's new navigator, was also interviewed on cassette by the Imperial War Museum, and they have again been gracious enough to allow us to have use of his words. Sadly Reg is no longer with us, but he left a wonderful account of his training and subsequent association with Tom Cooke:

Having joined the RAF my original training was at the ITW at Paignton, Devon where we learnt how to march, some basic history of the Service, rudimentary navigation theory, before sailing to Canada, where I ended up at No. 33 Air Navigation School at a place called Mount Hope, Hamilton, Ontario. I was there about four months and had about 100 hours of flying, 70% being in daylight, 30% at night.

I arrived in Canada on my birthday in August 1941 and about Christmas we moved on to No. 31 Bombing and Gunnery School, which was at Picton, Ontario. I spent about six weeks there, flying in Fairey Battles.

Lewis had, before he joined up, been bombed out with his family twice during the Blitz. Firstly this happened in Plaistow, where a bomb landed close by and severely damaged their house, forcing them to move out. At a new home in East Ham, four weeks to the day after the first house had been hit, a land mine completely destroyed the second house and the family lost virtually all their possessions. Little wonder he had no love for the Germans and admitted later that the idea of revenge was somewhat embedded in his mind. He continued:

Our Course finished on 2 February 1942 with an 'average' pass and I got my Observer's Wing,[1] became a sergeant and soon sailed back home, arriving in Liverpool. In May I went to No. 9 Air Observer Advanced Flying Unit in North Wales and for about a month did around 30 hours learning to navigate around England in wartime conditions. At the end of that we moved to No. 26 OTU at Wing, in Buckinghamshire, about July, flying now in Avro Ansons. This lasted until mid-September and it was here we began to form into crews.

At some time during this Course, there were a number of navigators, wireless operators and pilots, and left alone we were expected to form ourselves into crews of five. We were more or less left to ourselves to do this, and fortunately there was an equal number of each trade. In due course I found myself as part of a five-man crew, with Sergeant Bob Kidd, a New Zealander from Christchurch, as pilot, a bomb aimer, Sergeant Bell, who had been trained as an air observer, he and Sergeant Reed WOP/AG, both Geordies, plus Sergeant Beattie, a Canadian who was to be our rear gunner. While I continued to fly around learning to navigate, Sergeant Kidd was being trained to fly Wellingtons.

Then, on 9 September, to our surprise and shock, we found ourselves being briefed for an attack on Düsseldorf, in the Ruhr. We were going to carry four 500lb bombs, but in the event we suffered engine problems and had to abort after two hours, 45 minutes, and bring our bombs back. A week later we found ourselves briefed again, for a raid on Essen, with another four 500 pounders. We carried out this mission although I had some difficulty with my navigation on the way back and landed at Castle Camps, near the Suffolk/Cambridgeshire border. I had been flying back on dead reckoning and when I estimated we were somewhere in the area of Abbeville, I probably steered north-west in order to hit the English coast but we must have been a little east of that because I'm certain we flew up the east coast of England and had to seek the help of wireless stations to get on some sort of course. We landed very low on fuel and I later got a rocket from the CO.

Despite the number of embryo crews from various OTUs being ordered onto this operation, it was not another 1,000-bomber effort. In fact, this raid on Düsseldorf would only embrace the efforts of 479 bombers. Of these, thirty-three failed to return, including fifteen from the OTUs. No.16 OTU lost five Wellingtons and Lewis' No.26 OTU lost two, only one of the ten men in them surviving – as a prisoner. Lewis made no mention of this but continued:

Next we moved to No.149 Conversion Unit, then to No.1657 Conversion Squadron at Stradishall. Here the pilot had quite a lot to learn while navigators worked on learning about the Gee Box.[2] We had also picked up two more crew members, a flight engineer and a mid-upper gunner because we were now going to fly Short Stirling bombers. Sergeant Kidd then began an intensive training programme, and the rest of us were given a new pilot who had already become proficient on the new aeroplane. We got Flying Officer Cooke who by that time had already completed a tour of operations on Whitleys so knew what it was all about. He had been instructing at an Operational Training Unit, so I suppose we were very lucky to have an experienced pilot, and it was probably his bad luck to be given a crew who was not.

Cookie, as we later called him, had by that stage already been decorated with the DFM, and we spent two or three weeks flying with him going through various exercises. I was now using the Gee Box as a navigational aid, the only really accurate instrument that could, with limited range, give precise information on one's ground position at any time. It was very exact and a great boon to navigators. It was very simple to work, for it gave a series of positions indicated on a sort of cathode ray tube, rather like a TV screen, which could then be transformed into position lines on a map. It didn't require any skill at all really, but it was a great help in navigating the aeroplane.

At the end of the period of instruction we found ourselves posted to No.15 Squadron at Bourn, on the Cambridge/St Neots Road, in 3 Group, equipped with Stirlings, about 7–8 miles west of Cambridge. While our pilot was an officer the rest of us were sergeants, but we were extremely lucky to have Sergeant Collins as our Flight Engineer. He had been a boy apprentice in the RAF, trained at RAF Halton (therefore being known as a Halton Brat) before the war, so knew a lot about what made an aircraft fly. He had also completed a tour of operations, in Stirlings, so along with our pilot, while not an experienced crew, we had the makings.

★★★

The Cooke crew were not on the operational roster for the night of 18/19 November, which was just as well for the squadron had a problem. The target was Turin, Italy, but Stirling BF384 R crashed on take-off due to a severe crosswind, effectively blocking the runway at Bourn, fortunately without injury to the crew.

Finally, on the 20th came the crew's first mission. Cooke recorded in his log book that it would be his thirty-third in total and the target was Turin. This time 15 Squadron did not have a runway problem. They took N3669 LS-H. Eleven aircraft were on the line but in the event one went unserviceable and one failed to take off on time. All nine began to lift off at 1802hrs (S/L G.M. Wyatt DFC), the last at 1847hrs (P/O Hopson). The first six carried incendiaries, the last three large 2,000lb land mines, things that could cause massive devastation. Cooke was away at 1832hrs and was through the Alps and over Turin at 2222hrs. Coming in on a course of 125 degrees, he let go his bombs from 11,000ft, having followed the River Rip to the aiming point. They saw both bombs explode on target and as Cooke turned the Stirling for the trip home he could see the town covered in smoke from numerous fires. Eight aircraft landed back between 0145hrs and 0239hrs, except Cooke who did not touch down until 0305hrs, after some eight and a half flying hours.

The one that didn't make it was BK595 LS-A flown by Wyatt, the first one to take off. As Wyatt had approached the Alps one of his engines failed but he pressed on and managed to clear the mountains, then continued on and bombed Turin. It was doubtful if they could gain enough height to re-cross the Alps so it was decided to set course for Spain. They reached it safely but had to force-land shortly after midnight at Playa de Aro (Gerona), 10km south-west of Palamos. Here, after a brief internment, they were taken to Gibraltar and returned to England by sea, arriving on 26 January 1943. Wyatt had earlier flown with 57 Squadron. There was a change in flight commanders following Wyatt's loss, Cooke's 'A' Flight being taken over by Acting Squadron Leader H.T. Miles DFC RCAF. Later in the war he received a Bar to his DFC whilst operating with 408 (RCAF) Squadron. Reg Lewis again:

> We were only with 15 Squadron for a short time during which we flew just five operations. The first two were quite long trips for an inexperienced navigator like me. They were some 8½ hours duration. One was to Turin where we brought back a photograph plotted only ¾ of a mile from the aiming point, which in those days was deemed excellent. We then had two aborted trips, one to Stettin then one to Stuttgart.

An air test on the 22 November heralded another briefing for a night operation, this one being a further attempt to raid Stuttgart, flying W7581 *C*. Of the eleven aircraft scheduled, four were later withdrawn so just seven took off. This began at around 1800hrs, Cooke lifting off at two minutes past the hour. With him he took a new skipper, Sgt Ripley, to give him experience. Cooke carried two 1,000lb bombs and loads of incendiaries. Almost exactly four hours later he was running into the target from 10,000ft from the north over some broken cloud. During this run-up, he and the navigator pinpointed the River Neckar and the railway line, so were quite happy about bombing the correct spot, although more cloud covered the area as they let go their load. Everybody returned home despite the efforts of two Ju 88 night-fighters attacking, which damaged the starboard outer engine of F/Sgt W. McMonagle's BF355 *F*, forcing him to land at RAF Manston in Kent. He had been caught by searchlights so the Ju 88s found an easy target but not an easy victory. Cooke also noted in his log book that a night-fighter made an attack on his aircraft, but with no mention in the squadron diary it must have been slight. Cooke later recalled how landmarks helped locate the target:

> One problem we had was how to locate a particular target within a city – how does one do that? If you happened to have a lake handy or something prominent like that one could recognise in the dark, then you could do a timed run from it. You'd know from the briefing in the first instance if there was something to spot, and studying a map yourself, how long it would take from such a recognisable landmark, then steer a course for so many seconds, until, counting with your thumb on the control column, know when the estimated number of

seconds had elapsed. I would then ask the bomb-aimer if he could see anything as we should now be over the target area. It worked most of the time – good for those days anyway.

Targets near estuaries were a good deal easier, but at Hamburg the Germans had covered the two lakes there, but nevertheless, you still had the run up from the estuary. One was doing that sort of thing all the time. Lorient I remember, when bombing submarine pens, I went over Belle Isle and made a timed run-in from there. We actually saw the whole thing quite clearly, it was a moonlit night and at that time we were bombing from only about 7–8,000 feet.

When on Wellingtons we were told not to bomb above 10,000 feet and we were supposed to be all experienced chaps. At first we were told we'd all be fire-raisers and we would only carry incendiaries. Anyway it didn't come to anything and most chaps went in at 7–8,000 feet, almost balloon barrage height, so a bit dicey.

★★★

Losses on the Stuttgart raid were light, with just ten bombers failing to return. One of them was the first Lancaster Mk I lost from 460 Squadron RAAF from RAF Breighton. However, although four of the crew became prisoners of war, the pilot P/O D.T. Galt and two others evaded capture. David Galt was helped into Spain and returned from Gibraltar in January 1943, his two companions also getting home three months later. Galt's DFC was announced in February 1943, after his return, and the citation is both brief in length and in content: 'This officer displayed great gallantry, coolness, and presence of mind in hazardous circumstances when his aircraft was hit and set on fire by anti-aircraft gunfire.'

Another pilot who evaded this night was Sgt E.A. Coates RAAF, flying with 115 Squadron from East Wretham. His Wellington (BJ842 KO-W) was shot down by a Ju 88 night-fighter from IV./NJG4 over France and two of his crew were killed, with three others taken prisoner. Coates made a solo escape through France and into Spain, then Gibraltar, after fifty-five days on the run. He was home by mid-February 1943.

★★★

On 27 November there was to be a raid on Stettin and 15 Squadron put up six aircraft, but when they had just left the English coast there was a general recall. Cooke had again been taking a new pilot out for experience, a F/Lt Chave. The next night, 28/29 November, it was back to Italy, and this time he was to take

Sgt G. Ware too. Seven Stirlings were going from the squadron but it didn't turn out that way. Two aircraft were withdrawn at the last minute and two others aborted, one being Cooke's W7518. As Cooke wrote in his log book: 'Starboard engine failed and port inner throttle stuck open after take off. Bombs dropped in [the] Wash.' One supposes that this was experience of a sort for the understandably nervous 'second dickey'.

★★★

On the Turin raid, Bomber Command had another of its heroes receive the Victoria Cross. The pilot of a 149 Squadron Stirling (BF372 OJ-H) was Australian F/Sgt Rowden Hume Middleton, aged 26. By this time most of his crew had completed the required thirty trips of a bomber tour, but Middleton was still a couple short, so they decided to continue on until he had reached his thirty. Over the target they were hit by AA fire and Middleton was severely wounded. They struggled back to England, Middleton insisting on staying at the controls. Reaching the south coast of England, his aircraft barely staying in the air, he ordered his crew to bale out but only five did so before the Stirling crashed into the sea off Dymchurch. Middleton was awarded a posthumous VC and three of his crew received DFMs.

★★★

The next day, the 29th, Cooke took up R9192 for an air test but the undercarriage became unserviceable when the retracting jacks snapped. He makes no mention of a landing or taking off problem despite this happening, so one must assume he took it all in his stride. Cooke did not fly his old W7518 again, his next regular aircraft being BF411, although his next night mission, on the 2/3 December, was in R9168, the target being Frankfurt. Actually it was only 3 December really, as the three aircraft that left 15 Squadron's base did so at around 0200hrs. As all three reached the target they were aided by spotting a particular bend of the River Rhine near Mainz. All three were carrying loads of incendiaries and each aircraft dropped at differing heights: 12,000ft, 13,000ft and 14,000ft (Cooke). All three crews saw fires started after their incendiaries went down and one crew heard the master bomber giving aiming-point directions. Cooke took F/O J. Welford out for experience.

★★★

Losses for the 2/3 December raid were light, just three Halifaxes, one Lancaster, one Stirling and one Wellington. Another Stirling was badly damaged by flak and a night-fighter on the way back but the pilot got back only to have his undercarriage collapse on landing, although nobody aboard was hurt.

The three Halifaxes came from 102 Squadron, based at Pocklington. One came down on the outskirts of Mannheim and the other two were both shot down by night-fighters. S/L J.G.G. Walkington in W7916 crashed in France and was killed along with two others of his crew. Three others were captured but two evaded. One of these was W/C J.R.A. Embling, the commanding officer of 77 Squadron, who had decided to fly with 102 Squadron in order to '... assess the performance of some new photographic equipment'. In his report he says they were hit by flak but another suggestion is that they were shot down by a Ju 88 night-fighter. In any event, the aircraft was on fire and most of the crew baled out. P/O R.A. Haines RCAF, the navigator, evaded and got home by ship from Gibraltar in early 1943. Those captured were taken away by train but, during some confusion over carriages, W/C Embling managed to escape through a window and get away. He was later helped into Spain by the Resistance and once at Gibraltar was flown back to England in March 1943. He was awarded the DSO.

The other 102 Squadron crew was commanded by Sgt H. Morrissy DFM RCAF, shot down by Unteroffizier Ericher of II./NJG4, over Belgium. All eight men aboard were killed. Harry Morrissy, an American in the RCAF, had received an immediate DFM for his actions during a raid on Turin on 18/19 November 1942. When taking off, the top hatch over his head flew open and despite attempts by others of his crew it could not be properly closed and secured. Deciding to carry on despite the intense cold blast of air, especially when crossing the Alps, he continued on for an eight-hour mission and bombed the target rather than abort. It had been his twelfth operational sortie and, although notified of the award, the promulgation of it in the *London Gazette* dated 18 December, he did not live to read it.

Bomber Command's 2 Group of mainly light twin-engined bombers was always operating, either over the sea against shipping or against specific targets in occupied France, Belgium or Holland. Often these low-level missions against targets that really needed to be hit hard and destroyed, involved dangerous sorties in the face of fierce opposition by the Germans. One such mission worthy of note came on 6 December 1942, an attack on the Philips radio and valve factories at Eindhoven. Ninety-three aircraft were assigned the mission: forty-seven Lockheed Venturas, thirty-six Douglas Bostons and ten DH Mosquitoes, one being a photographic aircraft.

Severe damage was caused to the factories and full production did not reoccur for six months. However, nine Venturas, four Bostons and one Mosquito failed to return. Author Norman Franks knew one of the Ventura crew members, Sgt J.A. Wallis, wireless operator with 464 Squadron RAAF. Jack Wallis told Norman about this raid and about the Ventura, which was not a favourite RAF aircraft. The crews called it the 'pregnant pig' and, although it carried two machine guns in the forward nose section of the fuselage, they tended to cause the Perspex to become damaged if fired. Jack also said that this Australian squadron generally had Australian pilots and gunners, while navigators and WOps were British.

On the raid, Jack's aircraft was heading for home and had reached the Walcheren Island before being hit by flak. He thought they were flying especially low and would not have been surprised to have been brought down by a German bayonet! They crash-landed and all four aboard were captured, Jack having a large piece of shrapnel from an exploding shell embedded in his face. He ended up in Stalag Luft VI, where he met Larry Slattery, POW No.1 (see Chapter 1). Jack's parents had no sooner received the telegram that he was missing, when they received a second, informing them that their other son, Peter, mid-upper gunner in 158 Squadron, had been killed. He and his crew had taken off for a raid upon Mannheim on 6/7 December, but the undercarriage had failed to retract and, in trying to land, they had crashed. Two of the crew died, the rest were injured. Happily they did not have to wait long to know that their son Jack was alive.

Another Ventura lost on the Eindhoven raid was that of the CO of 487 (New Zealand) Squadron, W/C F.C. Seavill. Although he was an RAF officer he hailed from New Zealand. They were also downed by flak, crashing on Woensdrecht aerodrome, all four men being killed.

★★★

Cooke's squadron lost a crew on the night of 8/9 December. Sgt J.J. Blignaut, flying W7635 V, went on a mining trip and failed to return. Jochemus Johannes Blignaut is listed as British and has no known grave, although two of his crew were buried in Denmark.

Cooke now took over BF411 for his next mission, which occurred on 16/17 December. According to the squadron diary just three experienced crews were selected for this raid, which was against Deipolz aerodrome. Just to add some sparkle, Cooke was again asked to take a new pilot on this one, P/O W. Moffat. According to Martin Middlebrook's *The Bomber Command War Diaries* (Viking, 1985), eight Wellingtons attempted to bomb this aircraft depot on this date and one of them failed to return. In fact, it was Stirlings that made the attack, or at least the three from 15 Squadron did, and they did indeed lose one of their number.

Cooke took off at 1722hrs carrying small bombs and incendiaries, and bombed at 1937hrs on a heading of 270 degrees from 7,000ft, well below a large area of cumulus cloud at 15,000ft. He and his crew saw numerous fires started. The second aircraft, again with Sgt McMonagle in command, went in at 7,000ft too and as he bombed he came under attack from night-fighters. Cannon and machine-gun fire slashed by and into his bomber but his mid-upper gunner, Sgt E. Clark, opened fire and claimed one of the Me 110s shot down before he was badly wounded. A second Me 110 also scored hits before the gunners drove it off. McMonagle got back but landed at RAF Coltishall.

The crew that failed to return was that of Sgt F.S. Millen RCAF. He was flying R9168 *T*, the Stirling Tom Cooke had taken to Frankfurt two weeks earlier. The aircraft came down at Gortel, Holland, claimed by Leutnant Werner Rapp of I./NJG1, which was his first night victory. Only the rear gunner survived as a prisoner. Millen and one other member of his crew were American.

★★★

The Italian town of Torino (Turin) was Bomber Command's target for the night of 11/12 December 1942 and although only seven aircraft casualties were reported, two experienced crews were among them.

A Stirling of 7 Squadron (BF379 MC-D) flown by F/Lt W.T. Christie DSO DFM was hit by flak over the target, flying at 7,000ft, setting fire to the starboard outer engine; heading back they found the bomber would not climb sufficiently for them to get over the Alps, so he flew south and ordered his crew to bale out, after which the Stirling crashed near Fossano, Christie being killed. The rest of his crew were taken into captivity.

A Wellington III (BK514 EX-T) of 199 Squadron was being flown by the squadron commander, W/C C.R. Hattersley DFC. The bomber was hit soon after crossing the French coast and a fire started in the port engine. They began to lose height rapidly so Charles Hattersley ordered his crew to bale out. All did so, south of Paris, but one crew member died. The rest were taken prisoner, the skipper ending up in Stalag Luft III. Hattersley had received his DFC whilst with 44 Squadron in August 1940 against an aircraft factory at Dessan.

The New Zealanders of 75 Squadron suffered on the night of 17/18 December, losing four aircraft on a raid on the Opel works at Fallersleben, in the Ruhr. Three of the crews died and the fourth was all captured. One of the losses was the squadron CO, W/C V. Mitchell DFC, in Stirling BF396 AA-X. Victor Mitchell was a Scot from Elgin who had joined the RAF in 1936; he was 27 years old. Mitchell had decided to lead this small raid, going in low before climbing to 5,000ft for the bomb run. He took a new crew out with him. Victor Mitchell had won his DFC with 37 Squadron in 1940.

★★★

The squadron also suffered two casualties on the night of 17/18 December following some mining operations. W/C Menaul crashed BF356 *D*, while Sgt A.S. Forbes crashed BF380 *B* on landing. Both crews got away with it, suffering no injuries of note.

That was it for 1942, as far as Cooke and his crew were concerned. Their last flight came on 29 December, making an air test. That day, on another air test, W7585 *U* crashed near Bassingbourne, with three crewmen killed and the pilot injured. Before we leave this year there came news of a second award for Tom Cooke. In the New Year's Honours list would be his name as the recipient of the Air Force Cross. The citation read:

> Pilot Officer Cooke has been a flying instructor in the Conversion Flight of No. 22 OTU for the past fifteen months, during which time he has completed 500 hours instructional flying, 252 hours of which have been completed in the past six months. Throughout this period his keenness and energy have never flagged and he has been an excellent instructor and an inspiration to his pupils. This officer has displayed exceptional devotion to duty.

★★★

Before we leave 1942, mention should be made of two losses by 106 Squadron on the night of 21/22 December, during a raid on Munich. Lancaster R5574 was captained by F/Lt G. Cooke DFC DFM and came down over France with the loss of all but one of the crew. Grimwood Cooke had been awarded the DFM as a sergeant pilot after only thirteen operations, these being marked by his propensity for making low-level attacks after bombing, allowing his gunners to open fire on targets of opportunity. His DFC was awarded mid-1942, still operating with 106 Squadron. Two of his crew when shot down had won DFMs. Cooke had a twin brother Harold who was killed in action on a raid to Bremen as a rear gunner (sergeant) with No. 10 OTU.

No. 106 Squadron's second loss was Lancaster R5914, piloted by Sgt J.D. Brinkhurst DFM. John Brinkhurst had been returning from a raid on Düsseldorf in July 1942, acting as second pilot, when all four engines of their Lancaster failed over East Anglia. His pilot ordered everyone to bale out but Brinkhurst remained to assist his pilot in making a successful forced landing on an aerodrome without damaging the machine.

By the time of the 21/22 December raid Brinkhurst was first pilot, but over Belgium they were attacked and shot down by a night-fighter. They had been aware of the night-fighter's approach and had taken avoiding action, but the Me 110 got beneath them and a burst from its *Schräge Musik* – a night-fighter's upward-firing guns – set the Lancaster on fire. Despite attempts to put out the flames, it was soon apparent that the machine was doomed, so Brinkhurst ordered everyone out. Most did so but three of the crew did not survive, Brinkhurst being one of them.

Two of the survivors, after release from captivity, made it known that Brinkhurst had helped release the forward escape hatch that was jammed, then went back to the controls. Shortly afterwards the flight engineer sorted out and checked Brinkhurst's parachute harness then went through the hatch being aware that Brinkhurst had again returned to the controls to try to keep the bomber in the air until all had gone. Sadly he left it too late and was killed in the crash, but like so many pilots, died courageously making sure his crew had every chance to survive. He was on his twenty-first trip. He had previously made a name for himself as a bomber pilot, his DFM citation noting that as a war pilot he was '… unsurpassed and has set a magnificent example to his fellow captains'.

The victorious pilot was Leutnant Heinz-Wolfgang Schnaufer of NJG1, and this was his seventh victory. Schnaufer, 28, was to end the war as the highest-scoring German night-fighter pilot, with a total of 121 kills during 164 missions. He had risen to the rank of major and had received the highest awards that could be bestowed: the Knight's Cross with Oak Leaves, Swords and Diamonds. He died just over five years after the war ended, having been fatally injured in a road accident.

Cooke's Squadron suffered a sad loss on 29 December. F/Lt C.B. Ordish DFC had taken up Stirling W7585 (LS-U) on an air test but the aircraft suffered an engine fire and crashed near Bassingbourne. All four men aboard died, including S/L D.E.G. Ashill, the squadron's padre who had gone along for the ride, and LAC J.D. Hunt, one of the aircraft's ground crew. Charles Ordish had only just been awarded the DFC. The other fatality was the flight engineer, Sgt F.C. Jackson, who had just received the DFM. He had completed thirty-six operations and must have just about been tour-expired.

★★★

The year of 1943 began for Cooke and his crew on the second day, with a flight to Stradishall and then a height test to 14,000ft which took them nineteen minutes. As mentioned earlier, the Stirling suffered a lot of concern and bad press about its ability to climb to height. In 1987 Tom Cooke wrote an article for *Aviation News* in which he made several comments about flying the Stirling. The section about this height business is worth recording here, although he wrote some of the article in the third person:

Being based in East Anglia means that he [the pilot] has only reached about 11,000 feet as he crosses the Dutch coast. Searchlights and both heavy and light flak are on to him. Instinctively he eases the stick back to climb higher but the 99 feet wing and higher loading defeat him. The aircraft settles into a tail-down 'mushing' attitude, gaining neither height nor speed. He and his contemporaries will flounder on, well under the main force stream and easy pickings for flak and fighters.

The more experienced pilots, however, are up there at 18,000 feet tucked into the main force stream and carrying 18,000 lbs of bombs to the target. These pilots knew that when they reached 10,000 feet, it was important to keep the indicated speed at a good 150 mph and ignore the rate of climb. At about 12,000 feet the high speed blower could be usefully engaged and the aircraft would happily climb all the way to 18,000 feet if required.

Because of the period between 10,000 and 12,000 feet where the medium speed blower is to be effective, the Stirling climbed slowly and the new boys trying to make it climb got into this tail down mushing attitude, and complaining it would not climb any higher. My log book is full of entries 'aircraft number, war load, climb with Sergeant X 16,000 feet in 30 minutes'. In spite of this, the word soon got around that the Stirling was under-powered and would not go over 11,000 feet. This was joyfully taken up by the pseudo-historians and is now accepted as fact!

Although I have never seen it in any of the information on the Stirling, by the time I was finishing my tour we were operating with an all-up weight of over 72,000 lbs. Since by this time I was approving fuel and bomb loads, I am very certain of this and none of the old hands had trouble with the climb.

The aircraft performed admirably in the hand of the experienced. Unfortunately, the majority were inexperienced and the Stirling could not fit into the minimal training pattern used to build swiftly a vast strategic bombing fleet. Let the historians record, however, that the Stirling could perform well, if handled well.

There was little activity in early January because of the weather, but one entry in the squadron's diary for the 10th is of interest. No operations were detailed so the air crew were given a lecture on escape by F/Lt Picklin, a recent escapee. In view of Tom Cooke's future adventures, one has to wonder if he sat through it and also if he took some of it in. There is nobody by that name listed as an escapee but there is a F/Lt L.C. Pipkin DFC, an evader who baled out of a Halifax of 103 Squadron after being shot down on 6/7 September 1942. On his way down he lost a shoe and once on the ground – he was in Germany, near Duisburg – he took the time to make a square search in the darkness and found it. He was almost caught by German soldiers who discovered him loitering about and when a little later one man-handled him whilst demanding he show his papers, Pipkin overpowered the soldier and killed him by holding his head in a water-filled ditch by the side of the road. He eventually walked into Holland and was helped by a farmer and a priest who put him in touch with one of the escape lines run by the Resistance. In due course he found himself in Spain and then Gibraltar by October, from where he was flown back to England. Sadly he was killed in a shooting accident in August 1944.

The target for 14/15 January was the German U-boat base at Lorient. Six aircraft were assigned to the mission and five located the target and bombed, but one was forced to jettison its load over the Brest peninsula due to severe icing. Cooke took off at 2230hrs and was over the target at 0110hrs at 15,000ft on a heading of 10 degrees. Visibility was good and several fires could be seen in the nearby town. At this stage of the war it was required that a flash photograph be taken shortly after dropping the bombs, necessitating several more anxious moments flying straight and level – not something anyone particularly liked. This was so the backroom boys back home could see if the bomb load was dropped effectively and had produced some damage. On this occasion three crews brought back good photographs, Cooke's being one of them. There was often a sense of pride if a crew managed to get a good photograph on the bomb run, something that was not that easy to achieve. These pictures were usually pinned up in the crew room the next day and on this operation Cooke's crew had done well. So well that he felt obliged to make a note of it in his flying log book: 'Operations Lorient. U-boat base left burning; photograph of aiming point.'

Eight of the squadron's Stirlings went back to the same target the next night, bombing after the main force squadrons had left. This was noted as an experiment and, while the crews claimed a successful attack, nobody knew why it had been done. At least the boffins must have been happy with the results for the crews thought they had done better than the previous night. Cooke and Co. were not on this one.

During the operation to Lorient on 15/16 January, 214 Squadron lost S/L P.W.M. Carlyon DFC and all his crew. Paul Carlyon was a Canadian serving in the RAF and had received his DFC whilst flying with 140 Squadron in 1941. It was this flight commander loss that resulted in Cooke's next posting.

On 19 January he was posted to 214 Squadron, at RAF Chedburgh, Suffolk, as the flight commander of 'A' Flight and quickly settled into his new appointment. January continued cold and certainly 214 Squadron did little flying, or at least Cooke didn't. Cooke himself just made two air tests, an acceptance test for a newly arrived Stirling and a flight in an Oxford down to Tangmere with a Sgt Forbes. This NCO must have flown the Oxford back for Tom Cooke didn't. He was on leave with his wife, and returned to Chedburgh by train a week later.

★★★

Bomber Command's 2 Group had started to receive a new twin-engined light bomber, the North American B-25 Mitchell, named after the famous US general, Billy Mitchell, pioneer of America's military aviation. It was these aircraft, taking off from the deck of an aircraft carrier, that had bombed Japan in a daring raid in April 1942, led by the equally famous Jimmy Doolittle. With the RAF these bombers equipped 98 and 180 Squadrons in September 1942.

On 22 January 1943 came the first two losses of Mitchell aircraft. Nos 98 and 180 Squadrons, flying from RAF Foulsham, were tasked to attack the Purfina and Sinclair oil facilities, situated alongside the Ghent to Terneuzen canal in Belgium. No.98 Squadron had one bomber shot down by flak, while 180 Squadron lost two. One of these was piloted by the squadron's commanding officer, W/C C.C. Hodder AFC. His B-25 was hit in the starboard engine by AA fire and in struggling back he was attacked by Unteroffizier Vorhauer of II./JG1 and crashed into the sea off the Belgian coast. Hodder was 29 years of age and a married man from Cambridge. Two of his crew were DFM holders of long standing with 2 Group.

The other Mitchell, flown by P/O W.H. Cappleman DFM, was also shot down by Fw 190s off the Belgian coast. Walter Cappleman had been with 150 Squadron in 1941–42 and his DFM had been gazetted almost exactly a year earlier – 30 January 1942. He was 28 and a married man too, from Morden, in Surrey.

An incident on 29/30 January is worth a mention following a raid on Lorient. No.419 Squadron had a Halifax crash-land shortly after midnight having had undercarriage failure. The pilot was F/Lt A.P. Cranswick DFC and fortunately there were no injuries to him or his crew. Alec Panton Cranswick had flown a tour of twenty-nine operations with 214 Squadon in 1940, long before Tom

1 A young Thomas Cooke shortly before the war.

2 Tom and some friends playing with model
aircraft.

3 F/Lt John Cope outside Buck House with
DFC.

4 Would-be aviators being taught service drill on Hastings seafront 1939.

5 Below, left: Tom keeping fit along Hastings seafront. The background has not changed.

6 Below, right: Tom more suitably attired on a windswept Hastings seafront – with stripes!

7 DH Tiger Moth G–ADWB at No.12 EFTS, Prestwick, 1940.

8 End of course photo, No.12 EFTS, Prestwick, 27 April 1940. Those identified are, back row, left to right: Saul?, T.C.S. Cooke, John P. Wilkins, E.S. Osgood, –?–, Tom Weir, Ted Farmer, Don M. Vine, H.E. Puplett, Stan D. Graves; front: A.S. Ogilvey, V. Gray, T.D. Robertson, George P. Bain, D. Stein, A.J. Gibbs, Norman A. Welch, Don S. Edwards.

9 According to Tom, this picture proved prophetic, as they were the only two to survive the war from the course, Tom Cooke and Don Edwards.

10 Airspeed Oxford L4615, one flown by Tom at No.5 FTS in 1940.

11 Airspeed Oxford N4754 flown by Tom in May 1940, No.5 FTS.

12 The *Daily Sketch* did a piece on trainee pilots at Sealand, Tom managing to get himself in one of the pictures.

DAILY SKETCH, FRIDAY, JULY 26, 1940.—Page 7

F HISTORY'

13 Tom Cooke showing off his 'wings', May 1940.

14 At No.11 OTU Tom was introduced to the Vickers Wellington bomber, August 1940.

15 With 78 Squadron, Tom began his operational career on the Whitley at RAF Dishforth ...

16 ... which they shared with Whitleys of 51 Squadron in 1940.

17 Whitley bombers being 'bombed up'.

18 With 104 Squadron he had Wellington W5435 EP-F as his personal aircraft in 1941.

19 Wellington EP-F photographed from another aircraft, although almost totally obscured by the other's engine.

20 Tom's crew with 104 Squadron. He is seated in the cockpit, while his rear gunner, Sgt Stevenson, sits on the front turret. To his left is Sgt Haynes and, with his head sticking out of the cockpit roof is navigator, P/O Verver. Almost obscured inside the cockpit is Sgt Simpkin.

21 A more traditional grouping of Tom's 104 Squadron crew in the early days of the tour. Left to right: Tom Cooke, Sgt Haynes, Sgt Stevenson, P/O Verver and Sgt Simpkin, in front of W5435.

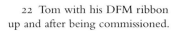

22 Tom with his DFM ribbon up and after being commissioned.

23 S/L Ray K. Glass DFC, 214 Squadron.

24 At No.22 OTU, Tom was sent on the first two 1,000-bomber raids. Here a ground crewman makes sure the Wellington's rear turret is totally clear.

25 At the other end the armourers begin 'bombing up'.

26 Tom is now flying the Short Stirling.

27 Tom Cooke looking very Churchillian, obviously pleased to be back on operational duty, 15 Squadron, November 1942.

28 Stirling aircraft being 'bombed up'.

29 Some of the senior officers on 214 Squadron. Left to right: squadron engineering officer and bombing leader, F/Lt E.W. Bitmead DFC, T.C.S. Cooke AFC DFM and George Wright, the adjutant.

30 With 214 Squadron his crew are, left to right: Reed, Lewis, Bell, Cooke, -?-, Beattie, -?-. (The two not identified would be A. Collins, and J. Harrison.)

31 Tom might well bite his fingernails – he now sits 22ft off the ground …

32 … but the cockpit is bigger and more roomy.

33 Tom's crew on 138 Squadron, 1943. Left to right: Cooke, Len Gornall, Stan Reed, Reg Lewis, A.B. Wethercombe, Ernest Bell and Bob Beattie. The dog belongs to Len Gornall.

34 Slim Beattie RCAF, rear gunner.

35 Tom's crew in North Africa buying oranges. Left to right: Bell, Lewis, 'trader', -?-, Gornall, Beattie, Withecombe and Reed.

36 P/O Reg Lewis DFC, Tom's navigator on 138 Squadron.

37 The crew and dog. Left to right: Wethercombe, Reed, Beattie, Lewis, Cooke, Bell, Gornall.

38 Unknown bombing by Lancasters on Germany, 1944.

39 Two bombing photos of Cologne, before and after.

40 Capt. Peter Ortiz of the OSS.

41 Tom C. Seymour Cooke DFC AFC DFM as a pilot with British European Airways after the war.

42 The house Reg Lewis knocked on the door of after baling out over France on 8 February 1944.

43 Lt Francis Cammaerts, the agent they took to France on the fateful night and who later helped them to evade capture. Post-war picture.

44 Tom Cooke's last photograph as a professional pilot upon leaving BEA.

Cooke arrived on the scene. He then went to the Middle East, flying with 148 Squadron, where he received the DFC. Back in England he joined the Canadian-manned 419 (Moose) Squadron but after just five operations he volunteered for Pathfinders and was sent to 35 Squadron of the Pathfinder Force (PFF). He made a further thirty sorties with this unit, bringing his overall total to ninety-six. Following a period with PFF HQ, he returned for another tour with 35 Squadron in April 1944. On the night of 4/5 July, he and his crew were shot down by flak, with just one of his crew members surviving. He had received the DSO and was lost on his 107th operation. He was only 24 years old. No.35 Squadron lost two flight commanders on the same July night, with S/L G.F. Lambert DFC and three crewmen also dying. Three others became prisoners and one successfully evaded capture.

On the night of 30/31 January 1943, the first Mosquito IV was lost during an attack on Berlin. Its crew of S/L D.F.W. Darling DFC and F/O W. Wright were both killed. Don Darling had earlier been a night-fighter pilot with 151 Squadron and was 24; he came from Balham, south London, while William Wright was a 34-year-old married man from Bedford.

While experience helped pilots and crews to survive, it was no guarantee of longevity on bombing operations. On the night of 2/3 February 1944 an experienced crew from 7 Squadron ran out of luck during a raid on Cologne. The pilot was S/L W.A. Smith DFC, whose DFC was gazetted a year earlier for operations with 7 Squadron, so he would have been on his second tour by this time. He had also been Mentioned in Dispatches. F/Lt Barry Martin DFC RNZAF had also received his DFC a year earlier, while Flight Sergeants R.N.B. Brooker DFM (flight engineer) and W.J. Dempster DFM RCAF (bomb aimer) were both very experienced air crew. Robin Brooker, when he was decorated, had flown twenty-nine sorties, while Bill Dempster had at least thirty-seven ops under his belt. Unfortunately, their Stirling (R9264 MG-L) carried one of the newer H$_2$S sets which the Germans found in the wreckage of the bomber. Both gunners had managed to bale out.

H$_2$S was a new type of ground radar originally introduced in 1942. The early sets were limited in nature but gave the navigator a good idea of the ground over which they were flying. Certainly coasts and rivers could be seen, as well as towns. H$_2$S sets were constantly improved and the one lost on 2/3 February was the latest design.

Dempster and crew had been brought down by Hauptmann Hans-Dieter Frank of II./NJG1, his eighteenth victory of an eventual fifty-five. He was killed as Kommandeur of I./ZG1 following a mid-air collision on 27 September 1943. He held the Knight's Cross and Oak Leaves.

No.214 Squadron lost two aircraft on a raid on Hamburg on the night of 3/4 February 1943. S/L W. Clarke in R9282 Q and P/O D.H. Smith in R9197 V were downed by German night-fighters over Holland. Clarke, one of Cooke's fellow flight commanders, and two of his crew were killed, with four others taken prisoner. All eight of Smith's crew perished. German pilots from NJG1 were to claim seven Stirling bombers this night out of the thirteen kills they made it total. Unteroffizier Christian Költringer is believed to have shot down Clarke, south-west of Utrecht, for his second victory.

Reg Lewis continues with his story:

In mid-January 1943, Cookie was promoted to flight lieutenant and became available to fill any flight commander vacancy. One did open up, with No. 214 Squadron, based at RAF Chedburgh, [on the A143, south-west of Bury St Edmunds]. He was then promoted to Acting Squadron Leader, and had recently been awarded the AFC. He was allowed to take his crew with him, so we went over to 214 Squadron and began operations with him during February and March.

No.214 Squadron was known as being affiliated to the Federated Malay States, which is why it had 'FMS' in its title. The squadron had a nightjar on its badge with the motto 'Active at Night'. Another air test on 7 February heralded operations that night; this time the target was once again the submarine base at Lorient. Cooke was now flying R9258 as his regular Stirling.

Six aircraft were detailed to attack Lorient 'Z', and two to attack Lorient 'A'. Cooke was one of the latter two, take-off for him being 1805hrs. They reached the target at 2030hrs, running in on a heading of 200 degrees at 14,500ft. The weather was good and the point of aim definitely identified by the estuary. As he came in Cooke could see markers from the Pathfinders going down and his bomb aimer let go their bomb load right on target. A number of fires were burning, the glow from which could be seen on leaving the Brittany coast. Cooke landed at 2316hrs and marked this raid in his log book as number thirty-eight. Once again they had achieved a good photo, Cooke noting: 'Operations Lorient. Credited with photo of aiming point.'

Lorient 'A' was on the menu again on the night of 13/14 February, Cooke and crew taking off at 1730hrs, with incendiaries in the bomb bay. Eleven Stirlings of 214 Squadron reached the target in bright moonlight and no cloud. All aircraft made a timed approach from the Ile de Croix, and the river, docks, estuary and bridge across it were easily visible in the light of the moon and flares dropped by the Pathfinder aircraft. Tom Cooke was on a heading of 48 degrees at 14,000ft and bombs went down on what seemed to be the centre of the dockyard area and many incendiaries could be seen burning in the town and docks. A huge flash was seen as a 4,000lb bomb exploded on the Keroman peninsula. Cooke, again in R9258, landed back at 2330hrs.

On this raid to Lorient, Bomber Command used only main force squadrons for the first time (i.e. no supporting sorties from OTU aircraft) and dropped 1,000 tons of bombs. It cost the Command eleven aircraft, including two lost in a collision on return to England, and another later written off after a crash-landing.

Three days later, 16/17th, it was Lorient again. On this raid 214 Squadron put up eight Stirlings, taking off around 1900hrs, including that of the CO, W/C A.H. Smythe DFC AFC. Alfred Smythe had been a flight commander with 214 Squadron in 1941 and was now back as its boss. The bombers reached Lorient, bombing between 2052hrs and 2103hrs, dropping thirty-one 1,000lb GP bombs and almost 8,500 incendiaries. There was no cloud and the moon again helped the crews to locate the target. The run-in was clear, the bomb aimers clearly seeing the River Scorff, its bridges and the docks, although aircraft that came in later found the dock area burning and by this point it had started to become obscured by the smoke and flame. One very large explosion was seen in the town itself, creating a huge ruddy glow and a mushroom cloud billowing upwards.

Cooke had lifted off from base at 1850hrs, carrying eight 1,000-pounders plus some incendiaries. He made his run-up from 14,000ft on a course of 160 degrees, and those crewmen able to look out saw many explosions, fires and smoke in the target area, especially around the aiming point. The crew could also see bombs exploding in another area of the docks, the target of other main force bombers. Cooke landed at 0005hrs and he wrote this up as his fortieth operation.

This raid was less costly than the one previously flown, with just three aircraft lost, but one Wellington, hit by ground fire over the target, had all its navigational aids destroyed and in consequence it crash-landed in the Republic of Ireland. Although the crew survived to be interned, the aircraft was destroyed by fire.

Cooke and Co.'s next trip was a mine-laying sortie. These operations again needed precise navigation in order to lay mines in specific areas off of ports, harbours or estuaries where enemy shipping was known to operate. They may seem less dangerous than bombing a city or factory complex but they could be highly dangerous, for apart from having to fly low to drop their mines, the bomber crew were vulnerable to shore-based flak fire as well as night-fighters. If they were unlucky they could suddenly fly over or near a flak-ship and, as this name implies, would come under intense AA fire. Many squadrons had newly arrived crews who were sent out on this sort of operation to give them an easier introduction to their tours, but it was not always a 'milk run'. Cooke and crew flew one such mission on the night of the 17/18th, to the mouth of the Gironde River off the west coast of France. The code for the area they were given this night was known as 'Deodars'.

Three Stirlings were assigned from 214 Squadron, each taking four sea mines, most of which went into the water from below 1,000ft. Pinpoints used were from the Ile d'Oleron and the Pointe de la Negade. Visibility was good, and Cooke, having left at 1805hrs, spread his mines at seven-second intervals starting at 2125hrs, having flown on a timed run from this latter point. They were back home at 0100hrs. However, one Stirling didn't make it. Upon return to England, Stirling R9163 C, flown by Sgt J.R. Rundle RNZAF, began to run short of fuel and Rundle ordered his crew to bale out some 4 miles north of Alton, Hampshire. Sadly he must have left it too late to get out himself and he was killed when the bomber crashed near Winchester. This crew probably found the dropping area covered in patchy cloud, whereas the first two had found it clear. No doubt trying to make certain of the position in which to mine, Rundle spent more time over the area which caused his fuel problem.

This same night 214 Squadron sent three other Stirlings to lay mines in the area coded as 'Furze', again in the southern area of Biscay. Two were successful but one crew brought their mines back, and one bomber had to land at Exeter. These sorties were called 'gardening' missions, and the mines were referred to as 'vegetables'. Therefore, crews would be sowing vegetables (mines) in the garden. Tom Cooke didn't fly too many of these types of operations and on the next mission he flew it was back to Germany.

Notes

1 Later changed to a half-wing brevet with the letter 'N' in the centre. However, early recipients of the 'O' brevet continued to wear them, being protective of their status in doing so. It also showed they had been serving in the early days of the war.

2 Gee radar was a system that enabled the navigator to calculate the aircraft's position by observing the time it took to receive pulse signals from three different ground stations in England. He had a chart showing the curves of distance from those stations.

6

PRESS ON REGARDLESS

The German port of Wilhelmshaven, situated right in the north of Germany along its limited coastline and access point to the North Sea, was frequently visited by Bomber Command during the Second World War. Emden, Bremerhaven and Cuxshaven were other ports along this section of coast, with Bremen just inland from Bremerhaven, along the Wesel Canal. To the east, again inland, was Hamburg, reached by navigating the River Elbe. Another nearby target was Kiel to the east, an additional important German port. Tom Cooke had been to some of these places before, but he went to Wilhelmshaven for the first time on the night of 19/20 February 1943.

A total of 338 bomber aircraft headed for this target: 52 Lancasters, 110 Halifaxes, 120 Wellingtons and 59 Stirlings. All available aircraft of 214 Squadron were among the latter, sending out ten Stirlings, although one had to abort due to an overheating engine, the crew jettisoning their bomb load into the sea. These aircraft carried a mix of 1,000lb bombs and incendiaries and they began lifting off from Chedburgh at 1800hrs, which was the exact time Tom Cooke left the ground. They reached the target shortly after 2000hrs but found 9/10ths low stratus cloud and haze which obscured the ground detail. One aircraft made a timed run-in from Altemilum but the others could not see the target and so they bombed on the Pathfinder's ground markers that were ringed with a good concentration of fires. However, the markers proved to be fairly scattered so the concentration of bombs became equally scattered.

Cooke took R9258 in at 15,500ft at 2016hrs on a heading of 160 degrees, dropping his load of incendiaries. Visibility was good and picking out Wangeroog Island gave Reg Lewis a good course to the drop zone. They saw the Pathfinder's red markers that seemed to be in the right place and bombed on those. On the way back, one Stirling was attacked by a Ju 88 night-fighter over the North Sea but the Stirling's gunners appeared to damage it, and no hits were scored on the Stirling.

As one might imagine, the damage to the target was poor and most of the raiding force's bombs fell in open country west of the target. Some bombs did fall on the town, causing some casualties, and a number of buildings were damaged. Two Lancasters failed to return.

Tom Cooke:

The Mark 14 bomb-sight was the first real bomb sight we had, otherwise we were operating on the old 1918 one, with very little modification on it. The bombs seemed an old design too. We then started getting properly designed bombs which were able to maintain their trajectory and not suddenly turn and go off at 90 degrees or something.

The real thing for Bomber Command was, in 1942, when we got a real 'punchy' leader – 'Bomber' Harris. Everybody I knew said that at last we've got a real leader here, and one thought we were now going somewhere. Word soon got around that he was going to get us the stuff we needed and very soon it began to arrive, and it became clear just how old our previous equipment had been. Everyone thought that back in 1939 Bomber Command was a powerful force but it wasn't. It was weak and ill-equipped, without any sensible objectives for the equipment we were using.

When you take into account when Bomber Command really got going, the Germans had to have over a million men manning their anti-aircraft defences, with all those deadly 88mm guns withdrawn from the battle fronts, not to mention all those thousands of people repairing the place, clearing the rubble, an so on, it took workers away from the factories producing guns, bombs, tanks, aircraft, etc.

Flying bombers was quite heavy work. You might be at 16,000 feet and the temperature might be minus eight degrees, but you are sweating like a pig up in the cockpit. Some aircraft of course were worse than others. The Whitley was a very heavy aircraft to throw around, so one needed a lot of physical strength. The Stirling was rather better.

This raid cost Bomber Command fourteen bombers and was a failure, due mainly to poor target marking by the Pathfinders. For some reason the Pathfinder crews were issued with out of date maps that failed to indicate recent town developments, so most of the bombs fell north of the town and port.

No.15 Squadron suffered the loss of three of its aircraft, including the first Stirling Mk III to be lost from the squadron. It appears that all three were shot down by Oberleutnant Hans-Joachim Jabs of II./NJG1, who thereby achieved his eighth, ninth and tenth victories. Jabs had started out as a day-fighter pilot flying Me 110s. As the Battle of Britain was ending he received the Knight's Cross after nineteen day victories. He was then trained on night-fighters. He survived the war with twenty-eight night kills, plus two Spitfires on day actions, bringing his total to fifty. He was given Oak Leaves to add to his Knight's Cross in March 1944. No.90 Squadron, which had previously operated with the Flying Fortress, lost two Stirlings on 19/20 February, one probably to the guns of Leutnant Wolfgang Küthe of the same II./NJG1. It was his sixth kill.

Another casualty was to 156 Squadron, which lost its first Lancaster III on this night, with a very mixed crew – three Canadian, one Australian, one New Zealander and two British. The Australian, Sgt Hugh Alexander McLennan, had been awarded the DFM in August 1942 for an act of heroism during a raid on Duisburg the previous month. On approaching the target the pilot had to make a sudden dive to avoid a collision with another bomber, and some incendiaries broke loose from their storage, ignited and filled the aircraft with sparks and smoke. With his bare hands, McLennan picked up one of them, which was burning furiously, but was unable to throw it out of an escape hatch. He then pushed the burning incendiary right through the wall of the fuselage and, despite burns to his hands, picked up a second burning incendiary and rammed this through the fabric too. Although his only reward was a DFM, the AOC of 3 Group in endorsing the recommendation for the award made the comment that in his view McLennan's action should be rewarded with the George Medal for his prompt action rather then the recommended DFM; however, obviously this was not acted upon at a higher level. McLennan came from New South Wales and was 26.

Bearing in mind Cooke's future posting, 138 Special Duties Squadron also lost an aircraft this night, Halifax W1012 (NF-Z). Shot down by flak over France, all eight members of the crew ended up as prisoners, the pilot, P/O R. Kingsford-Smith RAAF, among them. He and another crew member had evaded as far as Bordeaux before being captured.

★★★

Cooke and his crew went to Nürnberg on 25/26 February. This time a total of 337 bombers were on line, sixty-four of which were Stirlings. No.214 Squadron had twelve aircraft on the operation, but only nine were effective. Two failed to get airborne, one getting itself bogged down, the other damaging its starboard undercarriage. The third aborted due to icing, and jettisoned its bombs into the sea. It then crashed attempting an emergency landing at Stanstead, but the crew was not injured.

Cooke was off at 1955hrs but this time he had a different rear gunner, P/O D.B. Gaunt relieving 'Slim' Beattie. He reached the target, the home of the Nazi Party in the 1930s, where all those famous rallies had taken place, at 2330hrs. It was very dark and although there was no cloud there was a ground haze. Yellow marker flares were seen at Speyer – route markers – and over Nürnberg itself red and green ground markers were easily picked out. Cooke ran in on a 90-degree course at 15,500ft, the bomb aimer toggling the 152 30lb incendiaries, plus some leaflets. Fires could be seen springing up around the markers with others off to the south. When he got home, at 0305hrs, Cooke reported that the PFF marking was good, although at the turning point the markers were dropped too high. What he didn't mention, or at least what is not recorded in the squadron diary, is that they were caught by searchlights, for Reg Lewis recalled that they were coned over the target. Cooke also related what it was like to be suddenly exposed by searchlight beams:

> I was coned many times, so I just turned. The first time was when I was on Wellingtons on a Kiel raid. I almost went into a spin on that one because I was still relatively inexperienced. You're blinded by it at the start and then I got into a situation where I wasn't quite sure what the instruments were trying to tell me. The gyro was spinning madly and it took me a little while to ease out of that, but we eventually got out of it.

Reg Lewis also made mention of searchlights:

> Everything is brilliantly lit up when coned. One moment you are flying along in pitch darkness, perhaps a bit of moon about, and suddenly it is just like being held on a stage with all the spotlights holding you. It's an extraordinary sensation. Then the pilot would begin to weave about, trying not to lose too much height while doing so. Of course, the pilot is generally weaving to some extent all the time, but when coned he certainly becomes a little more animated.

***

One Lancaster lost that night was flown by F/Lt D.J. Curtin DFC and Bar RCAF of 106 Squadron. Among his crew, who were all killed, was a Sub Lieutenant P.M. McGrath RNVR on attachment from HMS *Daedalus*. Donald Joseph Curtin hailed from New York City and had been decorated with his first DFC following his very first operational flight. This had been in July 1942 while still finishing his training at No.14 OTU, flying a Hampden. Nearing the target his aircraft had been attacked by a night-fighter but he managed to evade it, but after bombing another fighter attacked, wounding two of his crew. Curtin was then momentarily blinded by an exploding AA shell and the Hampden lost a good deal of height before he regained control. Approaching the Dutch coast they were hit again by flak and sustained more damage, but Curtin got home, making a forced landing in a field. Helping his wounded comrades out of the aircraft he then set off to get help.

In February 1943 he received a Bar to his DFC following numerous sorties to both Germany and Italy. During a risky daylight raid on Milan on 24 October 1942 – fortunately with heavy cloud cover – he was attacked by two enemy fighters but he skilfully evaded them, allowing his gunners to destroy one and drive off the second. During a raid on Berlin in January 1943 he had remained over the target for half an hour to make certain of hitting his assigned target.

Danger on raids was not restricted to flak and enemy fighters. On 26 February, two 105 Squadron Mosquito aircraft collided over their target, a naval stores depot at Rennes. All four men involved were killed. One was the CO of the squadron, W/C G.P. Longfield. He and his navigator, F/Lt R.F. Milne, were long-serving RAF officers, both having joined the service in the 1920s.

★★★

On the last day of February 1943 it was back to the Biscay coast. Since the fall of France in May 1940, which allowed the German Kreigsmarine to use the Biscay ports of Brest, Lorient, Bordeaux and St-Nazaire to keep its U-boats, the RAF had been almost constantly bombing them. On their part, the Germans had built amazingly secure U-boat pens, so much so that the RAF's bombs of whatever size continued to bounce off them. Only collateral damage to port installations caused headaches, but the submarines themselves remained virtually untouchable. The Lorient attacks of mid-February had all but destroyed the facility and St-Nazaire was now on the RAF planner's list for some attention.

Cooke took off in R9258 and headed for St-Nazaire and its U-boat pens. For once all eleven Stirling bombers that went out bombed the target. The night was very dark with no cloud but smoke and haze didn't help. In all, 437 RAF bombers were on their way, sixty-two of them Stirlings. No.214 Squadron carried a mixture of 1,000lb and 500lb GP bombs, plus the inevitable incendiaries. The squadron's aircraft reached the target at 2115hrs and it took just three minutes for them to pass over and bomb. The estuary was clearly visible in the light of flares, and the bombs went down on the PFF's markers. There was a smokescreen in operation but this did not hinder the RAF bomb aimers overmuch. As the force headed out the fires from the target could be seen far out from the coast of Brittany.

Tom Cooke had taken off at 1820hrs and arrived over St-Nazaire at 2145hrs. Picking out the green TI (target indicator) markers, the incendiaries were let go. As he ran towards the target a huge orange-coloured explosion erupted ahead. Pulling round to head out, he congratulated himself on his forty-fourth operation, and, looking back, he too could see the base burning from 80 miles away.

One apparent change is noted by reading Cooke's log book. He had recorded upon his arrival at 214 Squadron that he was in command of 'A' Flight. However, on signing the book at the end of the month of February, it clearly shows that he is now in command of 'B' Flight. His flying hours were fast approaching 1,200.

★★★

March 1943 began with a raid on Berlin on the 1st. The squadron was now operating with some Stirling Mk IIIs, and on this night it put up eight Mk Is and two Mk IIIs. In the event, one of the Stirlings developed an engine fault and did not go (BU-C), one aborted due to its mid-upper gun turret failing (BU-N), but the other carried on (BU-K). Then one Stirling could not maintain height so turned back but did manage to bomb a last resort target (BU-Z). At least five of the others bombed the primary target, Tom Cooke and crew being one, who once again carried only incendiaries. Cooke reached Berlin and went across it at 16,000ft on a heading of 140 degrees at a speed of 150mph. The night and weather was clear and Cooke was able to make out red warning TIs so that crews would ignore what looked like the correct flares dropped earlier but may well have been bogus flares ignited by the Germans. He then spotted the proper green TI markers and the bomb aimer unloaded their cargo on them at 2220hrs. Cooke remarked upon his return: 'The PFF did their job well. I think the Berlin fire services had enough work given them to last them some time.'

Seven of the squadron's aircraft landed away from base, five at Swanton Morley and two at Lakenheath. Cooke was one of the latter two, having struggled along with his dead-reckoning compass and the gyro compass becoming unserviceable. In his log book he also commented that upon leaving Berlin 'target was burning well'.

One Stirling failed to return. F/Sgt J.M. Lyall RCAF had his R9145 K hit by flak at 2144hrs and had to order his crew out. The Stirling crashed near Königreich on the south bank of the Elbe. All his crew, which included three New Zealanders, baled out and became prisoners, except one of the New Zealanders who was killed by a splinter from an exploding AA shell as he descended. Lyall ended up in Lamsdorf prison camp.

Of the 302 aircraft that went to Berlin, seventeen failed to return, including four Stirlings, but it is on record that this night Berlin suffered more damage than on any previous raid. This in part was due to larger raiding forces and also better aircraft were carrying larger bomb loads. The combination of large bombs, such as 1,000-pounders and the 4,000lb 'cookies' that shattered buildings, factories and houses, allowed the incendiaries to ignite the debris and cause fires that often overwhelmed the firemen and other workers trying to extinguish them. One interesting fact emerged from this raid: bombs hit the Telefunken works in the city where a captured H_2S set taken from a previously shot down RAF bomber was being reassembled in order to discover its secrets. However, this same raid saw a Halifax of 35 Squadron brought down over Holland, in which the H_2S set was recovered, enabling the Germans to continue their research.

At this time, Tom Cooke assumed temporary command of 214 Squadron, due to the absence of the CO. In his log book Cooke glued in a copy of a memo he stuck on the noticeboard from Group HQ: It read:

Serial No.	26
Page	1
Date	3.3.43

No.214 (F.M.S.) Squadron Detail
By
S/Ldr T.C.Cooke AFC DFM
Commanding No.214 (F.M.S.) Squadron.

The following signal has been received from A.O.C. on handing over No.3 Group:-

'I WANT TO THANK ALL FOR THEIR EFFORTS OVER THE LAST SIX MONTHS WHICH HAVE ENABLED A STRONG FORCE TO BE BUILT UP IN READINESS FOR THE SPRING AND SUMMER CAMPAIGNS.'

No.3 Group's AOC, Air Vice-Marshal the Hon. R.A. Cochrane AFC, who had commanded the Group since September 1942, was handing over to AVM R. Harrison, who would lead it for the rest of the war. Group HQ was situated at Exning, in Suffolk, and had been since March 1940. Ralph Cochrane had been in airships in the First World War while serving with the RNAS. Among several important post-war jobs he had been seconded to the New Zealand

Government to advise on air defence and became first Chief of the Air Staff of the RNZAF between 1936 and 1939, when he became ADC to King George VI. Richard Harrison DFC AFC had served in the First World War and later in the Middle East. He retired in 1945 with the CBE and CB to his name, plus the French Legion d'Honneur, as well as the Croix de Guerre.

★★★

Tom Cooke flew back from Lakenheath on the 2nd and did not go on the squadron's next mission, a raid on Hamburg on 3/4 March. One Stirling failed to get back, P/O C.W.V. Pepper being shot down in ER329 *C* by flak. Everyone was killed except Sgt F. Mangleson RNZAF, who baled out and become a prisoner.

Cooke did not fly again until the air test on the 5th heralded operations that night. The target was Essen. No.214 Squadron detailed six Mk Is and four Mk IIIs, and again there were mixed results. Seven aircraft bombed the primary target, dropping six 2,000lb and four 1,000lb bombs, plus two 500-pounders and almost 5,900 mixed incendiaries. They bombed from between 2115hrs and 2124hrs and, even though there was no cloud, the haze and smoke didn't give them an easy target to spot. Red TIs were bombed and large fires could be observed, visible as far back as the Dutch coast.

However, one aircraft was caught in searchlights and in evading them the pilot lost height and was forced down to 1,000ft after turning on yellow route markers at Dorsten. He decided to return, but bombed Gladbeck on his way. A second aircraft was also coned and was held for some two minutes, which resulted in some very close explosions from flak. Finding it difficult to maintain height, the pilot ordered the bombs to be jettisoned 5 miles south-east of Soesterberg.

One Stirling failed to get home. Sgt H.W. Baldock, flying BK662 *K*, was hit on his way home at 2210hrs and crashed into the sea west of Ijmuiden, Holland. None of the crew survived, and this was the first Stirling Mk III lost from 214 Squadron. Harry Baldock, from Grimsby, was 23 and a married man.

In his log book Cooke noted that his target had been the Krupp works and that he had seen large fires and explosions. He had taken off at 1923hrs, bombed the target at 2118hrs from 15,000ft and it was identified in the cloudless sky by both red and green TIs. For a change he wasn't carrying incendiaries, but three 2,000lb, two 1,000lb and one 500lb bombs. Beattie was still missing from the crew, P/O Gaunt continuing to man the rear turret. They were back home half an hour before midnight.

The Essen raid also saw the demise of another of Bomber Command's more experienced crews, this time from 156 Squadron at RAF Warboys. S/L S.G. Hookway DFC was brought down over Germany, the Lancaster (LM304 GT-J) falling near Mönchengladbach. All seven men were lost. Stanley Gordon Hookway had received the DFC back in 1941 flying with 51 Squadron. In his crew P/O Frederick W. Hart DFM, the navigator, had only recently been commissioned, having received the DFM after completing forty-one operations. He had been with 156 Squadron since October 1942 after a tour with 150 Squadron. He had also flown on four trips while still at No.22 OTU. Sgt Donald Heap DFM had been a gunner and had flown forty-four operations with this and a previous squadron. The average age of this crew had been 28.

★★★

Three days later, the 8/9th, it was another trip to Nürnberg. No.214 Squadron had eleven Stirling bombers at readiness, but two later aborted and another was withdrawn prior to take-off. The other eight all reached the target and bombed during the last half-hour of the day, again unloading 2,000lb, 1,000lb, 500lb bombs and almost 3,000 incendiaries. The nearby canal was clearly seen, despite some haze, which put the bomb aimers on track, and although it was judged that the PFF marking appeared scattered, bomb aimers used their common sense from glimpses of built-up areas to see where to bomb.

The Pathfinders did indeed have trouble, for with no moon to help and considerable ground haze prevented accurate visual identification of the target area. These long-distance raids, of course, were outside the range of the Oboe radar system at this time, so this was another problem.

★★★

An interesting story emerged from that night. A 7 Squadron Stirling returned to England, where the mid-upper gunner, on leaving his turret prior to a hoped-for landing, had a shocking discovery. He was the only person still aboard! It seems that the crew believed they were short of fuel and would not make it back, so the skipper had ordered everyone to bale out, but the mid-upper gunner had not heard the order. He then baled out too over Kent and the Stirling crashed into the Thames estuary. It is suspected that the crew had believed they were still over France, so that is why they thought they wouldn't reach England. As it transpired they were over the sea and consequently all were drowned. Sadly, the mid-upper gunner only survived a further twelve operations before he was lost on a raid upon Wuppertal in June.

This squadron also lost an experienced crew, which crashed over France. All but one of the seven-man crew had been decorated and all were killed. F/Lt J.P. French had been awarded the DSO, and F/Lt C.L. Selman (navigator) and P/O L.G. Gosper RAAF had DFCs, while F/Sgt F.W.R. Cole, P/O H. Harwood and F/Sgt W.P. Hudson all had received DFMs. The citation for French and Selman (plus a Sgt I.J. Edwards DFM) appeared in the *London Gazette* on 16 October 1942, and read:

> One night in September 1942, Flying Officer French, Pilot Officer Selman and Sergeant Edwards were captain, navigator and wireless operator respectively of an aircraft of a bomber force which attacked Düsseldorf. Whilst over the target area, the aircraft was repeatedly hit by anti-aircraft fire. The petrol tanks were pierced, while some oil pipe lines were severed. In spite of this, Flying Officer Trench persisted in his mission and the target was bombed successfully. On the return journey, the aircraft lost height. All moveable equipment, even parachutes, were jettisoned in an effort to maintain height and the North Sea was eventually crossed between 100 and 200 feet. After crossing the English Coast, the aircraft was force-landed and, on impact with the ground, burst into flames. Flying Officer French and Sergeant Edwards were rendered unconscious but Pilot Officer Selman, with complete disregard of danger, extricated his comrades and pulled them clear of the burning aircraft. Throughout, these members of the crew of this aircraft displayed great courage, fortitude and devotion to duty in the face of extremely harassing circumstances.

Leo Gosper, for some reason, did not see his award gazetted until April 1945, with effect from 7 March 1943, for operations with 7 Squadron, presumably his death stopping a recommendation already in the pipe line. F/Sgt Frank Cole, the flight engineer, similarly did not have his citation gazetted until 19 October 1943, but it was again with an effected date – 19 February 1943. It recorded he had flown on thirty trips. Henry Harwood, WOp/AG, had been recommended for his DFM on 22 January 1943, having flown forty operations. F/Sgt William Hudson had been wounded earlier in his flying career, but by Christmas 1942 had been recommended for the DFM, having flown seventeen operations as mid-upper gunner. The rear gunner had been Sgt E.T. Beney. No.7 Squadron, of course, was part of the PFF, which generally meant longer tours of operations, especially if flown back to back (volunteering to continue after gaining the normally required thirty trips without taking a break before going on to do a second tour). While the risks were high in continuing to chance their luck without a long break, a crew who continued to fly did so in the knowledge that they were fully combat orientated and had that slight edge. It was sometimes difficult to begin another tour having been off ops instructing or some such for several months.

★★★

Cooke, who had left the ground for Nürnberg at 1950hrs on 8/9 March 1943, reached this distant Bavarian target at 2330hrs and bombed from 15,000ft three minutes later. Despite the problem of it being a dark night and the TIs being scattered, he located the green TIs and his bomb aimer let go their incendiaries. Operation number forty-seven was in the bag.

The next night he and his crew rested while others flew to Munich. Once again things did not go well. In the middle of take-off, a Stirling was allowed to get away on a training flight, but BF357 Q suffered an undercarriage collapse, right in the middle of the runway. With operating aircraft still waiting their turn to be off, they had to be switched to the airfield's short runway. To add to the problems, F/Sgt D.C. Moore RCAF, in R9358 A, had an oleo (shock absorber) leg fail to retract taking off from this runway and he clipped a tree and a house, crashing and bursting into flames. Everyone scrambled clear except one crew-man who became trapped, but he was saved by Moore and Sgt T.J. Wilson, both of whom were awarded George Medals.

Operation forty-eight for Cooke was a 'gardening' trip on the night of 10/11 March. Five of the squadron's bombers were assigned to this mine-laying sortie to the coded area of 'Deodars' again, each Stirling carrying four 'vegetables'. Cooke was away at 1840hrs, with another new gunner in the back, P/O E.K. Ward. On arrival off the Gironde estuary it was dark and hazy, making it impossible to see their drop zone, so Cooke approached it on a time and distance run from Grave Point. Then the bomb aimer released their mines at five-second intervals on a heading of 314 degrees at 180mph from 1,000ft at 2156hrs. They were safely back home at 0055hrs. The others had similar trouble but all made successful timed runs before dropping their mines and landing back without mishap. However, Cooke did have a further problem. He noted in his log book the small matter that they had returned on three engines.

Stuttgart was 214 Squadron's next target, on the night of 11/12 March. One Stirling failed to return, P/O A. Carruthers in BF469 M being shot down by a night-fighter over France. Oberleutnant Hans Autenrieth of VI./NJG4 claimed him south-west of Chalons. It was his tenth victory.

★★★

On this Stuttgart raid, the PFF 7 Squadron lost another crew, again one with experience. Stirling W7617 (MG-A) left RAF Oakington at 1929hrs and came down over the French countryside with all aboard being killed. S/L M.E. Thwaites DFC was in command, who had received his award with 50 Squadron in 1941. In his crew was F/Lt F.D.J. Thompson DFC and Bar, the crew's flight engineer. His first DFC had been awarded at the end of 1942 and the Bar came soon afterwards. His pilot on these occasion was Acting Wing Commander T.G. 'Hamish' Mahaddie DSO AFC, who also received the DFC at this time, as well as F/Sgt C. Stewart (navigator) being awarded the DFM. He was also part of Thwaites' crew on 11/12 March.

The event was a night in February 1943 during a raid on Cologne. Hit by flak over the city and then attacked by a night-fighter, the bomber was heavily damaged. With its aileron controls severed the Stirling went into a steep diving turn and, as the radio and intercom had suffered too, Mahaddie could not communicate with his crew. However, he regained control with expert use of the engines, stopped the descent and put the aircraft back on course for base. All three men 'displayed great, skill and initiative', read the awards citation.

From Edinburgh, Hamish Mahaddie had joined the RAF as a Halton apprentice in 1928, managed to persuade his superiors that he should become a pilot and by the mid-1930s had achieved this and was flying in the Middle East. He flew two bomber tours, one with 77 Squadron on Whitleys and then on Stirlings with 7 Squadron, before joining the staff of PFF HQ, where his main job was to seek out potential Pathfinder crews from main force squadrons and then help to train them. When going to Buckingham Palace to be officially decorated by the king, he created something of a record by receiving his DSO DFC AFC and Czech War Cross in one ceremony.

Post-war he sourced many aircraft for aviation films, most notably the ones used in *The Battle of Britain* in 1967 and especially the Luftwaffe's He 111s and Me 109s then being used by the Spanish Air Force.

Thwaites' crew also had other decorated airmen on board. F/O A.H. Bywater and P/O R.S. Luton both had DFCs, both in recent days, while rear gunner F/Sgt Alexander Clift had received the DFM, also a recent award.

No.83 Squadron also lost a good crew over Stuttgart. F/Lt N.A.J. Mackie DFC had his Lancaster shot down by a night-fighter over France and, although both his gunners died, the others all survived. Norman Mackie, who had been decorated in May 1942 on his first tour with 83 Squadron, was taken prisoner, as was two of his crew, one of whom, F/Sgt W.E. Barrett, had received his DFM after flying forty operations with 207 Squadron in 1942. F/Lt A.M. Ogilvie, a Canadian who had recently received the DFC, successfully evaded along with

Sgt R. Henderson, returning from Gibraltar in early June. Ogilvie received a Bar to his DFC but sadly Henderson, returning to operations, was killed in action in November 1943, still with 83 Squadron. Ralph Henderson had been on a 'second dicky' trip as a pilot gaining experience on the Stuttgart raid and it was only his third operation before operating with his own crew. Once home he received the DFM and was commissioned.

The mid-upper gunner who was killed, F/Sgt Alexander Lynch, had received the DFM after flying a tour with 144 Squadron in 1941–42. On his third operation he had successfully fought off three night-fighters and some nights later again successfully engaged a night-fighter that dived away steeply as if badly hit.

★★★

The next mission for Tom Cooke came on 22 March. Eight Stirlings took off for an attack on St-Nazaire, Gaunt being back once more in the rear turret. They were airborne at 1910hrs and had flown as far as the Channel Islands when they were recalled. They had to jettison their load and were back on the ground at 2235hrs. It was a disappointment but, because of the distance travelled, it still counted as an operation. It was Cooke's first mission in a Mk III – BK653. He had flown an aircraft acceptance test the previous day, making an hour-long flight to RAF Bourn and back.

On the 27th he flew a pre-operation air test and that night the target was Berlin again. On this night, there would be more Mk IIIs than Mk Is – six and five respectively Nine of these bombed the primary target, one jettisoned owing to a navigational problem and one failed to return.

Cooke had Ward back again in the rear turret and they were off at 1950hrs, carrying one 2,000lb, one 1,000lb and one 500lb bomb, as well as incendiaries. It was a starlit night with ground haze but the target was well marked by the Pathfinders, with red and green TIs easily seen by the bomb aimer. He toggled the bomb load from 15,000ft on a heading of 10 degrees at 2259hrs without problems and after the photo was taken it was 'home James'. They landed back at base at 0320hrs.

A total of 396 Bomber Command aircraft had been sent off to Berlin this night and nine did not get home, two of them Stirlings. The raid turned out to be a failure. The bombers came in from the south-west and, while the Pathfinders had established two separate areas with marker flares, both turned out to be well south of the city. Of the photographs taken none were plotted within 5 miles of the aiming point, and bombs fell anything between 7 and 17 miles short. Quite by chance, bombs had fallen in the middle of a concentration of buildings housing valuable radio, radar and other technical apparatus, much of which was destroyed. The Germans assumed this had been the main target for the RAF and were full of praise for the way some obviously special equipment had pinpointed and destroyed this target.

The Stirling lost from 214 Squadron was flown by P/O E. Challis (BF453 BU-L) and all crew members were killed. It was reported crashed at Finkenwerder on the south bank of the Elbe, which is around 8 miles from the centre of Hamburg.

Having landed safely back at Chedburgh, Cooke knew he had completed his second tour of operations. A second tour generally consisted of twenty operations, so this brought his total to fifty, and he would now be screened. For his devotion to duty he would soon be awarded the Distinguished Flying Cross, the award being gazetted on 11 June 1943.

The award was recommended on 7 April 1943 by 214 Squadron's CO, W/C M. V.M. Clube, a former pre-war auxiliary air force officer. Cooke had flown over to RAF Bourn in an Oxford III on 25 March and brought Clube back on the 26th. The recommendation read:

<u>CONFIDENTIAL</u>   <u>NON-IMMEDIATE</u>

<u>RECOMMENDATION FOR HONOUR AND AWARDS</u>

Christian Names	Thomas Charles	Surname	Cooke AFC DFM
Rank	Flying Officer	Official No.	103506
	(Acting Squadron Leader)		
Command or Group.		No. 3 Bomber Command	
Unit		214 (F.M.S.) Squadron	

Total hours flown on operations	340.30
Number of Sorties	50
Total hours flown on operations since receipt of previous award	133.50
Number of sorties since receipt of previous award	22
Recognition for which recommended	Distinguished Flying Cross
Previous awards	Air Force Cross
	Distinguished Flying Medal
Appointment held	Pilot and Captain of aircraft

1 This officer is the senior Flight Commander in the Squadron. He has flown a total of 50 sorties involving 340.30 hours against the enemy, including many on the most heavily defended targets in Germany. He has completed a total of 22 sorties involving 133.50 hours since he was awarded the Air Force Cross.

2 During an attack on Essen in May last year, he skilfully evaded five deter-mined attacks by German night-fighters, and on the 13th September, when Bremen was attacked, his aircraft was badly damaged by flak and a petrol pipe was severed.

3 Squadron Leader Cooke has at all times set an excellent example to his Flight and has contributed substantially to the success of the Squadron.

Date   7th April 1943   Signature of Commanding Officer

M V M Clube

Rank   Wing Commander

Remarks by Station Commander

I concur and strongly recommend this award.

Date   19. 4. 43   Rank   *A H Owen, G/C*

Remarks by Air or other Officer Commanding

Strongly Recommended for the award of the
Distinguished Flying Cross.

Date   28 April 1943   Rank   *R Harrison*

AirVice-Marshal

Commanding No.3 Group

Once approved the recommendation became reality and in due course the award was promulgated into the *London Gazette*, in Tom Cooke's case on 11 June 1943. Often the citation that came with it was also recorded in the same gazette, but sometimes, probably due to space limitations, it was not, instead just showing the name and rank within a list of other such awards for the DFC. However, the cita-tion is recorded elsewhere and reads:

Acting Squadron Leader Thomas Charles Cooke, A.F.C., D.F.M., Royal Air Force Volunteer Reserve, No.214 Squadron. This officer is the senior flight commander in his squadron. He has taken part in many attacks, some of them on the most strongly defended targets in Germany. During an attack on the Ruhr in May 1942 Squadron Leader Cooke skilfully evaded 5 determined attacks by enemy night fighters. Later, while operating over Bremen, his aircraft was severely damaged by enemy ground defences and a petrol pipe was severed. Despite this damage, Squadron Leader Cooke flew the aircraft safely to base. He has at all times set an excellent example to the squadron.

One final loss of a 214 Squadron Stirling took place on 29/30 March. EF362 N with F/O W.G. Cooper at the controls was heading for Berlin but was forced to abort due to severe icing. Over Suffolk the bomber collided with another Stirling, BK663 of 15 Squadron. Cooper was killed in a crash-landing but the others survived, with two injured. Cooper was on the first trip of his second tour.

On this Berlin raid losses had again been high, twenty-one out of a force of 329, which was not helped by the bad weather and icing. No. 106 Squadron once more suffered the loss of an experienced crew, shot down by Leutnant August Geiger of III./NJG1 over Holland. Geiger had a successful night, downing five RAF bombers (two Wellingtons, two Lancasters and a Halifax) and bringing his personal score to twenty. Geiger received the Knight's Cross with Oak Leaves and achieved a total victory score of fifty-three before being killed in September 1943, over Holland, when he was shot down by one of the RAF's top night-fighter pilots, W/C Bob Braham DSO DFC.

S/L E.L. Hayward DFC was on his second tour with 106 Squadron, having been awarded the DFC in early 1942 for his first. His navigator, F/O J.O. Young had been recommended for the DFC, an award not promulgated until after the war. One of the crew's WOp/AGs, F/Sgt E.H. Mantle, had received the DFM for a twenty-nine-operation tour with 144 Squadron in 1941, and a Bar just prior to his loss after forty-six missions flying with 106 Squadron. Twice he made repairs to his wireless and communications apparatus during raids where their aircraft had been hit by AA fire. Their Lancaster had been ED596 ZN-H – the first Mk III 106 Squadron had lost on operations.

A few nights later, going to Essen, twenty-one more failed to return, plus two that crashed in England. One aircraft lost on the Essen trip was a Lancaster III of 467 (New Zealand) Squadron, flown by S/L A.M. Paape DFC and Bar. Arthur Paape was a New Zealander from Dunedin serving in the RAF, and had won the DFC and Bar with 61 Squadron, the DFC in 1940 and the Bar in 1942. He was ten days short of his twenty-fourth birthday. On 12 February 1942, as three German battleships made their dash from Brest to Norway, once detected in the English Channel, bombers were sent out with the task of distracting the ships' AA fire whilst torpedo aircraft attempted to attack them at low level. Paape was in one of the Hampdens and in this action found himself 800ft above the ships, surrounded by bursting AA fire. With his gunners returning fire, he swept back to attack and by the time he had miraculously escaped from the withering fire his bomber had been hit several times. The Hampden's bomb doors were hanging down, the gun turrets were out of action, petrol was leaking from one fuel tank, and the hydraulics and trimming gear were useless. The Paape family also lost another son during the war.

Two other decorated crew members lost over Essen were F/O Thomas Dring DFC and rear gunner F/O J.M. Stewart AFC. Not all the crew were New Zealanders; the flight engineer was Canadian and another came from southern Rhodesia.

It was often this diversity of nationalities of Bomber Command crews that helped cohesion and, as can be seen, even in designated New Zealand outfits not all crew members necessarily came from this country. The mix of different cultures and backgrounds made for a good crew, but whatever the diversity, it made no difference to their chances of survival through luck and nor did experience. Crews could just as easily be lost on their first operation as on their last.

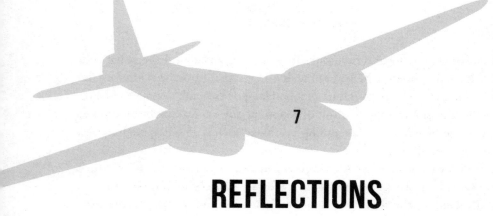

7

REFLECTIONS

Although Tom Cooke was now screened from further operational missions against the enemy, he remained on the squadron and in command of his Flight. While his former crew waited to be paired up with a new skipper, they made occasional flights with Cooke, who also began flying the squadron's Oxford III (EB787). There are a couple of interesting entries in his log book in early April 1943. On the 4th he took the Oxford up with Section Officer Ridley, presumably a member of the Women's Auxiliary Air Force. They were up for thirty minutes, his log book comment being: 'Inspecting the height of telephone wires.' While it might be that Section Officer Ridley had something to do with telephonic communications at Chedburgh, it seems more likely that Cooke was doing some playful low flying – very low flying – to entertain the lady.

On the 11th he was up in the Oxford again, in company with Squadron Leaders Watkins and Glass, 'searching for escapists'. They were up for ninety minutes and were probably the air side of an exercise where either soldiers or airmen were taken out into the countryside, dropped off and told to make their way home without being caught. The two squadron leaders were no doubt on a 'jolly' while watching out for the men on the ground. One of them, Ray Glass, a member of 214 Squadron, recalled this episode to Simon Muggleton in 1999:

> On perusing my log book I see Squadron Leaders Cooke, Wilkins, our C Flight Commander, and I, flew together in an Oxford aircraft for a one and a half hour flight on an escaped prisoner exercise. This was to give crews the experience of evading being caught if they were shot down. We used to take them 20 to 30 miles from the camp by coach and they had to be able to return without being caught.[1]

That afternoon Cooke and his old crew were out on a mission, searching over the North Sea in Stirling BF478. They were out for three and a half hours and all they found was an oil patch and an empty parachute. Later another squadron aircraft located a body. This mission was counted in the operational record in Reg Lewis' subsequent DFC recommendation, so we can assume that this was sortie number fifty-one for Cooke. On the 13th he and his old crew took up a Sgt James and his crew for an hour, showing them how to conduct a fighter affiliation sortie. A Spitfire made several simulated fighter attacks upon them, with the purpose of the gunners telling their pilot what sort of evasive measures should be taken.

In the meantime, 214 Squadron had continued operating and continued losing aircraft and crews. On 4/5 April, Sgt K.R. Burton DFM failed to get back from a raid on Kiel. Ken Burton's DFM had only just been awarded for gallantry during a raid on Stuttgart on 11 March 1943. It was an 'immediate' award, which means one given immediately for a specific feat of heroism, rather than a DFC or DFM awarded following a period of operations, even if one particular incident stood out in the citation. On the Stuttgart raid their Stirling had suffered engine trouble but the crew decided to carry on even though the target was still some 150 miles ahead of them. Once they had bombed and were on their way home a second engine failed and, although they were forced down to 3,000ft, well within range of all manner of AA fire, and despite being concerned with their dwindling fuel supply, Burton's skill got them back across the North Sea and home. Now he and his crew were dead. Burton's DFM was announced in the *London Gazette* the next day, 6 April.

***

Another loss to Bomber Command on the night of 4/5 April was from 156 Squadron operating out of RAF Warboys. Lancaster ED615 was captained by S/L the Honourable Brian Grimston DFC, the son of the 4th Earl of Verulam. His DFC had been awarded for a trip to Turin in December 1942, and his citation mentions the severe difficulties he encountered with the weather, which forced him to fly blind on the outward journey, especially getting over the Alps in thick cloud. His brother Bruce had won the DFC in 1941 flying with 149 Squadron during a raid on Bremen when attacked by a night-fighter. Bruce was killed in action flying with 524 Squadron of Coastal Command in July 1944, during anti-shipping operations. Two other of Brian Grimston's crew had received DFMs. P/O S.J. Volante had received an immediate award in November 1942 for the accuracy of his bomb-aiming duties during a raid on Cologne – important for a

Pathfinder crew. F/Sgt G.C. Stafford was rear gunner in Grimston's crew and his award came after flying thirty-one operations, fifteen with 156 Squadron. During a raid in August 1942 his aircraft had been attacked by a Ju 88 fighter and his turret had been knocked out, but he continued to give instructions to his pilot, thereby successfully evading the fighter's gunfire.

A 51 Squadron Halifax lost this same 4/5 April night was being flown by F/Lt A.A. Emery DFM. Alan Emery had started the war as an observer/navigator with 12 Squadron in France, flying Fairey Battles. On one occasion the Battle in which he was flying iced up, forcing the three-man crew to bale out. He then trained as a pilot and by the time he received his DFM he had flown seventeen operations. By this time Emery had risen in rank and became captain of the aircraft, and had been operational since the war began. At 29 years of age, one can compare this with his mid-upper gunner on 51 Squadron, lost with him in April 1943. Sgt Sidney George Adams, from East Ham, Essex, was just 17 years of age and amongst the youngest RAF air crew to be killed in action in the Second World War. He rests in Kiel War Cemetery.

W/O G.A. Davie of 214 Squadron and his crew were lost on the night of 11/12th during a 'gardening' operation to the Gironde estuary, flying BK612 Z, and two nights later Sgt L. Powell and crew were shot down and killed in EF331 H, claimed by a night-fighter over France during another raid on Stuttgart. This was NJG4's area of operations and this unit claimed eight Stirlings over France on that night.

Raiding Mannheim on the 16/17th, F/Sgt D.E. James RCAF was attacked by three *Wilde Sau* Me 109s, forcing the crew of BK653 *A* to bale out over France. The rear gunner was killed in the attack but the rest got out. Three crewmen were taken into captivity but the pilot and three others managed to evade. It had been this crew that Tom Cooke had shown the ropes to on fighter affiliation tactics just three days earlier. The four evaders were picked up by the Resistance and eventually were smuggled into Spain. James and Sergeants W.G. Grove, R.W. Adams and J. Hall arrived at Gibraltar in mid-July, sailing to England aboard the *Monarch of Bermuda* and reaching Liverpool on the 27th. Grove, who had been on a 'second dickey' trip, was later commissioned and, as a flight lieutenant, was killed in action on 24/25 March 1944 flying with 15 Squadron on a disastrous mission to Berlin. Seventy-two bombers failed to return that night, and was the last major raid on Berlin by Bomber Command. That same month in 1944, Bomber Command was to suffer its worst casualty rate of the war during a raid on Nürnberg on the 30/31st. Out of 795 aircraft sent, ninety-five would not return. On this night P/O C.J. Barton of 578 Squadron was awarded a posthumous Victoria Cross for bringing back his Halifax which had been severely damaged by a Ju 88 night-fighter. Obliged to make a crash-landing in England, he died soon after doing so, but three crewmen survived. Three others had baled out over Germany, including the navigator and wireless operator. Despite the damage, the loss of three crew members and with one engine knocked out, Cy Barton had continued on to the target and bombed before turning for home.

★★★

Cooke was finally able to get away with the arrival of a replacement 'A' Flight commander, and his next flight did not take place until 1 May, when he flew Reg Lewis to RAF Mildenhall and back in the Oxford. The next day he took leave of his Flight, squadron and crew, having been posted to command 'A' Flight of No.1665 Conversion Unit at RAF Waterbeach. He flew to his new command on 2 May with Sergeant Verral, who then brought the Oxford back to Chedburgh. Tom was back to instructing.

★★★

When Tom Cooke was interviewed at the Imperial War Museum about his war flying, he recorded a number of interesting events. It isn't always possible or easy to link some of them up with his flying log book, but nevertheless, we cannot let these stories go unread, so we record them here, and this excerpt concerns his time flying bombers:

> On one occasion I crash-landed with sea mines on board and fortunately they did not go up. That was at Bourn, on Stirlings, and we were bombed up to drop them off Bordeaux, when there was a lot of mining going on around the Gironde Estuary. Having taken off we had one of our undercarriage legs stuck in the down position and the other stuck in the up position. In those days we made our approach in Stirlings at 140 mph, so it was going to be an interesting proposition.
>
> Anyway, we touched down, with the whole squadron watching us after we had called up to say we were about to crash. The control tower used to use a Tannoy to call up the ambulance and fire engine, so everyone quickly knew something was happening. We actually cart-wheeled once we touched down and the aircraft broke into three parts. We all got out pretty smartly and started running, but the aircraft didn't blow up, sea mines or no sea mines. It had been, nevertheless, an uncomfortable feeling.
>
> Targets made little difference to us. We would prefer a town rather than a refinery in some field somewhere because we knew we would at least be able

to hit the town. We may miss the aiming point by a mile, but at least we'd hit the town. In a war you are out to do as much damage as possible, damage the enemy's war efforts, so other than that, I didn't normally care where the target was. Germany, France, Italy, it didn't really matter.

Germany was always much hotter of course. We had just as much trouble though over places like Brest for example, where the Germans had something in particular to defend, but personally I never considered the opposition. If I had a dislike for a particular target at all it was probably one which had a 10 or 12 hour trip. It was only about a four hour trip to the Ruhr Valley, which was far easier than grinding on hour after hour, such as to Stettin, Milan, Aosta and Berlin.

We used to have a naughty song about that. After sitting in the cockpit for hours I stuck it for as long as I could and then I'd say, f—— it, my arse is not made of wood, which we turned into our version of a popular tune of the day.

As far as I was concerned I was no braver than anyone else. Everybody was scared of course, knowing what could happen to you, but it was all part of the game. I found very few occasions where people showed their fear. Everybody was frightened but most people overcame it, and the one or two who didn't, in my experience, just went LMF [Lack of Moral Fibre] and quickly departed. We had a case of one friend of mine who started with me in Southampton and then we lost touch until we met up at Bassingbourne and crewed up – we always had two pilots at this stage. We then moved to Dishforth, then Driffield, then Mountford, Mildenhall and finally to Bourn. There we both got promoted and shot off in different directions. He then had an interesting experience. He later told me he had a navigator that whenever they got any-where near to the opposition he would immediately get on his knees and start praying while sighting the bombs. My friend had to get rid of him.

One should remember that all wartime air crew were volunteers. One could join or be conscripted into the Royal Air Force but if desired to fly operationally it was always on a volunteer basis. Of course, once a decision to fly had been made, whether as a pilot, navigator, flight engineer, wireless operator, bomb aimer or air gunner, and the training had been completed, there was a need for the man to carry on and fly on operations. One could unvolunteer, but it was not with-out difficulty and a certain degree of stigma. Cooke has mentioned LMF – the RAF's way of saying a man was a coward – and this generally meant a demotion, his flying badge taken away, and he might well end up as an AC1 sweeping out the aircraft hangars. Many times it was merely stress, but the RAF couldn't be seen to let people off operations easily. Generally a good CO or squadron medi-cal officer could spot the early signs and sort something out before it got to an

LMF charge, but this was not always the case. Every one has a breaking point. It was the same with completing tours. Anyone that did complete a tour of operations was not required to volunteer to do a second. Those that did were the more press-on types who wanted to get the war over with, or they had been bitten by the flying bug and felt the best way forward was to continue war flying in earnest. Those that went on to a third tour were those really mega press-on guys and either made it through or their luck ran out.

Many air crew thought that luck was a major factor. Many sailors and soldiers thought so too. These people pressed on in the spirit of fighting the enemy and if they were going to be killed, then there was little one could do to prevent it. Those who really thought about luck often carried some form of talisman with them: a rabbit's foot, a St Christopher's medallion, a lock of someone's hair, a fluffy toy of some description, a ladies' garter or a pair of stockings, it could be just about anything. It comes out in books and in films where someone temporarily loses his lucky charm and gets killed. That would be deemed bad luck and it didn't matter if it was thought to be inevitable that he would have been killed with or without it, those who read things into it knew it had been solely because of that bit of bad luck in losing his talisman. Cooke continued:

With my rear gunners I used to cut away the panel of Perspex right in front of the man's face, so that they could look out into the clear night sky. It would add to the cold but that was the least of our worries. German night-fighters generally tried to sneak up below us and to one side, trying to get themselves under one of our wings. They had upward firing guns that they would try to fire into our wing tanks. They wouldn't go for the belly of the aircraft because of our bomb load. The idea was for the rear gunner to spot them before they managed to formate on us. Sometimes after we'd left the enemy coast, Slim Beattie would ask if he could come out and have a stretch but I always said 'no' to him. 'Give it another ten to fifteen minutes till we get well clear.'

We had a couple of dust-ups with German fighters. Slim claimed one, one night, but you rarely knew if you'd got it or not. I liked the Stirling in many ways. For one, you could half roll it because it was so light on the ailerons, and with the wings having been cut down to 99 feet from the original 102 gave the pilot the advantage of a very quick roll. One night we were on our way to Stuttgart and Slim had a go at this chap as we were going down and it passed us and he claimed it.

Then we had another occasion, also while on Stirlings, when we were going to Berlin and we were somewhere over Denmark. I should make it clear, that if nothing much was going on at base, the radio operators used to go into a room and listen to a recording of previous German night-fighter instructions from the ground controllers, so, although they knew very little German, they could begin to understand what the final vector messages sounded like, and so on. So, this night over Denmark, our wireless operator was listening in to a German frequency and picked up this message, just at the right moment and called me to say that an enemy fighter was coming in on somebody. I did a very sharp 360 degree turn and as we went round in this circle, we saw a Ju88 coming in and then going off in the opposite direction. No shots were fired from either side, and no doubt he went off to try and find a less alert crew.

We also had a running fight with one of our own aircraft one night over the Ruhr! I was on Wellingtons then and if you think about it, the Wellington II had a high aspect ratio wing with two in-line engines, and this was a moonlit night. We spotted this chap coming at us head-on and thought it was a Me 110, so we opened fire on it and he opened fire on us. As we passed each other I saw the squadron letters on his fuselage which was EP-P for Peter – our own Sergeant Nichols I recall – and I was flying EP-F for Freddie.

When on Whitleys earlier, we never ever saw a night-fighter in those early days, for as the Germans thought we would never be able to bomb Germany, what defences they had were virtually all anti-aircraft artillery. Later of course it became more of a thing that you saw night-fighters fairly frequently, even if they weren't attacking you but were having a go at somebody else.

We feared night-fighters far more than AA fire of course. An AA hit was just the luck of the draw, more or less. It sometimes boxed you in which was a bind. I was once boxed in badly in a Wellington. The German gunners would fire up a box and try and close the area you were flying in and then when they realised that the box was the spot you were flying in, their guns really opened up. I was always gaining 500 feet, losing 500 feet, turning left so many degrees, holding it, turn right so many degrees, straighten up and then go through it all again. It was asking for trouble to simply fly ahead straight and level. It had to be carefully balanced of course, otherwise your poor navigator would get a bit upset about it. But I never stopped jinking about the whole time. Later we were told to stop this practise because with the increasing number of bombers heading out in our bomber stream there was liable to be collisions if everyone was weaving about madly all over the place. Anyway, I always did it, come what may. Colliding was one thing, but being boxed in by AA fire, perhaps with pre-dicted flak, or giving a German night-fighter the chance to sneak up on you with their airborne radar, were quite others.

We saw plenty of people shot down. In fact I had quite an amusing episode on Stirlings. One of my previous instructors from EFTS, who had been teaching me to fly there, turned up one day, and it was sheer luck of the draw that he was put down to fly as my second pilot. He was a bit long in the tooth really to be put back on Ops – 25 or 26 – something of that age, which we reckoned was too old.[2]

Anyway, we were flying across Germany when suddenly we saw an aeroplane going down in flames ahead of us. As we watched I told him: 'You'll see its tanks go up in a minute when it hits the ground.' Then the light flak began coming up as we reached the target, and he said, 'How pretty it all looks, and it all goes so slowly.' Before we knew it we were right in the middle of it with flak shells exploding nearby and these explosions were whipping by and then he was wondering what he'd got himself into. Flak always looked so harmless until you actually were there and it was coming close to you. It was quite an amusing experience to have this chap who had taught me to fly sitting next to me. It had been one of those nights where our take-off time had been continually postponed. It had started around 7.30, then put back to 8, then to 9 and then 10. We finally got airborne at 2 in the morning. By then the aircraft were covered in frost and I just rubbed away a little hole in the windscreen, peering out of this as we went thundering along the runway at something like 160 mph or so. He wasn't at all impressed by this. To him I was still the pupil!

Mentioning the name John, a friend who for the early years of the war seemed to shadow Tom Cooke with his postings, co-author Simon Muggleton traced him and in 1999 received a very nice letter from him. This, of course, was John Cope, mentioned in earlier chapters:

Dear Mr Muggleton,

Thank you for your letter concerning my late WW2 friend, T C S Cooke. I can give you a brief run-down of my association with Tom from 1940 to 1943 in the RAF.

He and I joined the RAFVR, he at Portsmouth and myself at Southampton, in early 1939 (aged 18). From September 1939 we were called up and went through the training centres up to our 'Wings' standard, he at Prestwick and Sealand, and myself at Hatfield and South Cerney. So we did not actually meet until after our 'Wings' Course, and then at RAF Bassingbourne (No. 11 OTU). We had by then flown DH Tiger Moths and Airspeed Oxfords. We crewed up for OTU training on Wellington ICs in August and September 1940 and then were posted in October to No. 78 Squadron at Dishforth, Yorks, on Whitley bombers. We then endured a horrible winter of snow and ice, operating at first as second pilots (with sergeant ranks) and then after about ten trips, became captains of aircraft on the Whitley V.

When we had done about twenty operations the squadron moved to Middleton St George but we were there only for a few weeks and were then posted to newly formed 104 Squadron at Driffield, flying Wellington IIs with Rolls-Royce Merlin engines instead of the usual air-cooled Pegasus engines then used.

After thirty operations we were posted 'on rest' to No. 22 OTU at Wellesbourne Mountford as instructors on Wellingtons. We also both were commissioned as pilot officers and received the award of the DFM. After about fifteen months, having taken part from there in the '1,000 bomber' raids on Cologne and Essen, we were posted to No. 1657 CU at Stradishall, Suffolk, prior to a second tour of operations on Stirling Is, and after crewing up, we and our crews were sent to No. 15 Squadron at Bourn, Cambridgeshire, in November 1942.

Up to this time Tom and I had been together on the same units from August 1940 and then proceeded to operate on Stirlings. However, we were destined to be separated in early 1943 due to promotion, first to flight lieutenant and then squadron leader. I remained on 15 Squadron and subsequently moved with the squadron to Mildenhall, whereas Tom was posted to 214 Squadron to complete his second tour of operations.

I did not meet him again until after the war when we bumped into each other near Heathrow. I had joined BOAC and he had, after demob in 1946, joined BEA, so our paths did not coincide much due to the different routes flown by these two corporations at the time.

After a pretty full career, on both our parts, he finally got in touch with me again in 1989, just as he was moving to the Isle of Wight.

With best wishes for your research,

John Cope

Cope and Cooke, both being in 104 Squadron in 1941 and already friends, were both flying operations at the same time. Upon their return they would look to see if the other had returned. A nod and a smile was enough to acknowledge that they had. These were always difficult moments on any bomber squadron, looking around to see who hadn't made it. Empty chairs at the breakfast table spoke volumes. Yet few made any comment about the missing faces. Perhaps they would turn up later, having been forced to divert to another airfield. If they did not ever reappear, their faces soon became a blur in the memory. There was nothing to be gained by dwelling on those who had not returned. To do so would start them thinking about their own mortality and that would not be good.

John Cope was awarded the DFM, gazetted in September 1941, not only for nearing the end of his first tour but also for a specific mission flown on the night of 4/5 July, the same day that Tom had been posted to became an instructor. His citation tells the story about what had happened on his twenty-eighth operation:

> A first class Captain who has carried out 28 exceptionally good operational sorties, always determined to get his attacks over the target, displaying the greatest zeal and courage. Recently on an attack on Brest on the night of 4th/5th July, 1941, his aircraft was hit by flak prior to the run-up. His starboard engine was severely damaged and caught fire. He, with great determination, switched the engine off, extinguished the flames and continued the attack using the port engine only. On the return home from the target, he re-started the starboard engine which again caught fire. He switched off the petrol and ignition and successfully flew and landed his aircraft and crew back at Exeter on the port engine. It is entirely due to this NCO's exceptional determination and skill that he brought his aircraft and crew back safely.

Following his tour on 15 Squadron, Cope, having been commissioned and reaching the dizzy heights of flight commander (squadron leader), was awarded the DFC, gazetted in April 1943.

John Cope assumed that because both their names began with the letters 'Co' was one reason why they seemed destined to be posted together for those three early years of the war. Cope's name certainly crops up time and again in Cooke's log book. The first time was at Bassingbourn, with No.11 OTU in August 1940. F/Lt Warner took them both up in a Wellington on a cross-country exercise, and then Cooke took over and flew Cope for another similar flight. They repeated this the next day and then for several days afterwards Cooke and Cope alternated as pilot, then doing the same on night flights.

Even when both were posted to 78 Squadron they had the occasion to fly together, taking Whitley bombers up on air tests in March 1941, for instance, followed by several day and night cross-country flying. Later at No.22 OTU they often worked together on various flights. They even got themselves an air-experience flight in a Halifax in July 1942, with S/L Tony Ennis DFC showing them the ropes. When with 15 Squadron, Cope, by now a flight lieutenant, is shown as flying together to RAF Gaydon and back in an Oxford in December. Cope's own crew at this time were Sergeants Klufus, Halcrow, Caveney, James, Clarke, Lousada and Hannah.

They got together in a Wellington III for a refresher on 25 August 1943 – Cooke's log book comment being: 'No trouble at all'. Both men were now squadron leaders. However, that's were it ends, with Cooke going to

138 Squadron for further adventures. Sadly, John Cope died in 2004, just a few years after Tom Cooke.

★★★

'One of the characteristics of the Stirling,' wrote Tom Cooke in *Aviation News*:

.... were the frequently produced wing tip contrails when the aircraft was flying under certain conditions. The Stirling came in for a lot of unfounded criticism from those who did not appreciate its qualities.

The long stalky undercarriage, low aspect ratio wings and lack of bomb racks capable of carrying more than 2,000 lb bombs, plus its alleged inability to climb, led to misconceptions that eventually meant the aircraft was assigned to secondary duties.[3]

The same wonder at the size led to the conclusion that the long throttle and pitch control runs would be too heavy for a pilot to manage. A decision was made to use 'exactor' controls. These were small pistons pushed by the levers which compressed oil in a pipeline leading to the engines where the pressure moved another piston, which in turn moved an actuating arm. It certainly required less force to operate but built in a considerable time lag and had an endearing habit of freezing up at altitude.

In addition to its built-in time lag and tendency to freeze up, exactors had the enchanting characteristic of constantly varying the control setting. One was constantly resetting boost and revs and trying to synchronise the engines. It did have the asset, however, of distracting your attention from all the hideous things going on outside of the cockpit.

Some of the take-off swings caused by the throttle lag were horrendous. The undercarriage legs did not always give, though, and I have seen fully laden Stirlings getting airborne at 90 degrees to the runway, causing the occupants of flight offices and control towers to be in good physical shape from constant running and dodging. I once saw a departing Stirling swing and hit a landing Stirling. The Stirling taking-off lost its nose back as far as the leading edge of the wing and then, with engines still running, trundled round and round the airfield like a headless chicken until the undercarriage finally gave up under the strain.

★★★

Reg Lewis and the others of Cooke's crew went on to complete their tour of operations by the start of July. After Cooke had departed, the crew made raids upon Dortmund, Duisburg, Bochum, Düsseldorf (twice), Krefeld and Cologne. This made a total of twenty-eight for Lewis, at which time he was recommended for the Distinguished Flying Cross. His recommendation form reads:

CONFIDENTIAL   NON-IMMEDIATE

RECOMMENDATION FOR HONOURS AND AWARDS

Christian Name	Reginald William	Surname	Lewis
Rank	Pilot Officer	Official No.	142873
Command or Group.	No.3 Group Bomber Command		
Unit	214 (FMS) Squadron		

Total hours flown on operations	155.15
Number of Sorties	28
Total hours flown on operations since receipt of previous award	N/A
Number of Sorties since receipt of previous award	N/A
Recognition for which recommended	Distinguished Flying Cross

1 P/O Lewis has completed 28 operational sorties against the enemy as Navigator.

2 He has successfully navigated his aircraft to targets in all parts of Germany, occupied France and Italy, including two attacks against Berlin and 7 against the Ruhr.

3 Throughout he has consistently maintained a very high standard of navigation, enabling his Captain to locate the target aiming points accurately.

4 On 3rd/4th July when the aircraft which he was navigating was hit by flak over Germany and petrol tanks were holed, causing considerable loss of petrol, it was largely due to Pilot Officer Lewis's accurate navigation that the aircraft was brought successfully back to base.

Date   19th July 1943.   Signature of Commanding Officer

M V M Clube

Wing Commander

Remarks by Station Commander

P/O Lewis has always displayed a high standard of devotion to duty throughout his 28 operational sorties.

Date   22/7/43   Rank   *K S Batchelor G/C* [DFC]

Remarks by Base Commander

Concur. Award recommended

Date   22.7.43   Rank   *A H Owen G/C*

Remarks by Air or other Officer Commanding

Recommended for the award of the Distinguished Flying Cross.

R Harrison
Air Vice-Marshal.
Commanding No. 3 Group.

Lewis' DFC was duly approved and it was promulgated in the *London Gazette* on 14 September 1943.

Notes

1   I once did this from the back seat of a DH Chipmunk two-seater, flown by a veteran RAF master pilot. We were out looking for ATC cadets, who similarly had been dumped in the middle of nowhere in the Cambridgeshire countryside and told to get back to a certain point without being discovered. Of course, it was not difficult to find many of them, usually bunched in small parties and waving madly at us. My pilot would swoop down and 'beat them up' and I can distinctly remember cadet berets being thrown up – and actually reaching some feet above us. Now that was real low flying!! Norman Franks.
2   Cooke was something like 22!
3   Such as transport, troop carriers and glider tugs.

8

REST & RETURN – THIRD TOUR

Officially leaving 214 Squadron on 2 May 1943, Tom Cooke was sent to No.1665 Conversion Unit at RAF Waterbeach, just north of Cambridge, to command the unit's 'A' Flight, where he remained for just four days. On 5 May he conducted an air test on Stirling BF330, which he combined with some local flying to Mildenhall, returning that night. The next day he was posted to command 'B' Flight of No.1651 Conversion Unit, operating from the same station, and managing to squeeze in a thirty-minute flight in a Tiger Moth (BB814) before conducting more various tests and local flying on further Stirlings.

With No.1651 Conversion Unit, he began testing officer and NCO pilots converting on to Stirling bombers, and occasionally managed to get himself up in the Tiger Moth to throw it about doing aerobatics. There is nothing like the freedom of a small single-engined biplane to sweep away the cobwebs and rigid routine of flying a large bomber aircraft. On 6 June he took up a couple of American second lieutenants and also Sgt Gornall, a flight engineer, who would later feature again in Cooke's flying life.

Flights continued on Stirling Is and also Oxford IIIs in June and there is an interesting entry in his log book for 24 June, flying an aircraft test with four passengers. These he named as F/Lt M.A. Brogan DFC RAFVR, formally of 149 Squadron, F/Lt N.A. Williamson DFC RNZAF, who had been on 214 Squadron during Cooke's time with it, P/O G. Watson DFM, another ex-149 Squadron pilot, and P/O Cullington.

These flights continued into July, mostly of short duration from an hour or so, down to a mere fifteen minutes. Then something a little out of the ordinary occurred on 26 July. Taking F/O Brace and crew, they became part of a large daylight exercise. Cooke noted in his log book: 'Daylight "Eric".

Attacked Waterloo Bridge, Docks at Portsmouth and Poole. Intercepted by Mosquitoes and Spitfires. Exercise carried out in formation with F/O Bird [in] 'E' No.3, W/O Mackie [in] 'U' No.2.'

Every now and again he would run a converted pilot through his paces by giving him a 'Flight Commander's Test', while on 6 August he took up some Air Training Corps (ATC) cadets for some air-experience flying. One of the longest trips he undertook was taking Sgt Dayton and his crew on a cross-country flight to Honeybourne, east of Evesham, Harwell, south of Oxford, Land's End, then all the way up to the Wash, and back to Waterbeach again, in four hours and forty minutes.

On 13 August he took Gornall up to Scampton in a Stirling to visit W/C Guy Gibson VC DSO DFC and S/L George Holden DSO DFC and Bar. Cooke knew George from earlier days, and Gibson had led 617 Squadron, the force that had bombed and breached the Möhne and Eder dams in the Ruhr back in May. Holden was also now with 617 Squadron and would take over Gibson's crew as well as the squadron when Gibson left later in August to take part in a tour of North America. Some give the date for his departure as early as 8 August, but Cooke clearly notes his visit to see him being on the 13th. Holden was killed in action against the Dortmund-Ems Canal on the night of 15/16 September 1943, along with four of Gibson's famous 'Dambusters'.

Gibson, of course, was himself killed in action flying in a Mosquito of 627 Squadron, as master bomber on a raid on 19 September 1944. Uncertainty as to how he died was never satisfactorily resolved. All that is certain is that the Mosquito crashed near Steenbergen, Holland. Thinking today tends to support accounts of him being shot down by gunners in a British bomber who suddenly saw a twin-engined aircraft appear behind them. Apparently it was not unknown for Gibson to sneak up behind RAF bombers returning from a raid to see if they were alert to his presence. On this occasion they were, and rather than order their pilot to take evasive action, merely opened fire.

The next day, 14 August, Cooke was up doing some two-engined flying – feathering the other two engines – while also doing some fighter affiliation with a Bristol Beaufighter. On the 15th there was more fun, in which he flew S/L Stafford Clark, the station medical officer, and a surgeon lieutenant from the Royal Navy. Cooke had been asked to demonstrate how evasive action affected members of air crew. On the 16th it was another Operation Eric. This time he flew with F/Sgt Riley and his crew. Cooke left Waterbeach and headed down to Brighton on the Sussex coast, then east along to Southend, before heading north-west to Swindon in Wiltshire. From here he pointed the Stirling south to reach the Isle of Wight at St Catherine's Point. He then carried on to Portsmouth before heading for London and making a 'bombing run' on Waterloo Station. Then he flew to 'bomb' Rushford, near Thetford, and finally the air gunners did some sea firing off the Norfolk coast before going home. Another long four hours and forty minutes of flying time.

Testing a Stirling on the 17th, he and Gornall suffered severe and violent juddering, possibly due to an airframe fault, but they got back safely. On the 19th Cooke flew four 'new' second pilots up to RAF Mepal where they were to join 75 Squadron. No.75 Squadron was a unique outfit, for soon after war was declared a bunch of New Zealand airmen who had come to England to fly back with some Wellingtons for the RNZAF stayed on. Shortly afterwards several New Zealanders in the RAF started to be moved to it and it became known as 75 (New Zealand) Squadron. After the war, in the form of thanks and gratitude, the RAF gave the RNZAF the squadron number, the only time the RAF gave up one of its squadrons, and today it is still officially 75 Squadron RNZAF.

The next two log book entries are of interest. Firstly on the 24th Cooke flew a Stirling up to RAF Tempsford, east of Bedford, by the A1. Along with Gornall, they flew a circuit for W/C R.D. Speare DFC and Bar, the CO of 138 Squadron which was based there. Richard Speare, a pre-war airman, had received the DFC in 1941 whilst flying with 7 Squadron, and a Bar whilst operating with 460 Squadron RAAF. He would also receive the DSO. Exactly why this flight was made is unclear, although as readers will discover, Tempsford was about to feature greatly in Tom Cooke's flying career.

The next day he took up his old pal John Cope, now a squadron leader with the DFC and DFM. Cooke's log book merely says it was a refresher flight for his old mate. Later that day, Cooke went up with Cope for another flight, but this time it was in a Wellington III (BK337) of No.29 OTU.

However, there was obviously something in the wind. Exactly what it was we can see from the words of Tom's former navigator on 214 Squadron, Reg Lewis DFC:

> By the time we had got to the end of March 1943 we had flown 20 operations and Cookie had flown his 20 that fulfilled his requirement for a second tour contract. In total he had done 50. At that stage he left the Squadron after a few weeks while we still had some more to do. Cookie received the DFC and eventually went off to a Conversion Unit to instruct new pilots onto the Stirling, as a flight commander. A Squadron Leader Bilton took his place as flight commander on 214 Squadron and we flew with him to complete our tour. He did not have the operational experience of Tom Cooke and I don't think he quite had the operational skill or was able to handle a Stirling as well as Cookie but we had some eventful and uneventful last few trips with him.

However, we did have one with him which was probably the most exciting of our tour because we managed to get attacked by a fighter and we returned from Düsseldorf on three engines. Unbeknown to us our tyres had also been punctured in the attack so we crashed on landing. I was actually hit by [gunfire from] this fighter and spent a while in hospital but was back on operations again some 16 days later. We were also hit by flak going to Cologne on 3 July, so it was an exciting little time overall. However, that trip proved to be our last on the Stirling. In fact it was also the end of our bombing efforts.

By this stage, Cookie, stuck into his instructing job at a Conversion Unit, was itching to get back into action.

In all probability Cooke would have found it difficult to have himself posted back to a bomber squadron after only a couple of months, but he had obviously come into contact with the people at RAF Tempsford, whose operations were somewhat different to night bombing. Lewis continues:

We hadn't yet left 214 Squadron when Cookie came over and asked us if we'd like to see what else we could do. We said yes, while ordinarily, of course, we would have been posted to some instructing jobs somewhere. He told us he thought it might be possible for us to get posted to RAF Tempsford. This was that Station from which Special Duty flying was carried out, and by Special Duties, I mean this was where the aegis of SOE [Special Operations Executive] where various secret operations were carried out. This involved dropping agents, and or supplies, in all areas of Europe, from Norway to Czechoslovakia, or further still into Poland and to the most southern parts of France, and so on, from Halifax aircraft. The supplies were dropped to Resistance fighters and organisations, and Tempsford also used Westland Lysander aircraft to actually land in occupied territory to deliver and retrieve agents.

I have to say we were enamoured with the idea of going to Tempsford and once the paper work had been completed, most of us found ourselves posted to Tempsford, to join No. 138 Special Duties Squadron, on 9 September 1943.

I should also record that when Group HQ heard of our plans, in their doubtful wisdom decided that we were the right types for the Special Duties set up at Tempsford. We did lose our flight engineer, L Collins, who got his dearest wish to undertake a pilot's course, so we needed a new bod. Cookie managed this by bringing along Len Gornall who had been flying with him at Waterbeach. He had also, we discovered, already flown a tour on Stirlings. Len hailed from the Merseyside area. He ran a Ford 8 h.p. car, but I dare not commit to paper some of the pranks we got up to in that.

At RAF Tempsford, our Nissan hut, in which we were all domiciled, always had a supply of petrol which was stored in large cans on a shelf above the entrance door. Len also had a mongrel dog which often came up on air tests with us – but never on Ops. Len was an extremely brave character.

For the record, Tom Cooke's crew on 138 Squadron were as follows:

Navigator: F/O Reginald William Lewis DFC, aged 21, a former clerk from Upminster, Essex. He had joined the RAF in February 1941 and had been at No.26 OTU before going to No.1657 Conversion Unit.

Flight engineer: F/O Leonard John Gornall, a former apprentice engineer from Birkenhead, Cheshire, aged 21. He had joined the RAF in August 1939.

Wireless operator: F/O John Stanley 'Stan' Reed, a former salesman from Sunderland, Durham. Aged 30, he had joined the RAF in September 1940 and had also gone through No.26 OTU and No.1657 Conversion Unit.

Bomb aimer: P/O Ernest Bell came from Newcastle-upon-Tyne and was 21 years old.

Rear gunner: F/O Robert Leslie Beattie, from Londesboro, Ontario, Canada. A former salesman, he was 30 years of age and had joined the RAF in February 1941. He too had been to No.26 OTU and No.1657 Conversion Unit.

They were soon joined by F/O A. Bruce Withecombe as dispatcher. He was 22, from Northam, near Bideford, North Devon, and had been a dental mechanic prior to joining the RAF in June 1941.

★★★

Special Operations Executive (SOE) had come into being during 1941, at a time when Winston Churchill, Britain's prime minister and outstanding war leader, wanted to, as he put it, 'set Europe ablaze'. His idea was to maintain the hostile pressure on German occupation troops in France, Holland and Belgium by helping those Resistance movements then being organised in these countries. Specially trained agents were selected because they were either native to these countries or were British volunteers who had both the language skills and knowledge. The agents would be parachuted or sometimes landed into the occupied zones in order to help the local Resistance groups and, on occasions, help to disrupt the German war efforts by sabotage. This might involve blowing up bridges and railway tracks, cutting telephone wires, etc. It was always going to be a dangerous occupation for anyone engaged in these activities and the Germans were not worried if they came down heavily on the local population. Often people were arrested, sent to concentration camps or even shot if it meant they might curtail these irritating habits of civil disobedience.

This obviously meant it was necessary to have a special RAF unit formed to deal with these operations and initially this came in the shape of 419 Flight (later 1419 Flight), which was formed at RAF North Weald as early as 1940. The Flight grew so rapidly that it soon became necessary to have a larger unit, and in consequence it was decided to form a full squadron. Therefore, in August 1941, 138 Squadron was formed at Newmarket from the nucleus of 1419 Flight, and was designated as 138 (Special Duties) Squadron.

Equipped at first with Whitleys and Lysanders, then with Halifax aircraft, it began operations from Newmarket, then Stradishall and finally from Tempsford. Its first CO was W/C E.V. Knowles DFC, and later, in November 1941, it was led by W/C W.R. Farley DFC, who had been awarded his DFC for work with both the Flight and the squadron. By September 1943, when Cooke and his crew arrived, 138 Squadron was commanded by W/C Speare. The squadron had moved to Tempsford in March 1942. There was also a Lysander squadron based at RAF Tangmere on the south coast. Lysander pilots would fly night sorties across the Channel taking agents and landing them in the middle of nowhere, with the help of local Resistance groups who would secret the agent away so he or she could begin their support work. This squadron would also use Hudson twin-engined aircraft for similar operations where a larger aircraft was needed to take not only agents but supplies. No.161 Squadron also operated Halifax aircraft from Tempsford.

If anyone thinks that operating with these Special Duties squadrons was an easier option to bombing sorties over Germany, they should think again. Dropping agents by parachute into precise places in the middle of nowhere in any of the occupied countries necessitated low flying, and before they could let their passenger go, the crew needed to be sure they were in the right place and the correct signals had been observed from the reception parties on the ground. German fighters and flak might be less of a hazard, except when flying into or back out of these countries, but flying comparatively low in a totally blacked out countryside, only sometimes aided by a period of moonlight when cloud per-mitted, caused just as many casualties amongst the crew of 138 Squadron as with a main force bomber squadron. Care had also to be taken in case the Germans infiltrated a Resistance group and were now acting as the reception committee for an agent about to be either parachuted down or landed by Lysander. No.161 Squadron was commanded by W/C L.M. Hodges DSO DFC and Bar. Lewis Hodges had gained his first DFC with 49 Squadron in 1942, and the Bar in May

1943 while flying with 161 Squadron. He later became an air vice-marshal with a Bar to his DSO as well as French decorations.

Once posted to 138 Squadron, Tom Cooke became officer commanding of 'A' Flight and after arrival he and the others spent several days being given instruction about what their duties were, how they should operate and how important their jobs were within the overall scheme of things. There was also a great need for secrecy. Loose talk was always heavily discouraged by RAF personnel in all units, but with 138 Squadron it was even more imperative and the lives of their agents, whom they called 'Joes', could be seriously put at risk if loose talk was overheard at a local pub, cinema or dance hall.

On 24 September 1943, Cooke had his first flight in a Halifax II (BB364 R) since that air-experience flight with John Cope back in July 1942, with F/Lt R.E. Wilkinson in the captain's seat. Reg Wilkinson had just been awarded the DFC for his work on the squadron. With him on this 'air experience and dual on type' flight was P/O Gornall, P/O Bell and Sgt Shaw. Later, Cooke took off again in this aircraft for his first solo on type, taking Gornall, Bell and P/O Beattie with him. On the 25th he was off in another aircraft (LW375), this time on a two-hour and fifteen-minute cross-country flight via Andover, Pershore, Cambridge, Peterborough, Hitchen and back to base. On this trip he took a five-man crew, Bell, Lewis, Reed, Gornall and Beattie, and they carried out 'Rebecca' training. The same crew made another practice flight on the 26th and again on the 27th, although this time they flew a fighter affiliation sortie, with F/Lt Stiles as co-pilot.

Rebecca (and its associated 'S-phone') was a blind homing aid where an airborne station – Rebecca – was used in combination with a ground station known as 'Eureka'. This enabled people on the ground, either soldiers in action or, in 138 Squadron's case, Resistance people, to give an aircraft a pinpoint for the dropping of agents or supplies. It used a form of cathode ray tube. Invented by Dr R. Hanbury-Brown and J.W.S. Hope of the Telecommunications Research Establishment (TRE) in 1941, it was modified several times during 1943–44 and was now used regularly by the RAF, where accuracy in locating people on the ground was paramount.

After a flight on the 28th, flying a night practice drop using Rebecca, Cooke recorded in his flying log book that they had flown once again LW375, coded NF-O. Although during his time on 138 Squadron he would fly a number of Halifax aircraft, eventually he would settle down with *O-for-Oboe* as his main aircraft, and fly most of his operational missions in it. Once he had started writing down LW375 in the log book he continued to do so as a matter of routine. However, Halifax LW375 did not serve with 138 Squadron, but operated with

425 and 296 Squadrons, and then with No.1355 Conversion Unit and finally with No.1 Ferry Unit. What he should have written down was that *O-for-Oboe* was LW275.

★★★

The Handley Page Halifax was the second four-engined bomber to fly with the RAF after the Stirling. This was only three months after the Stirling, but it was the Halifax that first bombed a German target, during a raid on Hamburg in March 1941. With the coming of the Avro Lancaster in early 1942, it and the Halifax became the two main bombing aircraft to serve with Bomber Command until final victory in 1945.

Just as with RAF day-fighters, the Spitfire being better known than the Hurricane, so the Lancaster was far better known than the Halifax. Nevertheless, the Halifax did wonderful service with the RAF, not only with Bomber Command but also with Coastal Command, Transport Command, and it also saw service in the Middle East and the Far East. Just like the Lancaster, it had a normal crew of seven and was powered by four Rolls-Royce Merlin X engines. Its range varied depending on bomb load, but, of course, with 138 Squadron there were no bombs carried, so the range could be as high as 2,500 miles. With some of the far-flung places 138 Squadron had to fly to it was just as well. When dropping agents, they used a hatch in the floor of the fuselage – the agents did not just fling themselves out of the side door. They would sit over the hole with a red warning light on the fuselage side. When the pilot was happy they were over the correct spot and had received the pre-arranged signals from the ground, he would press a 'tit' and the green light replaced the red and out would go the Joe.

★★★

There is no way of knowing just how Cooke and his crew felt about their upcoming sorties with their new squadron, but one can easily imagine how they might have reacted within a week of their arrival. On the night of 14/15 September, four Halifax aircraft did not make it back to Tempsford. One, HR666 *E*, with F/Sgt W.H. James in command, went out on a mission to Poland, code-named Flat 12A. They were shot down into the sea off the Danish coast. James and four of those aboard were killed, and two became prisoners of war. JD154 *V*, with F/Lt F. Jakusz-Gostomski DFC PAF at the controls, flew a Flat 22 operation. Flying low, it crashed into a building at Nowe Skalmierzyce, south of Kalisz, dived into the ground and exploded.

All seven Polish air crew died. Franciszek Jakusz-Gostomski had won his DFC with 300 (Polish) Bomber Squadron in 1942. There was, in fact, a Polish Flight as part of 138 Squadron known as 1586 Polish Special Duties Flight.

Halifax JD269 Q, with F/Lt A.J.M. Milne DFC, also went to Poland and was shot down by AA fire south-west of Mińsk Mazowiecki. They were carrying three Polish agents who were believed to have been killed along with the seven RAF men. Angus Milne had won his DFC on Cooke's old 214 Squadron in August 1943. Finally, F/O E.C. Hart, flying JN910 K, also out on a Flat 22 mission to Poland, dropped his agent but was hit by flak on crossing the German coast on the way home and crashed into the Baltic. Seven men died, one was taken prisoner.

In all, the squadron had sent out eleven aircraft that night, so with four missing and at least two others damaged by AA fire, the odds of survival did not look good for Cooke and his crew. It looked decidedly worse after the night of 16/17th, as two more squadron aircraft did not make it back. Again Poland was the area of operations. Halifax JD156 W, flown by F/Sgt L.A. Trotter RAAF, was shot down by a night-fighter and crashed into the sea off Jutland. The pilot and three of his crew became prisoners; the other three died.

Halifax BB309 T, with F/Sgt T. Miecznik PAF in command, was also shot down by a night-fighter on his way back from Poland after dropping two agents into area Obraz 108. Only the pilot survived by evading; five of his all-Polish crew were killed and one captured. Five civilians also died when the aircraft crashed into a Danish farmhouse at Slaglille, north-east of Soro. Both aircraft had been intercepted and shot down by pilots of 11./NJG3, Oberleutnant Johannes Hiedlmayr and Leutnant Richard Burdyn, each claiming their first night victories.

Things did not improve. Two more Halifaxes were lost on 19/20 September. First BB317 N, with F/Sgt N.L. Sherwood in command, was damaged on a trip into Holland and was forced to ditch. Sherwood and two of his crew were killed, four being rescued and taken prisoner. It might have been five but one man was washed overboard just hours before being rescued and drowned. Norman Sherwood was 21, married and came from Morden in Surrey.

The other loss was of S/L R.P. Wilkins DFC RCAF and his crew, who had also been awarded the Czech Military Cross. This was a highly experienced crew for, apart from Richard Wilkins whose DFC had been won with 138 Squadron, two of his crew had received DFMs with 138 Squadron too; another had the DFM following a tour with 58 Squadron in 1941, while yet another had also received the Czech Military Cross. P/O G.A. Berwick DFM had been the flight engineer and when awarded his decoration in January

1943 he had flown over twenty sorties. F/O J.W.H. Brown, navigator, won his DFM flying with 58 Squadron during 1940–41, having then flown twenty-one bombing ops. F/O H. Burke, WOp/AG, had won his DFM in 1942, having flown forty trips, mostly with 58 Squadron, then with 138 Squadron, so was an extremely experienced wireless operator. The rear gunner, F/Sgt A. Hughes, had received the Czech Military Cross. The Halifax went down into the sea off the Frisian Islands and there were no survivors. They too had been operating over Holland on a Catarrh 14/Leek 9 sortie.

One of these aircraft was claimed by Major Werner Streib, Kommodore of NJG1, as his sixty-fifth victory. As his score shows, Streib was a very successful night-fighter pilot and, at 32 years of age, he was no youngster. He would gain one more kill before becoming the Inspector of Night-fighters.

September 1943 ended for Cooke and his crew with a flight in LW274 *E*, dropping a sea marker on which his air gunners could practice their firing skills. He ended this trip by feathering inner and outer engines in turn to see how the aeroplane handled, and how quickly they could get the engines running normally again. Cooke also ran his flying hours total to 1,309 in this week.

★★★

If there was any hesitation by Cooke and crew as they became operational in view of the recent losses it hopefully did not show. October began with an aircraft acceptance test on the 1st, Cooke recording in his log book that it was DJ921 *B*, although there is no such serial for a Halifax II. He continued with this error when he flew to Chedburgh and back on the 3rd. On the 4th came the crew's first operation with 138 Squadron, in *O-for-Oboe* (LW275). Reg Lewis:

> There were certain skills required at Tempsford, that were rather different from those we used with Bomber Command. It called for a great deal of accuracy from the navigator and a high degree of flying skill from the pilot, and certainly the bomb aimer, who was called in to assist in helping the navigator.[1] Accuracy was essential because wherever we were going, be it Poland or the South of France, one was carrying precious cargo in the form of human cargo, who we were going to drop in the middle of an occupied country and at a pre-arranged appointed place.
>
> So, in deep contrast to bombing a place in the Ruhr, for instance, where even if we missed the actual aiming point, the bombs would hopefully be recorded as a 'near miss', now we had to locate the corner of some field

somewhere, and only when ground signals had been passed between us in the air and those on the ground, could we comfortably let out the agent who would parachute down.

This was achieved mainly by flying at fairly low levels, rarely much above 1,000 feet, at night, and because it was necessary to fly at such a height, we only operated during the moon periods. That is to say, full moon; or, say, from half full moon, or a little less, so during perhaps in all a twelve day period. This also assumes we had fairly cloudless nights. We never dropped blind and careful consideration was always made to the weather forecasts of the areas we were going to before taking off.

One navigated mainly by map-reading. On some nights every aircraft in the Squadron would be flying to a different point on the compass and we had to keep low for if we flew at normal heights we were very vulnerable to anti-aircraft fire or night-fighter attack and almost certainly shot down. Low heights also helped keep night-fighters away for it was difficult for enemy radar to locate us and therefore completely impossible for controllers to vector a Messerschmitt 110 or a Junkers 88 towards us, and even if one did come close, we would be lost in the ground clutter on the fighter's own radar.

Personally I was to find the work extremely interesting and we also had other aids to help us with navigation. Two were called *Rebecca* and *Eureka*. Once in the area of our drop zone we were able to pick up a transmission from a reception party on the ground and we could home-in on that beacon. This was not commonly used, for not every ground party had this apparatus but they were a marvellous means of identifying a correct dropping point. We also had an instrument known as an 'S-phone' and that enabled the pilot to have a conversation with the reception party, using his normal intercom, and when sufficiently close, one could speak to them and exchange whatever coded messages were necessary. There was always the danger that the Germans had captured a ground party and were hoping to convince us to drop our agent into their eager hands, so it needed care to ensure those on the ground were the actual people we were meant to contact.

It was necessary when dropping agents or indeed supplies to people on the ground, that we flew into the prevailing wind and at the minimum height to get either or both onto the ground as quickly as possible, so we were often down to 700 feet or so for the run-in. The reception party would identify themselves and also provide us with the best course to approach them. They would do this by a series of, maybe, four or five lights, mostly hand-held torches, arranged in such a way as to make a rough shape of a cross. We would then fly up the stem of the cross and drop at the intersection.

Due to the secret nature of 138 Squadron's activities, it is difficult to find very much information on the operations Tom Cooke and his crew carried out. The squadron's war diary Form 540 gives little away either.

Their first operation on the night of 5/6 October 1943 was one of three the squadron undertook. Cooke took off at 2014hrs in *O-for-Oboe* and all that is recorded is that it was to France and given the code word Wheelwright 30. The code 'wheelwright' meant a trip to the Bordeaux-Basses Pyrenees area. The squadron diary records that the Halifax landed back at base at 0253hrs. Cooke merely noted in his log book, 'Operations as ordered, somewhere in France' with Lewis, Bell, Reed, Gornall and Beattie, and that the flying time was six hours and forty minutes.

The other two operations that night were Wheelwright 42, flown by F/Sgt B.L. Gregory (later warrant officer DFC), and Grebe 1, flown by F/Lt J.V. Perrins (later DFC), to Norway (Grebe or, to be correct, Grebered, were Norwegian trips). Both aircraft returned safely having completed their drops successfully. There were lots of code words used at this time: Apollo, Capricorn, Feather, Tablejam, Cottage, Harr, Bob, Scientist, Paul, Trainer, Tom, John, Peter, Marc, Spaghetti, Fieldfare, Asnvil, Osprey, Goldfinch, Pelle Fleu, Mine, Gendarme, Osric, Stockbroker, Detective, Parson, Jockey, Tybalt, Rigi – the list seemed endless. Some had different numbers after them and, of course, the names were repeated as further operations to these coded areas came along. Most of these were French trips: Parson, for instance, concerned the Rennes area and Jockey was for the Apt-Nice areas. Tybalt meant Belgium and Rigi, Germany.

Cooke's next operation was flown in LW276 *E* on the 8/9th. Four sorties this night, beginning at 1805hrs with Cooke and crew heading for Norway on another Grebe sortie. Again it is frustrating not to know more but the squadron diary says nothing and Cooke only noted in his log book: 'Operations as ordered, somewhere in Norway.' It was an eight-hour and forty-five-minute mission, with eight hours on instruments in thick cloud.

Three days later, on the night of 11/12 October, they were off to Norway again, this time in LW278 *T*. Two aircraft and crews were going to Norway, S/L C.W. Passy on operation Tablejam 12 and Cooke on operation Bundle. Cooke took off at 1756hrs and both sorties were completed, with both pilots being diverted to land at RAF Kinloss, Cooke noting an eight-hour and five-minute flight, most of which was in cloud and flying on instruments. This bad weather continued into the next day, for Cooke noted that upon his return to Tempsford the cloud was down to 400ft and visibility no more than 800yds beneath it. All but the ten minutes for the actual landing was on instruments. On the 14th he put on his flight commander's hat and tested DJ921 *B*, which had been fitted with a new port outer engine.

Cooke's next operation, his fifty-fourth, was not completed. On the night of 17/18th, no fewer than eight Halifax aircraft of 138 Squadron headed out on a variety of operations, all to places in France. Cooke took off in aircraft *S-for-Sugar* on Operation Trainer 96, but a fire started in the aircraft mid-Channel. The crew managed to put it out and they carried on to the French coast, but the fire was still smouldering and in danger of flaring up again so they reluctantly had to abort and bring their agent back to base. They had left at 2016hrs and were down by 2317hrs.

S/L Cyril Passy DFC was lost on 18/19 October in LW281 *W* on a trip to Belgium. The aircraft was attacked by a night-fighter and crash-landed east of Antwerp. While one of the crew was captured, Passy and the remainder of his crew, as well as the agent, M. van Schell, evaded. Passy had won his DFC as a night-fighter in North Africa with 89 Squadron, so now he knew how it felt to be on the receiving end of a night attack. Helped by the Resistance, Passy eventually ended up in Gibraltar via the famous Comet line and was back in England before Christmas. One of his crew, F/O G.H. Ward DFM, had been Passy's radar operator in 89 Squadron as a flight sergeant. George Ward was also passed along the Comet line with his pilot. Most of the others also went along with other parties on the Comet line, although one, Sgt J.P. Healey RCAF, fought with the Belgian Resistance until September 1944. They were possibly brought down by Feldwebel Günther Bahr of III./NJG6, who also claimed a Lancaster, his fifth victory.

By early November, Tom Cooke and his crew were back flying LW275. On the 3rd they had a short flight, testing the aircraft by feathering the two starboard engines. That night 138 Squadron lost a crew. P/O H.F. Hodges in Halifax DT726 (NF-H) were on a John 13 operation. All on board except the rear gunner, Sgt J.F.Q. Brough, were killed.

★★★

Two days before Tom Cooke's next operation with 138 Squadron, Bomber Command had another of its pilots awarded the Victoria Cross. William Reid was serving with 61 Squadron operating out of Syerston, near Newark, which he had joined in September 1943. By November he had a reputation for determination during raids over Germany and it was this determination that led to his bravery on the night of 3/4 November 1943.

Flying Lancaster LM360 QR-O, he and his crew set off for Düsseldorf. They were a reasonably experienced crew; in fact, F/Sgt A.F. 'Joe' Emerson in the rear turret was on his second tour. It would be Bill Reid's tenth operation and Emerson's thirty-eighth. His mid-upper gunner was F/Sgt C. Baldwin.

Soon after crossing the Dutch coast they were attacked by a Me 110 night-fighter; one cannon shell blew out Reid's windscreen and others damaged both gun turrets. Reid was wounded by splinters to the body and face – even his eyelids, but his eyes were not touched. Pulling his goggles over his eyes to help deflect the howling wind coming through in front of him, he decided to carry on despite the damage, which also included a smashed port elevator and the loss of several instruments, including the compass. With his foot jamming hard down on the rudder bar to keep the Lancaster straight, they were then attacked by a Fw 190, which raked the whole of the fuselage, killing his navigator and seriously wounding the wireless operator, Sgt J.J. Mann. Reid was also hit, as was his flight engineer, F/Sgt J.W. Norris. The oxygen and hydraulics systems were also hit.

Despite their wounds, Reid and Norris struggled with the controls, Reid calmly continuing their track to the target, although they were now down to 17,000ft. Keeping his eye on the Pole Star until he finally spotted Cologne off to starboard, Reid approached Düsseldorf, which he reached a good hour after the second night-fighter had attacked. The bombs went down and, with Reid now folding his arms around the control column, they turned for home.

Reid was suffering. His position with left leg pushed down on the rudder, his arms gripping the control column with fingers linked, was sapping his strength. Reaching the Dutch coast again they came under AA fire but got through without further damage. By the time they got close to the English coast, Reid was aware of their low fuel state, ruptured hydraulics and bomb doors hanging down, and that there was only partial control in direct flight. Nearing an airfield, he had to get the wheels down by using the emergency bottle, but now at a low, and warmer, altitude, his head and facial wounds were opening and he was in danger from blood flowing into his eyes at these crucial moments.

Preparing his crew for a crash-landing and with his bomb aimer, F/Sgt L.G. Rolton, standing behind him in case he should black out, Reid put the aircraft down at a USAAF base at Shipdham, Norfolk. The undercarriage collapsed and the crippled Lancaster screeched along the runway until it finally stopped after some 60ft. Not long afterwards F/Sgt Mann, the wounded wireless operator, died of his injuries.

Bill Reid received the VC, while Norris was given the Conspicuous Gallantry Medal (CGM) and Joe Emerson the DFM. Reid later returned to operations with 617 Squadron in January 1944, flying a number of operations before being shot down on 31 July to end the war as a prisoner at Stalag Luft III and later in Stalag IV. Joe Emerson also returned to operational flying but did not survive the war. Les Rolton was later commissioned and received the DFC while with 61 Squadron. In June 1944 Cyril Baldwin's DFM was announced.

On 5 November, Cooke got the chance to return to the skies over Germany, but dropping an agent this time rather than bombs. Four aircraft were on operations this night and Cooke was the first off at 1925hrs on a Rigi/Tybalt operation. They returned at 0050hrs but had only managed to complete the Rigi part of the mission; however, the other part was carried out successfully by the other three crews.

Two nights later, 7/8th, it was back to France for operations Posse and Bob 18. Nine squadron aircraft were out this night and, while Cooke noted those unhelpful remarks in his log – 'Operations as ordered, somewhere in France' – the squadron diary notes that his operation was not completed, so one assumes he brought his 'cargo' back, being unable to contact the Resistance people on the ground. However, with seven hours' flying time, six being flown on instruments, the operation counted – his fifty-sixth. Of the others this night, four crews did not complete their mission either, so it was a bad night for 138 Squadron.

Yet another loss occurred on this night of 7/8th November. F/Sgt K.R. Copus in JN921 *B* flew a Tom 6 mission and crashed near Liesse, north-east of Laon. There were no survivors. Anyone still thinking that being on Special Operations was less dangerous than flying bombing ops would be wrong.

There was another failure to drop on the 11/12th, on Operation Parson 17 to France. Taking off at 2054hrs and landing back at 0055hrs, weather must have been the main problem, for Cooke only recorded three hours and fifty-five minutes of flying, so must have aborted over France. While it counted as operation number fifty-seven, it would have frustrated Cooke and his men that they had put themselves in harm's way for no return for their efforts.

However, it was a better result on the 17/18th with a trip to Norway – Operation Curlew. Three aircraft went there, a fourth going into Belgium. One Norway flight was not completed but the others were. Cooke was off at 2107hrs and back at Tempsford by 0450hrs, so there was another seven hours and forty minutes for the log book.

A leave period now came up, Cooke starting it off on the 19th with a flight to Bruntingthorpe to pay a visit to his old pal John Cope; then he was off to spend some time with his wife. He did not return until early December, making his first flight on the 4th. It was just as well he had had a breather, for his next operation would take nearly two weeks to complete.

Notes

1 Lying in his bombing blister in the front of the Halifax, Ernie Bell needed to spot landmarks and report them back to Lewis in order to help maintain exactly where they were.

9

THE FINAL MISSIONS

Tom Cooke was still recording in his flying log book that he and his crew were operating in Halifax LW375 O rather than LW275. His first entry upon his return from leave was an air test in this aircraft on 4 December 1943. The winter weather was making flying difficult, but the next flight, dated 10 December, would take them all away from Britain's icy grip.

Taking off on what is recorded as his fifty-ninth operational trip, Cooke flew from base, across France, dropped supplies and then, instead of returning home, continued on to Blida in North Africa. Amazingly it only took six hours and five minutes on little else but instruments and Reg Lewis' skill in navigation.

Blida is situated just to the south-west of Algiers and about 8 miles from the Mediterranean coast. They stayed here until the 14th and then took off in daylight, heading north-east out across the Mediterranean and towards southern Italy, landing at Brindisi on the east coast of the heel of Italy's 'boot'. Another four days here, where they were briefed for an operation to a location in Poland and back, a flight of nine hours and fifteen minutes. After another two days' break, Cooke headed back to Blida, again in daylight, and on the 22nd flew direct from Blida to base in six hours and twenty minutes. These long flights took his total flying hours to over 1,400. Reg Lewis:

Our trips from Tempsford also included flights to the south of France, Norway, and one into Germany. I remember this one surprised me because we carried an agent dressed up in a German uniform. Then somebody had the bright idea of going to Poland via the Middle East and we flew out to Algiers and thence to Brindisi a few days later. Finally, from there we flew an operation across the Balkans to a spot somewhere near Warsaw and back. That in fact took over nine hours, and the whole trip involved a total of 15 hours. Apart from the danger of the flight itself it was almost at the complete endurance of a Halifax and a number of crews were being lost, particularly over the Baltic, from night-fighter attacks.

It was a navigational nightmare because we had no knowledge of flying over these territories, but nevertheless we certainly navigated to Poland. Our bomb aimer did a brilliant observation up the Vistula I recall, and we made our way back on what turned out to be an uneventful trip.

After these long trips there was no flying over Christmas; in fact, Cooke did not fly again until the 29th – twice – followed by some S-phone practice on the 30th and another flight test on the 31st. January began as December ended: cold. Cooke tested a new Halifax on the 4th which he turned down as being 'duff', but once the ground crew had done some work on it he passed it as okay on the 5th. On the 6th and again on the 8th he took Bell, his bomb aimer, up for some dual instruction in the squadron Tiger Moth. Bell was obviously going to be the man to fly the Halifax in case Cooke was wounded or killed, if only to get the aircraft back to England. To ensure there was extra cover in case this event ever occurred, he also took up Reed, his WOp/AG, in the Tiger on the 19th. Reg Lewis:

In January 1944 all we did was a couple of air tests the whole month because the weather was so appalling. Then as February began there was a bit of a flap on because with all this bad weather there was a back-log of agents itching to get going. Obviously the top-brass knew that the invasion was on the cards for early summer and it was important to get as many agents into position as quickly as possible to get the Resistance people fully prepared. However, February began bad and some crews were going out and being forced to return with their passengers still aboard.

There was a training centre for these agents not an awfully long way from Tempsford and I believe they had training courses there. At the end of these courses there would be agents ready for dropping during the next moon period. It was not uncommon for this centre to throw parties prior to this moon period and a number of us aircrew would be invited over. I know I went on a couple of them and they proved good evenings. Agents were there of course, but we didn't know them personally, or even their nationalities but we talked and had drinks with them.

At our base itself I particularly remember Yeo-Thomas coming to see us and talk to us, telling us something about what he and the others were doing in France. Nothing too detailed naturally, but he did emphasise how desperately important it was for us as air crews to drop these agents as accurately as we possibly could. Thomas was a very forceful and dynamic character. Many of our drops were blind, so the agents were relying on us completely to place them in the right spot.

***

W/C F.F.E. Yeo-Thomas came from London, born 1902, but his early life was spent in Dieppe, France. As a young man he saw active service as a dispatch rider in the First World War, having lied about his age, and later fought with the Polish Army during the Polish–Soviet War of 1919–20. Captured by the Russians he avoided action by escaping, strangling a Russian guard in the process.

Between the wars he worked in a Paris fashion house but after the fall of France in 1940 he escaped to England, becoming an interpreter with Free French forces. He then moved to SOE, initially in an administrative job and on liaison work. Volunteering for more hazardous duty, he was parachuted into France in early 1943. After a period back in England he again parachuted into France that September. After another period working with the Resistance he was back home, only to be parachuted into France a third time in February 1944, about the time same as Cooke and crew were lost on their final mission.

Thomas was betrayed and taken to Paris by the Gestapo where he was subjected to repeated and horrendous torture. Later sent to some equally infamous prison camps, he eventually escaped and when recaptured passed himself off as a French national, ending up in Stalag XX-B near Marienburg. He was finally freed in April 1945. His war service brought him the George Cross (1946), the Military Cross and Bar, the French Croix de Guerre and finally he was made a commanduer of the Légion d'honneur in June 1963. He was known by his code name of 'The White Rabbit'.

Post-Second World War he was a witness during the Nürnberg War Trials and a key witness against German guards who had been at Buchenwald and Dachau concentration camps. He died in Paris in February 1964. His first names were Forest Frederick Edward, but inevitably he was known as 'Tommy'. His story is told in the book *The White Rabbit*.

***

Throughout the war, 138 Squadron with its various aircraft dropped some 995 agents into occupied territories, plus over 10,000 supply packages. The Lysander pilots also brought out many VIPs and RAF evaders, and they were not averse to bringing back bottles of cognac or champagne if there was room. In all the squadron lost eighty aircraft.

A couple of these losses had occurred when Cooke and crew were on their trip to North Africa, Italy, Poland and so on. On the night of 10/11 December F/Lt A.C. Bartter failed to return. They had taken off from Tempsford at 2150hrs on Operation Tablejam 18 and 19, setting course for Denmark. They encountered a Me 110 night-fighter and in the exchange of fire both aircraft were hit. The Me 110 was seen to go down but Bartter was forced to crash-land his Halifax somewhere between Tostrup and Bonderup, 15km south of Holbaek. There were nine men aboard, for another pilot had been flying with the crew for experience, and of course the 'passenger', named as Dr Flemming Muss. He is noted as 'safe' so he must have been dropped before the encounter. Five crew members were subsequently captured, while three successfully evaded and reached Sweden with the help of the Danish Resistance, the pilot being one of them.

On 17 December F/Sgt J.G.A. Watson and his crew were off on a Detective 3 operation. Setting out towards France they encountered severe weather conditions and had to abort. Trying to land at the emergency airfield at Woodbridge, Suffolk, the Halifax hit a tree and crashed at Capel Green. Watson and four others were killed, and three injured. LL115 *A* was a write-off. That same night, F/O R.W. Johnson and crew were going out on a Wheelwright 36 trip over France. Bad weather also caused them to abort, but rather than attempt a landing in such appalling conditions, the crew baled out and the Halifax went into the sea off Felixstowe.

A third crew, that of Sgt H.D. Williams (BB364 *R*), were all killed on the 19th during a training flight. The Halifax collided with a tall factory chimney at the Arlesey brickworks, south-east of Henlow, Bedfordshire. They had been practising the dropping of supply containers over nearby Henlow airfield.

The night of 16/17 December was a bad one for the Special Duties squadrons, for apart from the two from 138 Squadron, three Halifax aircraft of 161 Squadron, also at Tempsford, had problems. All three were flying Wheelwright operations to France. DK206 MA-V was forced to return early and in attempting to get down at Woodbridge, the emergency airfield, it hit some trees and crashed in Tangham Forest, near Capel St Andrew. The two agents aboard suffered no injuries but the pilot and two crew members were killed, with the other three injured. LK889 MA-T hit a wooden radio mast west of Bawdsey, Suffolk, and crashed on to mudflats in the River Debden. The pilot and one other were injured while a third crew member was thrown clear but suffocated in the mud. LL120 MA-W was also forced back early and eventually the captain had to order everyone to bale out near Spilsby. All got down safely, with just one man injured, and the Halifax went into the sea off Skegness, Lincolnshire.

As if this was not enough, 161 Squadron, operating from Tangmere, had a Lysander crash into a ploughed field returning from picking up two agents in France, whilst trying to get down at base. The pilot was killed but the agents, a man and a woman, scrambled clear. This same night another Lysander pilot was killed trying to land at Ford airfield in Sussex. One of the two agents aboard was also killed and it is understood the other died later of his injuries.

★★★

No.138 Squadron had lost a crew while Cooke was on leave. W/O H.M. Kennedy in a Halifax V (LK743 BF-J) was on a Tybalt 3 and Thersites 4 operation on the night of 7/8 January, over Belgium. Returning five hours after take-off the machine crashed at Tetworth Hill, near Bedford. All were killed.

On the night of 14/15 January, two senior officers had been killed operating to Braunschweig. W/C N.R. Mansfield DFC was flying Lancaster ND357 GT-G but was shot down by a night-fighter over Holland. Nelson Mansfield, a 31-year-old New Zealander, had been awarded his DFC whilst flying with 156 Squadron since June 1943. He had flown some fifty-three operational sorties. He had a wife in London. W/O C.H. Lawrence, the flight engineer, had received the DFM in the autumn of 1943 after twenty-nine operations with 156 Squadron, but, being on a Pathfinder squadron, was on an extended tour of forty-five ops. S/L E.S. Alexander DFC DFM (navigator) was RCAF and had received an immediate DFM in May 1942 following a raid on Kiel with 149 Squadron. His aircraft was damaged by night-fighter attack, slightly wounding him, and had jammed the rear gun turret, trapping the gunner inside. Edward Alexander freed him with an axe and got him out. For his continued good work he received the DFC, gazetted in January 1944. Another decorated crew member had been F/Lt C.R. Swinney DFC, his award being gazetted in October 1943.

Lancaster DV404 AS-Z of 166 Squadron was being flown by the squadron commander, W/C C. Scragg MBE AFC. Colin Scragg was an American serving in the RAF since the 1930s. Believed to have been shot down by night-fighter attack, he was the sole survivor, ending up in Stalag Luft III.

A well-decorated crew from 514 Squadron was also lost on this raid. S/L E.F. Sly DFC had gained his decoration with 218 Squadron in 1943. Four of his crew each had received DFMs. Wireless operator W.L. Harvey RNZAF gained his DFM with 149 Squadron in 1943, an immediate award, on his twenty-second operation. During a mine-laying task he was severely wounded in the head but continued his job of getting bearings in order for the crew to get home, even though two important navigational aids had been knocked out. P/O E.H. Thomas RCAF, the bomb aimer, had been with 218 Squadron since 1942 and received the DFM in 1943 after twenty-eight operations. Another RCAF crewman was F/O J.A. Sneddon, mid-upper gunner. His DFM had been awarded for his work while flying with 115 Squadron, as rear gunner. P/O F.G. Rosher was, unusually, awarded the DFM whilst a flight sergeant gunnery instructor with No.1651 Conversion Unit in 1943, but he also volunteered for several operational flights when Maximum Efforts were called for. Tom Cooke had been with No.1651 Conversion Unit at the same time.

As already mentioned, the length of a first tour was generally thirty missions, although this did vary slightly from time to time. Also mentioned was that experience did not guarantee survival over Germany; a crew on its first operation could easily fall victim to flak or fighters as a crew on its final mission. Such an event took place on a raid on Berlin on 28/29 January. Lancaster ND382 AS-Z, flown by P/O J. Horsley DFC, from RAF Kirmington, was shot down and crashed at Fretzdorf, south-east of Witterstock. Joseph Horsley came from York and was 22 years of age. All were killed. They were on their twenty-ninth sortie, so were just about finished, especially if their war flying hours were about to exceed 200. Sometimes the criteria were thirty ops or 200 operational hours, whichever came first.

Joseph Horley had won his DFC for an earlier raid on the German capital in December 1943. Soon after crossing the enemy coast one of his engines failed but Horsley decided to continue on even though he would not have been questioned if he had turned back, especially with the target at such a distance. Over Berlin, amidst intense AA fire, Horsley made three bomb runs in order to make certain they were targeting the correct aiming point. Then he lost another engine to flak and having also lost the use of the directional gyro and artificial horizon he, with the help from his navigator P/O K.F. Cornwell, reached home on two engines. Ken Cornwell also received the DFC for his actions.

★★★

After more aircraft tests, Cooke and his merry men were selected for operations on the night of 4/5 February. Again we face the same dull 'Operations as ordered, somewhere in France' in his log book, with an equally bland: '20.46. Halifax aircraft "O" took off on operation Marc 1B, captained by S/L Cooke, target France, carrying Agent, containers and packages. Operations completed, landed base at 0404 hours.' Operation number sixty-three took seven hours and twenty-five minutes.

On the night of 5/6 February, F/Sgt Styles took his Halifax out on a Thrush Red operation to Norway, with containers and packages. They had one container 'hang up' (caught in the release equipment) and when Styles made another run over the reception area, there were no signals from the ground. Cooke and his crew were off again on the 7th, air testing LW275 for an operation that night. It was France again, but this time they would not make it home.

★★★

On 5/6 January 1944, main force squadrons were raiding Stettin and again some experienced crews were lost. No.35 Squadron had Halifax JP123 TL-F fail to get home, piloted by F/Lt R.R.G. Appleby DFC. Their last radio message said: 'On three engines, maintaining height, 5505N 0320E.' Robert Appleby had received his decoration the previous summer with 35 Squadron. Four of his crew had DFMs. F/Sgt B.L. Robinson, flight engineer, had just been recommended for his after thirty-five operations. WOp/AG F/Sgt I.C. Redfearn likewise had just been recommended after thirty-six sorties, while F/Sgt E.C. Nixon, bomb aimer, had his DFM gazetted in November 1943. P/O N.G. Emery DFM, navigator, was the only crew member to survive as a prisoner of war. He had received his decoration for his work in bringing home a crippled aircraft in October 1943 after it had been badly damaged by a night-fighter. The wireless was knocked out and most of the other navigational aids were not working, but he got them home.

A 207 Squadron Lancaster (ED586 EM-F) also failed to return, flown by F/Lt G.H. Ebert DFC. On board was W/C A.D. Jackson, who had twice been Mentioned in Dispatches. He had been attached to 207 Squadron to get operational experience prior to taking command of another squadron. All were killed.

★★★

Tom Cooke and his crew took off during the night of 7/8 February 1944, on what was hoped would be another reasonably normal operation. They took with them one passenger, an agent that had to be dropped that night, and all they knew was that it was important for him to be parachuted down safely. He had already been thwarted on previous nights because of the weather. Quite naturally they had no idea of the identity of the agent, who was only referred to as 'Roger'. However, his name was Francis Charles Albert Cammaerts.

In February 1944 Cammaerts was 27 years of age and had been born in London, the son of Professor Emile and Mrs Helen Cammaerts, who was a Belgian poet and patriot. Francis became a pacifist in the 1930s whilst reading

English at Cambridge University and history at St Catharine's College, where he won a hockey Blue. He became a teacher, starting his career at Cabin Hill School in Belfast in 1937. Once war came he became a farm labourer in 1940, rather than undertaking any military service.

However, with the loss of his younger brother, Pieter Emile Gerald Cammaerts, aged 21, whilst serving with 101 Squadron RAF on 31 March 1941[1] as a sergeant/observer, Francis decided he had to have a more active role in the war, so with his fluency in French and a love for this country too he joined the SOE. For someone who was to become so successful with the SOE it is interesting to note that he was initially assessed as 'lacking in dash' and 'not suitable as a leader'.

His first mission to France occurred in March 1943 and was in a 161 Squadron Westland Lysander, piloted by another famous person associated with SOE operations, S/L H.B. Verity. Hugh Verity was about to receive the DFC (gazetted in May 1943), having by this time flown well over 100 operational sorties, firstly with Coastal Command, then as a night-fighter pilot and finally on clandestine sorties into occupied territory across the Channel from RAF Tangmere. He would later be awarded the DSO and Bar, the French Légion d'honneur and Croix de Guerre.

Cammaerts was assigned to the 'Donkeyman' circuit in southern France, one of several such groups within Vichy France control. Based in Cannes, his cover was as a teacher recovering from jaundice. He soon organised his own 'Jockey' circuit of eight men who set about recruiting potential saboteurs in readiness for the invasion. By late 1943 he had started to organise several other groups down the banks of the River Rhône between Vienne and Arles, and also towards the Isére Valley. His usual mode of transport was by motorcycle and while visiting his groups nobody ever knew his real name or his nationality, or where he was based. It is said that during his time in France he never slept in the same spot for more than four nights. Cammaerts was recalled to London in November 1943 to be briefed on how the Resistance would be able to help the invasion of Europe.

By early February 1944 Francis Cammaerts was ready to return to southern France to begin work on how his groups could help the upcoming invasion by disrupting telecommunications, rail and road traffic, and all the other irritating inconveniences his bands of saboteurs could put their hands to. It is recorded that once the invasion began on 6 June 1944, every train leaving Marseilles for Lyons was derailed at least once and in the Indre Department of France more than 800 lines were cut in June alone.

As mentioned in the Preface, Tom Cooke flew towards the south of France on the night of 7/8 February 1944, having taken off at 1945hrs for the 700-odd-mile trip south. While his Halifax may or may not have been hit by AA fire over the

French coast, which could have potentially affected one engine, the fact remains that an engine caught fire. The first instinct had been to abort over the French coast but Cooke knew the importance of getting Cammaerts to his destination, so they carried on, despite encountering worsening weather conditions.

They had reached a spot some distance into France when Cooke first became aware that he had a problem. An initial glow quickly turned to visible flame, but they were so near their assigned drop zone he decided to attempt to reach the spot and drop the agent. This is confirmed by Reg Lewis, who recorded:

It was important to get our agent down to the South of France. The weather had already frustrated the start of his mission and two trips had already been aborted. We were briefed on the 7th, having completed a successful trip on the 4th, which took us over seven hours, down to Bordeaux I think. We were told to get him to a spot close to Marseilles, not that we knew his name at that time, and gathered previous attempts had failed and that it was absolutely imperative we get him there. We had been chosen this night because we were an experienced crew.

We set off in appalling weather and I don't think I saw the ground anymore until I landed in my parachute. In our desire to do everything in our power to deliver our man, we probably pressed on too much. We were in continual cloud, having also to fly above some high ground en-route, so a good deal of ice formed on the aircraft, altering our aerodynamics, and then an engine caught fire.[2] Although this was put out with the graviner extinguisher, we were losing height rapidly, again over some high ground, in the area of Valence in the Rhône Valley, just below Leon, so we had to advise our passenger to get out.

We tried to throw out as much equipment as we could in order to lighten the aircraft, but in the end we had no alternative but to jump for it.

Simon Muggleton was in touch with Francis Cammaerts in November 2000, who said:

I was flown back to France on the night of 7/8th February 1944. I should have been dropped south of Castellane, near the road Castellane – Grasse, but my Despatcher told me the weather was too bad and we had to return home. Some five minutes later he let me know that the aircraft was on fire and we had to jump.

Seeing the starboard inner engine starting to glow and then burst into flames, the fire quickly eating into the wing, Tom Cooke knew they would not be completing their mission. Hopefully the dispatcher, Withecombe, would get their passenger out in quick time once he announced the order to bale out. Going down to the forward escape hatch, having clipped on his parachute, Cooke found the hatch cover jammed. Returning to the cockpit was a problem due to the aircraft starting to spiral but he made it and, looking out at the burning wing, decided that any idea of trying to correct the spiral and getting back into some kind or level flight was impossible. He returned to the front lower hatch and with brute force, helped by adrenalin and anger, managed to kick it out; within a second he was out in the freezing night air and grasping for his parachute release handle.

How much height he had before the ground arrived he had no real idea, but he knew he had to get well clear of the falling Halifax before pulling the D-ring, after which he would either feel the merciful tug as the parachute opened above him or crunch into the ground 'like a pound of strawberry jam', as the song went. Mentally he could respond to the former but would have only the smallest of split seconds to be aware of the latter. He had survived more than sixty operational sorties and no doubt suspected that he was on borrowed time. Would his luck hold a little longer? The next few seconds would tell.

★★★

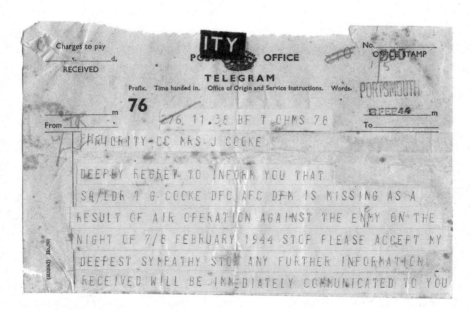

The telegram informing Tom's wife that he was missing on the night of 7/8 February 1944.

This same night 138 Squadron lost a second aircraft, Halifax LL114 NF-P, flown by F/O G.D. Carroll. They were also operating in bad weather over France on a John 35 sortie and crashed at Autrans, Isere, 14km west of Grenoble. All seven men aboard were killed and one assumes they had already sent down their agent. It is noted that the average age of these seven airmen was just 20.

★★★

After Tom Cooke and his crew were reported missing, acts of heroism continued to be made by men of Bomber Command, and so too did losses in air crew, experienced and inexperienced. Another raid on Berlin on 15/16 February saw the loss of S/L J.A. Hegman DSO DFC RNZAF, serving with 7 Squadron. He was aged 29 and lost with him that night was W/C James B. Tatnall OBE RAFO, a pre-war airman who had no doubt gone along for the ride. John Hegman came from Auckland and had been a farmer before he joined up in 1941. He had received the DFC in early 1943 whilst operating with 162 Squadron. In his 7 Squadron crew was P/O W.G.K. McLaren DFC, whose decoration had been gazetted in April 1944 for operations with this same squadron and so would have been on a second tour. Their Lancaster (JB224 MG-W) went down near Berlin.

Three DFM holders also died: Flight Sergeants D.E. Harrison (bomb aimer), A.K. Buchanan (wireless operator) and W.D. Nichols (air gunner). David Harrison had flown thirty-nine operations, twenty-six of which had been as marker to this Pathfinder squadron. Alexander Buchanan had just been recommended for his DFM after thirty-five operations, while Bill Nichols, from Huntingdon, was 40 years old and had similarly been recommended after forty operations as a mid-upper gunner.

No.7 Squadron suffered badly on this Berlin raid, with four Lancasters lost in all, and all with experienced men aboard them. F/Lt R.L. Barnes DFC captained JB224 MG-W, another to fall over the 'Big City'. Roy Barnes had received his DFC flying with 115 Squadron a year earlier, so had been recruited into the PFF. His New Zealand navigator, Frank Jones, got the DFC while with 149 Squadron. Bomb aimer James McLachlan had also been awarded the DFC for ops with 115 Squadron.

Lancaster ND365 MG-L was the third loss, flown by F/Lt P.K.B. Williams DFC. They were hit by a night-fighter and their bomber exploded, throwing out Peter Williams and F/Sgt G.S. Staniforth, the only two survivors who were taken prisoner, the latter with serious leg fractures. Staniforth was eventually repatriated in February 1945, having spent most of his time since capture in German hospitals. Peter Williams, whose DFC was awarded in December 1943 for bringing a severely damaged Lancaster back to England from Berlin, where he and his crew had to take to their parachutes, served out the war in Stalag Luft III. The others aboard were killed. They included P/O J.M. Alexander, holder of the Conspicuous Gallantry Medal (CGM), W/O Walter Hawkins DFC RCAF, another 7 Squadron veteran, awarded his DFC a year earlier, and F/Lt R.B.S. Ballantyne DFM. He had gained his DFM with 50 Squadron in 1941 as a sergeant WOp/AG, having flown thirty-one operations.

James Mitchie Alexander came from Wood Green, London. Born in 1920, he enlisted as the war began and he flew as navigator on sixty operations in the Middle East. Returning to England, he joined 7 Squadron and, having flown a further nine sorties, was awarded the CGM in January 1944. The CGM was only awarded to 110 airmen in the Second World War, it being the NCO equivalent of the DSO awarded to commissioned officers. He was buried on the Isle of Skaro, Denmark.

The fourth loss was Lancaster ND445 MG-D, captained by S/L R.D. Campling DSO DFC. Richard Campling was another stalwart member of 7 Squadron, having been given the DFC at the end of 1943, followed soon afterwards by the DSO. All but one of his crew had been decorated for bravery; F/Lt R.J.H. Clayton had just received the DFC, so too had F/Lt D.F. Langham and rear gunner W/O C.E. Quinn. Charles Quinn had won the DFM with 207 Squadron in 1943 after thirty-three operations. F/Sgt B.S. Cubbage had flown over thirty missions and had just been awarded the DFM. Lastly, F/Sgt C.H.L. Wright had also recently received the DFM after thirty-five operations, as flight engineer. His aircraft had been hit and damaged on one occasion and the petrol tank punctured, but his knowledge and expertise got them home, even helping to extinguish an engine fire as they neared home.

Not that Pathfinder aircraft were the only losses this night, for 50 Squadron lost F/O H.A. Litherland DFC and Bar, while 78 Squadron lost F/Lt R.N. Shard DFC DFM. Over the target their hydraulics were shot out and the wheels of his Halifax dropped and could not be retracted. Due to the drag that resulted, their fuel supply did not get them home and Shard had to order his men to bale out on nearing the English coast. All but one man were killed, mostly by drowning. Robert Shard had won the DFC in a recent operation to Magdeburg in January. Severely damaged by a night-fighter, he got his aircraft home despite losing an engine, the astrodome being shot away, both turrets being knocked out and damage to the flaps and burst tyres. Aged 23, he left a wife in Faringdon, Berkshire.

F/Lt K.H. Berry DFM, still only 20, was on his second tour with 103 Squadron and his navigator, S/L H.L. Lindo DFC RCAF, 27, hailed from Jamaica, British West Indies. They were shot down by a night-fighter on the 15/16th over Holland with everyone lost. They had become the victim of Oberleutnant

Heinz-Wolfgang Schnaufer of NJG1 – victory number forty-five – the first of three Lancasters he shot down that night.

Bomber Command crews certainly had a fear of night-fighters, and so they should; they were often deadly in air actions along the bomber streams. Take Schnaufer, for example. He often scored in multiples, almost as if it was too easy. He downed three bombers on 25 March 1944, four on 25 April, three on 13 May, five on 25 May, three on 13 June, four on 22 June and another four on 23 September. On 21 February 1945 he shot down nine Lancasters, perhaps even ten.

Author Norman Franks had a conversation with the late Mike Allen, who, along with his pilot Harry White and receiving the DFC and two Bars, flew night-fighter operations over Germany, endeavouring to intercept German night-fighters that were operating against RAF bombers, using Serrate radar with 141 Squadron. He said that it was not unusual to see dozens of RAF bombers in the night sky, all plodding along in the bomber stream and could see how relatively easy it was for German pilots to find targets with or without their airborne radar.

We will mention two more losses of note during February 1944. On the 15/16th too, a Mosquito of 169 Squadron (HJ707 VI-B), within 100 Group, was being flown by W/C E.J. 'Jumbo' Gracie DFC, an experienced day-fighter pilot who had fought in the Battle of Britain and on Malta. Like Mike Allen, he was flying bomber support missions. His aircraft was attacked by a night-fighter north of Hannover and set on fire at the starboard engine. Gracie, who had joined the RAF in the 1920s, was 32 years old. He ordered his navigator, F/Lt W.W. Todd, to bale out, which he did, but Edward Gracie didn't make it himself.

A few nights later, on the 19/20th, during a raid on Leipzig, Halifax III (HX325 TL-J) of 35 Squadron was attacked and shot down by a Ju 88. With a fuel tank on fire, the pilot, S/L D.J. Sale DSO and Bar DFC, ordered his crew to bale out; all did so, although the rear gunner was killed. Canadian Douglas Sale was badly injured and died from the effects on 20 March 1944. Sale, aged 30 from Toronto, had had an extraordinary war. On 12/13 May 1943, with 35 Squadron, his Halifax (DT801 TL-A) was shot down by Oberleutnant August Geiger of III./NJG1 over Holland. Geiger had claimed three kills this night, two Halifaxes and a Wellington, to bring his score to twenty-seven. Two of his crew were killed and four others were captured, but Sale evaded and after numerous adventures he got himself to Gibraltar in July, returning to England the following month. He was awarded the DSO.

In his crew that February night was fellow Canadian S/L G.H.F. Carter DFC and Bar, the squadron's navigation leader. Gordon Carter had also been shot down, over France, in raiding Lorient with 35 Squadron back in February 1943. He had also evaded capture, and so too did five of the crew, including his pilot, F/O J.C. Thomas RCAF. Carter was back in England in April. Thomas, an American in the RCAF, got himself into Switzerland in March. Returning to operations with 35 Squadron, Carter teamed up with Sale for further operations.

Another in the crew had been W/O G.H. Cross, the flight engineer, and holder of the DFC and DFM. Flight Lieutenants B.O. Bodnar DFC RCAF and H.J. Rogers DFC – both captured – were bomb aimer and wireless operator. Carter, Bodnar and Rogers all ended up in Stalag Luft III, a month before the mass breakout that ended so tragically.

Notes

1 Sgt P.E.G. Cammaerts was part of a Blenheim IV crew. Returning from an attack on Brest, his pilot overshot on landing at St Eval and crashed into a nearby field. Pieter Cammaerts and his pilot were killed, the air gunner injured. Oddly enough, Tom Cooke had been on a raid to Brest the night afterwards.
2 Lewis actually says two engines caught fire, but this is uncertain.

10

EVASION

The parachute opened and Tom Cooke's fall was jerked to a gentle drop. Within a short space of time he saw a brief glimpse of the snow-clad ground before he crunched down in a heap. He had heard the explosion as his aircraft had gone in and been aware of the instant flash that lit up part of the sky a short distance away. Then he was once again in darkness, alive, but alone and apprehensive. Reg Lewis recorded the start of his adventure after baling out:

> I landed in the small snow-bound area, just a few miles north east of Valence. [After burying his parachute in the snow] I walked for a while, saw I was in a very remote area but suddenly found a house. I didn't knock at first but began to explore the general area for an hour or so, but as far as I could discover, this was the only house around. Retracing my steps I went up to the front door of the house and knocked. It was eventually opened and I was allowed in by a very nervous lady and her daughter, they being aged around forty and twenty-ish. Explaining who I was frightened them even more. Not that they were afraid of me, but they knew, having been under German occupation for nearly four years, what the consequences would be if they were found to have given shelter to a British airman.
>
> Nevertheless, Bless them, they allowed me to stay the night and I gathered that their respective husbands had been directed by the Germans into some kind of factory work. I was given one of their suit of clothing and a pair of French civilian shoes, then they went out, once I had told them where I thought I had buried the parachute, and they found it and brought it into the house. They seemed very glad to have it. Taken to a bedroom I was quickly asleep, knowing that nothing much was going to happen to me now, and felt

determined to try and get back to England. I think what worried me most was that my mother, who I had never dared tell I had gone back onto operations, was going to receive a nasty telegram informing her that I was missing.

In the morning the mother had vanished from the house and I must say I was wondering if she was going to turn me in, but eventually she returned with a man with two bicycles. After eating some breakfast we rode off together and travelled quite a few miles before landing up in a small village, where I was taken into the back room of a pharmacy. Within 48 hours I was joined by three other members of my crew. They had been collected from various locations and each given civilian clothes.

In his debriefing by MI9 back in England, Lewis reported:

I came down about 2300 hours (7 Feb) within a yard of a house in a very small village. As I could hear somebody moving about nearby I ran for about 400 yards, leaving my parachute for the time being. The person moving about eventually made off, so I returned and hid the parachute in a ditch.

I walked about for an hour to try and discover my whereabouts, and eventually knocked at the door of one of a small cluster of houses. A woman opened a window at the top of the house and after some discussion, during which she fetched her 14-year-old daughter, I was admitted. With the help of drawings I made them understand that I was a British airman. Another daughter of about 24 joined us, and it was decided that I should stay the night and that they would try and obtain help for me in the morning. I discovered that I was near, and south of, Châteauneuf D'Isér. In the morning at about 0930 hrs another girl turned up who explained that the mother had gone off on a bicycle to get help.

At 1130 hrs a man arrived with a Dutch lad, who was also in hiding, and I was taken to a house in the neighbourhood of S. Marcel, where I eventually linked up with Bell, Beattie and Reed.

Tom Cooke had a similar experience and he too recorded what happened to him. He, Len Gornall and Bruce Withecombe had all landed quite near to each other and quickly met up:

On the ground I found I was somewhere between Dijon (?), towards Valence, perhaps Lyon, but right in the middle of some open country. The main problem initially was to find out exactly where I was. I had some maps and the sky was cloudy, so there was no way one could look at the stars and get a direction. None of the road sign-posts had been taken down in that part of France but this didn't help unless you've pinpointed the area you were in. However, I eventually discovered where I was and set forth.

We decided our objective should be to get over the border into Switzerland. We knew that one place on the border, at Jura, was heavily patrolled and guarded and were not going to get over there. So we tried to go round and come up by Grenoble. The first thing that struck me, and I don't think the other two were totally aware of this, certainly Len wasn't – he wasn't really sure of what time of day it was – that in this Special Duties Squadron I was one of the few people, because I was a flight commander, to see the maps of France showing all the dropping places for our agents. I remember having the impression that France was an absolute maze of people waiting to help us. Therefore, we started to knock on doors. As I was the only one able to speak French, it fell to me to inform the occupants that we were English airmen and could they help us? The usual answer, much to my disappointment, was to have the door slammed in my face, or a very occasional: 'come on in'. However, the latter could quite easily be a prelude to someone nipping out the back of the house, and heading for the local gendarmerie, so we didn't tend to hang around long.

The other crew members were also interviewed by MI9 back in England. Slim Beattie:

I came down on a slope just beside a house at about 2300 hrs. I gathered up my parachute and carried it for about 100 yards into a wood. I took off my brevet and stripes and cut off the tops of my boots.[1] I stayed in the wood all night. At dawn I came out and watched the house by which I had landed for any move-ment. I could see two women and a child, so I approached them. They appeared unable to make out who I was, but gave me food and wine. I returned to the wood, as they could not help me, and started walking south-west by my compass.

I walked all the morning and, although I saw various farmers, I approached nobody. At about noon (8 Feb) I discovered I was near Châteauneuf D'Isér. I continued in the direction of a small village north of S. Marcel. Walking through the village I saw a man with some children. I beckoned him over and tried to get him to understand that I was a British airman. He appeared mysti-fied, so I walked away, but found he was calling me back. There were now some other men with him and one of these put some test questions to me. They appeared satisfied and took me into a house. I was given food, and one of them wrote a note and sent it off. I was given plain clothes and quite soon was taken away on a bicycle to a small place in the neighbourhood of S. Marcel, where I found F/O Lewis, and later was joined by Bell and Reed.

In this same report, James Reed's story appears as follows:

I came down at about 2300 hrs (7 Feb) on a bank side. My parachute had got caught in a tree. I cut it down and hid it and my harness in a cave. I started to walk south over fields for about three hours. I came across a wood, which I entered, and where I buried some personal wireless papers. Just outside I found a cave in which I spent the night.

At about 0800 hrs (8 Feb) I approached a nearby farm. I knocked at the door and made my identity known to the man and woman who came out. I was given a meal and I asked if I could stay for two days. I was given permission to do so.

In the afternoon the man, who had been out, told me that somebody would be coming to see me that evening at 2000 hrs. At the stated time about four de Gaullists appeared and said they had seen my Canadian friend. I went with them and we walked for about three hours, passing our own crashed aircraft on the way. At 2300 hrs we arrived at a house in what I discovered was a village near S. Marcel. I stayed the night in this house.

In the morning (9 Feb) another de Gaullist brought me a suit of civilian clothes and took me in a taxi to Valence. On arriving at the market square the de Gaullist and I left the taxi and walked to a small café where two men, speaking broken English, asked for my name, rank and number and identity discs.

After half an hour I was taken to a wine shop and then to a private house, where I met a man who told me that three of my crew were safe. At about 1900 hrs I left with him in a car and met the others in a house in the neighbourhood of S. Marcel.

The report by Tom Cooke, Len Gornall and Bruce Withecome, once back in England, appears to be a narrative by all three men, rather than individually, although one suspects it was mostly narrated by Cooke:

We came down together within a few yards of each other in a field on the edge of a wood, about four miles south of Hauterives. We dug a hole in the wood and buried our parachutes and harness. After deciding that the aircraft had come down south of us we walked north towards a road. Before we reached the road we hid our 'mae wests' and the tops of our flying boots in a quarry. Reaching the road, we continued north. We passed through Hauterives just as [the village clock] was striking midnight. The dogs started barking, but we ran through the village on tip-toe and were not seen by any of the inhabitants. We continued along the road until we found a track running north-east from just before Lens-Lestane. About 0500 hrs (8 Feb), we got into a tool shed between two farms and remained there till evening, keeping the farms under observation. Throughout the day we ate some of the food from our [escape] aids boxes.

At 1900 hrs we went together to one of the farms, but the woman here was too scared to give us anything to eat, and when she spoke of fetching someone from the village we left quickly. We followed a track running north-east towards the road to Marcollin. To reach the road we had to cross a firing range in a marsh, where there were many shell holes full of water, and the going was very hard. About half way across, Gornall fell into a shell hole and got his clothing soaked. It was snowing hard, and we had to keep going [at a brisk pace] to avoid catching cold. Near Lentoil, Gornall went to a farm, while the others hid in a barn. At the farm Gornall was given coffee and allowed to dry his clothes. He then fetched the others and we all had fried eggs, bread, and coffee at the farm. We stayed the night in the barn.

On 9th Feb it continued to snow all day. No-one came near us during the day and we left the barn at 1800 hrs. We began to walk towards Beaurepaire along a secondary track. We went in this direction because we saw from our escape maps that Beaurepaire was on the way to Lyons, where we knew there was considerable partisan activity and hoped we might get in touch with an organisation. As there was a blizzard blowing, we got into a barn at Marcollin. We stayed in the barn all night and all next day (10 Feb), when the blizzard continued. In the evening we asked at a farm for food. We were given food, but the people suspected us of being Germans in disguise, and a young man who was brought in cross-examined us in French as to our identity and wanted to see our papers. We showed him our identity discs, but he insisted that, if we were genuine, we should be carrying papers. We gave the farm people 50 francs for the food and we had had to set out for Beaurepaire.

The blizzard was still blowing. We went through Beaurepaire about 2215 hrs, a quarter of an hour after curfew. North of Beaurepaire we were so exhausted that we had to rest in a greenhouse. Eventually the snow stopped, but the wind was still strong and it was very cold. We went into a barn north of the village and hid there for the night, and the next day [11 Feb]. About 1700 hrs a farmer came to the barn for hay. He did not discover us, but noticed our water bottles hanging on the wall. He took them outside, holding them at arm's length, apparently fearing that they might be bombs. We saw him send a child off, and, thinking that he might have sent for the gendarmes, we came out, gathered up the water bottles, and made off across the fields.

We continued due west and reaching Pact, asked at a farm for food, and were directed to a café in the village. We went to another house, but the two old ladies here were too scared to help us. At the second farm the farmer took us in and gave us food. A woman visiting the farm recognised us as English and brought her son from the village. He questioned us as to identity and we showed him our discs and maps. We stayed the night at a farm and next morning [12 Feb] we were put in touch with an organisation. The rest of our journey was arranged for us.

For some odd reason Bell does not appear to have contributed to this report, although he was safe but not, apparently, with the others during the subsequent debrief. In the meantime, Reg Lewis was still evading, as he recalled:

I remember being nervous because of our Special Operations job and if caught the Germans would have a good guess as to what we had been up to, so we all decided not to become too involved in whatever these French people were planning and just to go along with it. I remember the name of the pharmacy was *Jean Chancel* – a name that has stuck in my memory.

Within 24 hours of arriving there, in walked a man dressed in the uniform of an American marine, in fact he was a Captain in the US Marines and his name was Peter Ortiz, an agent with the OSS,[2] who it seemed always walked around this part of France in his uniform. He was very wary of us, not at all certain we were who we said we were. He was a tough character, in fact a frightening character in a way. We discovered later that he was something of a soldier of fortune, and either we were a nuisance to him just turning up in his territory, or he was overly suspicious of us.

Pierre (Peter) Julian Ortiz was a larger-than-life character in many ways. Although born in New York in July 1913, of a Spanish/American mother and a French/American father, he spent his early years in southern California. After elementary school he went to France to continue his education at the College du Montcel in Versailles and at the University of Grenoble. He spoke ten languages including French, German and, later, Arabic.

In early 1932, aged 19, he had joined the French Foreign Legion for five years' service in North Africa, starting at the legion's training centre at Sidi-Bel-Abbes, Algeria, and later served in Morocco, becoming a corporal the following year, then sergeant in 1935 (he was wounded in 1933). During a campaign against the Rif Berbers he was twice awarded the French Croix de Guerre, with two palms, one gold star and one silver star. Once his contract with the legion came to an end with the rank of adjutant he turned down a commission if he re-enlisted and went to Hollywood, where he became a technical advisor for war movies with John Ford.

With the coming of the Second World War, and America being neutral, Ortiz re-enlisted in the Foreign Legion in 1939, taking his old rank of sergeant. During the Battle of France he was wounded in action and taken prisoner by the Germans, but escaped in 1941 and made his way back to the USA. He joined the US Marine Corps in June 1942 and, because of his experience and training, was commissioned as a second lieutenant after just forty days in the service. By December he had become a captain. With his knowledge of North Africa he was sent to Tangier, Morocco, prior to the US landings in Tunisia and conducted reconnaissance missions behind the German lines for the OSS. During a night mission, Ortiz was seriously wounded in a fight with a German patrol and was sent back to the United States.

Ortiz became a full member of the OSS in 1943 and in January 1944 he was parachuted into the Haute-Savoie region of France as part of the three-man 'Union' mission to evaluate the capabilities of the local Resistance groups in the Alpine region. It was then that he came into contact with Reg Lewis, Stan Reed, Bob Beattie and Ernie Bell of 138 Squadron.

Later he left France with his team and was promoted to major, then parachuted back into France on 1 August 1944 to command the 'Union II' mission. He was captured by the Germans on 16 August during a special mission to inflict casualties upon German reinforcements stationed in his area, and spent most of the remainder of the war as a prisoner. Despite numerous interrogations by the sadistic Geheim Staats Polizei, he was lucky enough not to be executed. He was imprisoned until 10 April 1945 when he and three others managed to escape from a marching column that was attacked by RAF Spitfires. After ten days on the run, cold and hungry, they got back to the camp to find the prisoners had virtually taken over and the guards that remained were not interested in their charges. The camp was liberated by the 7th Guards Armoured Division on 29 April.

He ended the war as the most highly decorated member of the OSS and a colonel. His awards included the American Navy Cross (twice), two Purple Hearts, the US Legion of Merit, Médaille Militaire, Croix de Guerre avec palms, the French Médaille des Blesses, Médaille d'Evades and the Médaille Coloniale. The British also made him a Member of the Order of the British Empire. The French later made him a Chevalier of the Légion d'honneur.

In fact, his first Navy Cross, for his work in France between 8 January and 20 May 1944, also involved some of Tom Cooke's crew. The citation for this award is as follows:

The Navy Cross is presented to Pierre (Peter) J Ortiz, Major, US Marine Corps (Reserve), for extraordinary heroism while attached to the United

States Command, Office of Strategic Service, London, England, in connection with military operations against an armed enemy in enemy-occupied territory, from January 8 to May 20, 1944. Operating in civilian clothes and aware that he would be subject to execution in the event of his capture, Major Ortiz parachuted from an airplane with two other officers of an Inter-Allied Mission to reorganize existing Maquis groups in the region of Rhône. By his tact, resourcefulness and leadership, he was largely instrumental in affecting the acceptance of the mission by local resistance leaders, and also in organising parachute operations for the delivery of arms, ammunition and equipment for use by the Maquis is his region. Although his identity had become known to the Gestapo with the resultant increase in personal hazard, he voluntarily conducted to the Spanish border, four Royal Air Force officers who had been shot down in his region, and later returned to resume his duties. Repeatedly leading successful raids during the period of his assignment, Major Ortiz inflicted heavy casualties on enemy forces greatly superior in number, with small losses to his own forces. By his heroic leadership and astuteness in planning and executing these hazardous forays, Major Ortiz served as an inspiration to his subordinates and upheld the highest traditions of the United States Naval Service.

Reg Lewis and the others had certainly come into contact with a very colourful man. After the war, Ernest Bell's son said that whenever his father spoke of his war experiences, he never failed to mention the bravery of Peter Ortiz. What had amazed him most was that throughout the time of their escape Ortiz wore his complete Marine Corps uniform under his coat, even in railway stations swarming with German soldiers, knowing that the Germans would have loved to have captured him.

In April 1954 Ortiz volunteered to return to active duty as a marine observer in Indochina but he was turned down. However, his active life was far from over and he appeared in several movies directed by John Ford. One of these was *Rio Grande* in 1950, which starred John Wayne, Ortiz playing Captain St Jacques. His son, Peter J. Ortiz Jr, who also became a marine lieutenant colonel, said of his father: 'My father was an awful actor but he had great fun appearing in movies.'

At least two Hollywood films were based on his personal exploits: *13 Rue Madeleine* (1947) and *Operation Secret* (1952). Peter Ortiz died of cancer on 16 May 1988, aged 74, in the Veterans Medical Centre in Prescott, Arizona, situated in his home town.

Ortiz drove the four airmen to a Maquis camp in the mountains above Chabeuil, about 8km south-east of Combovin. After about three days, the camp was moved to a small furniture factory on the plateau here. Ortiz also radioed

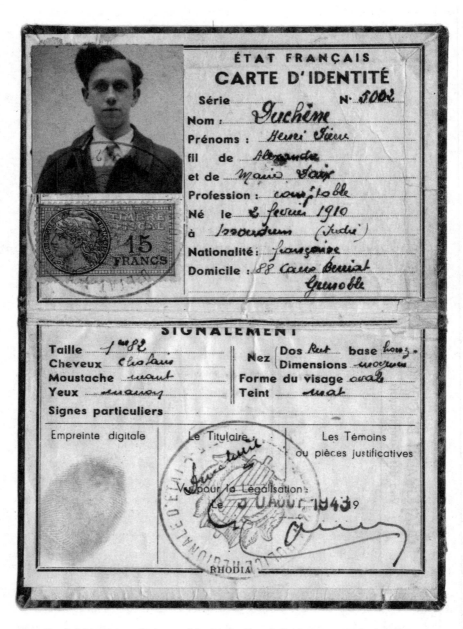

Tom Cooke's identity card, given to him by the French Resistance organisation that was helping him evade to Spain. As Tom noted later, this was useless without a work permit, and fortunately he never needed to produce it.

London, giving them the details of his four guests, not only to advise them of their safety but also to check that they were indeed genuine RAF air crew.

On 1 March news was received that the Germans were planning a raid on the camp, so Lewis and his pals were moved to the home of an elderly retired French army doctor by the name of Sambuc, and his wife, in la Paillette, near Montelimar, where they were confined to one room until the 26th. The Sambuc family included two nieces, who were Maquis couriers. In the meantime, Ortiz had been instructed to go to an address in Aix-le-Bains to contact someone who had connections to a Polish organisation. He was told that if he could get the four airmen to Carcassonne, his organisation would take them off his hands. Ortiz drove them to Valence where they could get a train despite the fact they had no identification papers. At one stage about a hundred German soldiers got on the train but nothing happened to endanger their journey, and the Germans got off at Narbonne.

The airmen had now been issued with fake identity cards. Cooke's shows him to be Frenchman Henri Duchin, son of Alexander Duchin, born at Issoudun (Indre) on 2 February 1910, but now living in Grenoble. As Cooke pointed out later, this was all very well but was virtually useless unless accompanied by a work permit. Perhaps the strain of flying made him look more like 34 years old rather than his 22, or it may have been his helpers, showing him much older, thought he would not be taken as a military man. However, his ID photograph did not make him look much older than 19.

Reg Lewis continued his recollections:

We were later put on a train, Ortiz coming too, and we were able to travel from Valence all the way to Carcassonne.[3] I have done that journey several times since those days, and it is certainly a long way. In 1944 it took us some ten hours or so and yet not once did anyone pass through the train to check either tickets or papers – not that we had any papers in any event! As far as I know this was just a one-off trip that Ortiz organised, and it was not part of any escape line or anything like one.

Once at Carcassonne the men were handed over to a guide who took them in an electric train to Quillan, where they were passed on to this organisation which dealt mainly with Poles. That evening, along with six Poles, they were driven in a taxi to a point where they would have to start walking. With two Spanish guides they left Axat and began the trek up into the mountains, and at a shepherd's hut met up with six American evaders, and shortly afterwards they were joined by another ten Poles.

Crossing eventually into Spain on the evening of the 30th, the group was hidden in the luxury of a sheep pen until the morning of 2 April, at which time a truck arrived. Told to scramble aboard, the four airmen were driven non-stop, straight through to the consulate-general's building in Barcelona. They had made it.

After a couple of days the four were driven by car to the British Embassy in Madrid, issued with false papers and found themselves once more on a train, this time travelling to La Linea, near the border with Gibraltar. At around 0700hrs the next morning, they crossed the border whilst making themselves as inconspicuous as they could amongst a group of Spanish dockyard workers, and then made their way to the RAF station on the Rock. Put on a cargo ship for safekeeping, they discovered that while they were stashed away in the vessel's hold German prisoners were housed in comfort in the ship's passenger cabins. A few days later they were taken to the airfield and flown to RAF Lynham, Wiltshire, arriving on 12 April 1944.

★★★

Tom Cooke, along with Len Gornall and Bruce Withecombe, now 'safe' in the hands of a Resistance organisation, began their journey towards Spain, Gibraltar and freedom, but it took a little time, as Cooke recorded:

Eventually we got in touch with somebody who likewise put us in touch with another person in the village of Beaurepaire, and in this way we were eventually put in touch with a chap in the Maquis, who turned out to be a communist. He and his friends sheltered us but they were constantly going out and doing little sorties and being able to understand the language I soon understood what was going on. I remember the first time they went out they went to a nearby farmhouse and bullied the occupants, in order to pinch cigarettes and bread, etc. After a while I asked why they weren't going out to blow up a few bridges and so on, but that didn't appear to be over popular with them.

After a period of time, the agent we had flown out with, later known to us as Lieutenant Cammaerts, but at the time just as 'Roger', turned up and spoke to this lot and very soon we began to be passed along to some other group, finishing up in the hands of a Monsieur Merle in Valence, close to the nearby airfield. He was a great old guy, who told us he was 85. He put us in a room at one end of his house while at the other end he was often entertaining German soldiers because they would bring him food which he then fed to us. When we eventually left he said that he hoped now we would drop him a machine gun when we got home, but I said that wouldn't be a good idea, but I would try to drop him some coffee if I could, knowing full well that was never going to happen.

From his house we were passed along and finished up at a house in Estagel, close to the mountains of the Eastern Pyrenees, not far from the border with Spain. There we waited for a woman who knew someone who might be able to help us further and eventually a chap turned up. He spoke English with an American accent, and also spoke Russian and Spanish. He said he would show us the way over the border into Spain if we helped carry some stuff for him. Fortunately, or perhaps unfortunately, we didn't ask him what the 'stuff' was. We made arrangements to meet him in a derelict house down a small road and we were to be there at the crack of dawn. We duly arrived and began to wait, but then began to hear this 'clank', 'clank', 'clank' up the road. We peered out and it was this chap who was walking towards us covered in sten-guns! We had been dropping these sorts of weapons by the canister load from time to time over France. He duly distributed these guns between us to carry and then we set off to climb across the Pyrenees, right alongside Andorra, before dropping down towards a place called Ripoll in Spain.

However, we had a bit of an argy-bargy at the actual border, as he thought he was only taking us to it. I don't know what his bosses had told him to do, but I said that if he took us onwards he would get money for our safe arrival at the British Embassy. This seemed to satisfy him and so we began our descent towards Ripoll.

We managed to cross the border, which of course was defended and patrolled, but once safely through our man told us to stay put and where was the money? I replied that he would have to go to Barcelona for that. Anyway, he told us to wait for 48-hours and if he was not back, we were on our own. We waited the agreed 48 hours – in fact some little time after that – and were just about wondering what we should do, when a car rolled up on the road below us. It was a Humber, so that looked encouraging, and a chap got out and began looking around. We started to walk down to the road in a nice casual manner and as we reached him he said equally casually, 'Oh, hello chaps, please get in. There's beer and some pies in the back.'

This guy actually had papers made up for us, even although he didn't really know if we were still going to be there. Apparently our guide did in fact go into Barcelona, turned up at the Consulate there, and they promptly chucked him out although they had listened to what he had to say. He turned out to be a known communist agitator who had all the sten-guns to start up his own little battle. The Consulate people just decided to come up and see if indeed we were about, and when we duly appeared they realised that he had been telling the truth. I asked if they had given him any money and the man said, 'No!'

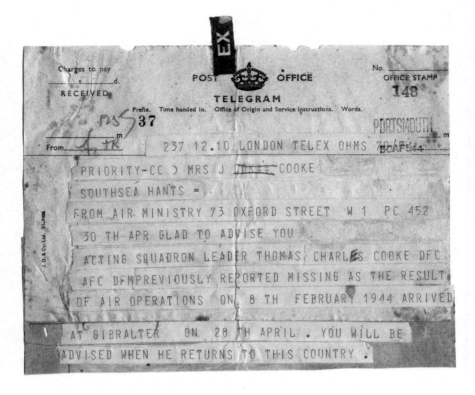

The telegram to Tom's wife informing her that he was safe and in Gibraltar on 28 April 1944.

Cooke's surprising meeting with Francis Cammaerts turned out well and it was due to him that the Resistance band got Cooke and the others started on their way south. Francis Cammaerts told Simon Muggleton:

I landed quite easily and quickly discovered that I was only about ten miles from one of my best teams, at Beaurepaire. I established a series of search parties and the whole of the crew were readily picked up. With the assistance of MI9 the seven crew were taken down to the Pyrenees, crossed into Spain and got back to their base within a few weeks. I remained in France till the Liberation and was appointed senior Allied liaison officer with French Forces of the Interior, headed by General Henri Zeller in the military regions of Lyons and Marseille.

What Cammaerts does not mention is that despite his meticulous security arrangements while assisting the French and American forces that had landed in southern France in August 1944, he and his two companions were picked up and arrested by the Gestapo in Digne, a town in the Alpes-de-Haute region. However, they obviously did not realise the significance of taking Cammaerts, but it was sheer nerve of his courier, Christina Skarbek, described as an alluring and dynamic Polish woman, who had avoided arrest, that the three were eventually released. Francis Cammaerts died in July 2006.

★★★

Once at Gibraltar, Cooke and his two companions were soon on a flight to England, although it was 4 May before they did so. In the meantime, he managed to wangle a flight in a Catalina flying boat of 202 Squadron (JX208), flown by F/O Hackman, and also some dual flying for one hour and ten minutes. The following day he and the others were flown to RAF Whitchurch in a BOAC Douglas Dakota (G-AGIX) – but as a passenger. It took seven hours and fifty minutes, but they were home. He would not fly again for over a year.

Notes

1 By this stage of the war very few airmen were wearing normal-type flying boots but a later design that in essence were civilian shoes to which were attached leather leggings that embraced the calves around thick socks. Should an airman land in occupied territory, he could easily cut away the calf section thereby making it look like a plain civilian shoe.
2 Office of Strategic Services, in other words the American equivalent of the SOE.
3 Midway between Toulouse and Perpignan.

11

APRÈS LA GUERRE

Upon his return to England, Tom Cooke's war was effectively over, at least the operational side of it. It was very rare for an escapee or an evader to be allowed back on war flying, especially in the same theatre of war where he had escaped from. He knew too much about people and places in France, about the Resistance, and so on, to risk capture. The Germans had ways of learning about men who had returned to England and would be only too pleased to have a 'chat' with them if they fell into their hands.

According to RAF records he was on the books of the personnel holding unit at Morecombe. In other words doing little more than reuniting himself with his wife and taking some well-deserved 'survivor's leave'. The Normandy invasion took place on 6 June 1944 – D-Day – but, of course, Cooke had no role in this. In fact he was in hospital, as he recalled:

> I was in hospital on D-Day, having ruptured myself when baling out, so I had to have it sewn up. Also my feet were in quite bad shape. After that I was posted to the Air Ministry and was in the ACSI's pool of intelligence officers. There were about eight of us, including two from Bomber Command, two from Fighter Command, two from Coastal. We went through every department in Air Ministry and then after that I got posted to Burma.

This began with a posting to No.2 Personnel Dispatch Centre on 22 March 1945, followed by a posting for him to go out to Burma, to HQ ACSEA – Air Command, South-East Asia. Saying farewell to his wife, in the full knowledge that he would be gone for some considerable time, he went to RAF Kinloss and No.302 FTU where he was to fly out to the Far East in a Catalina flying boat (JX376) that was going out to be a replacement machine for 205 Squadron.

Listed as a passenger, he was flown by F/Lt Waters, the long journey beginning on 19 July. First stop was Ceylon (Coggala) then on to the Cocos Islands in the Indian Ocean. Cooke managed to get two hours in as second pilot, and the overall trip was twelve hours and twenty minutes.

On the 21st Waters flew back to Ceylon for some reason. Cooke hung around for some days until he was notified of his start at HQ ACSEA on 12 August, although the next day he was flown by a Capt. Duvine, in a Dakota, to Madras, where they refuelled then headed on to Dum Dum – Calcutta. Cooke persuaded Duvine to give him some dual instruction, so he was able to log five hours and forty-five minutes of flying time in the second pilot's seat. On the 15th he was flown in another Dakota (Mk IV) of 267 Squadron to Mingaladon airfield, at Rangoon. Here he took up his intelligence duties and didn't get his hands on another aeroplane until 3 October.

On this date, F/Lt Ruggeroni, in a Beechcraft Expeditor, of HQ's Communications Flight, took him up for air experience on type for just over a couple of hours. A couple of days later F/Lt Dunbar gave him another trip flying circuits and overshoots. Having done this, he was then allowed up alone for two more hours, making a look-around trip to Zyatkwin–Waw–Hmawbi and back. Cooke had obviously got himself detached from a desk, for the rest of October he was tripping around. He flew an Expediter on a petrol consumption test on the 15th, then flew a Mosquito on the 17th up to Hmawbi (RF841). Between the 25th and 26th, W/O Wojowski flew him in a Dakota to Don-Muang (Bangkok), then on to Tan San Hnut (Saigon), and back to Rangoon. In October he was promoted to temporary wing commander, remaining at HQ well into December.

Another period of no flying ended on 4 December, taking two RAF officers up in an Expeditor on what he termed a 'photographic reconnaissance of Rangoon and Syriam'. His last flights in the Far East came on 17 December, in a 12 Wing Dakota (KN289) from Mingladon to Akyab on the Arakan coast, then on to Barrackpore, Calcutta – two three-and-a-half hour trips. These flights took his personal flying hours to over 1,050.

His time in Burma was now ended and like many thousands of his contemporaries his time for release from the service was fast approaching. On 19 December 1945 he was sent to the Release and Embarkation Centre at Worli where he spent Christmas. One month later he was posted to No. 104 Personnel Disposal Centre and returned to England by sea. Officially released with effect from 8 February 1946, his last day of service was noted as 15 April 1946. Like most wartime former air crew he was given the opportunity of speaking to a resettlement officer, to see if between them they could work out what Cooke should do now he was leaving the service after six years. Cooke had the idea of going to a university and to take up some form of education for the future, but there were no places available. The man suggested he might think about becoming a commercial traveller. That had no appeal so he fell back on the one thing he knew – flying.

From July that same year he became a civil airline pilot and over the next two and a half years flew Dakota and Vickers Viking passenger aircraft, during which time he amassed almost 1,100 flying hours of day and night flying, bringing his overall total to 2,540 hours and 47 minutes. He had come a long way since 1939. At some stage during this period he decided he wanted to be known as T.C. Seymour Cooke.

He ended his civil flying at the end of 1948 and applied to re-join the RAF, and received a permanent commission with the rank of flight lieutenant in the General Duties Branch with seniority from 11 October 1947. He became a supernumerary with 46 Group but within days he was sent to HQ Transport Command, on 1 January 1949. In March, still at this HQ, he took on some intelligence duties and just over a year later was responsible for work with flying accidents within the Command. By November 1950 his records indicate he was part of the Air Staff, again as a supernumerary, but in February 1951 he was posted to 31 Squadron for flying duties with the unit's 'B' Flight. It was also at this time he took up membership of the RAF Escaping Society. He was already a member of the Caterpillar Club, for people whose lives had been saved by using an Irvin parachute. This also brought him the privilege of wearing a small gold caterpillar badge on his lapel, its eyes being two small rubies. These badges were issued by Irvin on application to join the club.

No.31 Squadron was a long-established RAF outfit that had been the service's first squadron to fly in India during the First World War. For the interwar years it flew all sorts of aircraft over the North-West Frontier, often operating against dissident tribesmen with the general policing of the areas under British control. Soon after the Second World War began, and after seeing action in North Africa, it returned to India once Japan entered the conflict. For the rest of the war it saw distinguished service as a transport squadron, supplying ground troops with supplies during the bitter fighting in the Arakan, the Chin Hills, Kohima and the Imphal Valley, and later supporting the Chindits expeditions in central Burma.

When Tom Cooke was sent to 31 Squadron it had returned to England and was based at RAF Hendon, north London, having been temporarily disbanded in India. It had reformed in August 1948 when the Metropolitan Communications Squadron assumed the mantel of 31 Squadron. It was equipped with light communication aircraft such as Percival Proctors, Avro Ansons and later DH Devons. Most of the work entailed flying VIPs and senior staff from place to place.

Cooke remained with 31 Squadron until 1952, when he took voluntary retirement from the service on 19 July, retaining the rank of squadron leader. He later became a senior captain with British European Airways. His flights to Europe were a far cry from his earlier experiences with Bomber Command.

***

While we have now reached an entirely new phase of Tom Seymour Cooke's life, we have reached the end of his story as a Royal Air Force pilot. Joining BEA enabled him to keep flying and, as luck would have it, his old friend John Cope had joined BOAC post-war and both became BOAC captains when it and BEA amalgamated to form British Airways. However, their paths did not often cross in the early days because these two corporations flew to differing destinations, but they always tried to keep in touch. In the meantime, John had met Judy, a BEA air stewardess, whom he later married.

At one stage Tom Cooke and Connie lived in Woodburn town, Buckinghamshire, and later at Bourne End, Bedfordshire. When he left BEA they lived in Devon, but Connie was diagnosed with cancer, whereupon, in 1989, they moved to Freshwater, on the Isle of Wight, in her final year. The Macmillan nurse who looked after her later became Tom's second wife. This lady had a twin sister and between the three of them they purchased a flat in Majorca. It was while having a holiday there that Cooke suffered a heart attack and died in 2002.

***

Reg Lewis died in October 2009. Following his return from Gibraltar he became an instructor and, like Cooke, later saw service in South-East Asia, at one time on the personal staff of Air Marshal Sir Keith Park, the Allied commander. Lewis left the RAF in 1946 to become a successful investment manager in the City of London. In his spare time he also served on the executive committee of the RAF Escaping Society, and later became its secretary. As if this was not enough, he also became treasurer of the Bomber Command Association. He had lived in Gidea Park, Romford, Essex.

Lewis often thought of the people who had helped him and the others to get out of France. He once wrote:

After the war I tried to track down the people who had helped me, but because of the secretive nature of our work it was difficult. I didn't know the names of the people who had helped, because you just didn't ask.

Eventually, with the help of the RAF Escaping Society, I managed to find some relatives of Dr. Sarbuc, who had since died, and in 1970 I accepted an invitation from the French government to go to Paris for the 25th Anniversary of VE Day. Afterwards I drove south to seek out my helpers but I didn't make it because on the way down I had a car crash and my wife was killed.

Two years later the Escaping Society was going to the South of France, so I went along and met one of the doctor's nieces, and gradually managed to track down the places I had stayed, including the chemist's shop, where the pharmacist's wife was still alive. All that was left was to find the house where the lady had first helped me, and after days of searching, I found it. The lady who answered the door said the woman I was talking about, Madame Giraudin, no longer lived there, but to my delight she still lived in the village and I was overjoyed to be able to see her again. So many people had risked their lives to help me, and it meant everything that I could finally thank them in person.

★★★

Of the others, Len Gornall was one of the few air-crew members who had evaded that was allowed to return to operational flying over Europe, remaining with 138 Squadron. He was awarded the DFC, the citation for this being promulgated in the *London Gazette* on 15 September 1944: 'This officer has completed a large number of sorties. He is an extremely keen and enthusiastic flight engineer and has at all times displayed the greatest determination. He has imparted much of his technical knowledge to other members of the squadron with good results.'

Sadly, he was not destined to see the war's end. On the night of 26/27 February 1945 he was part of F/Lt P.B. Cornwallis' crew and flying a Stirling IV LK272 NF-P. They went out on an operation coded Crupper 37, setting course for Norway with four agents on board. The met AA fire which hit them and the aircraft crashed into the sea. All those on board were killed.

Ernest Bell also returned to operational flying with 138 Squadron and he too was awarded the DFC, gazetted on 16 January 1945. However, he survived the war. So too did James Reed, and he too received the DFC, his being gazetted on 2 January 1945.

Slim Beattie was another recipient of the DFC, the citation recorded in the *London Gazette* in October 1944: 'As air gunner has completed a large number of sorties. He is a courageous and resourceful member of aircraft crew and he has on more than one occasion contributed materially to the safe return of his aircraft. He has set a worthy example.'

APPENDIX A

RECORD OF SERVICE AND AIRCRAFT FLOWN

RECORD OF SERVICE OF SQUADRON LEADER T.C.S. COOKE DFC AFC AFM AE

Enlisted at Southampton	25 Aug 1939–2 Sep 1939
RAFVR, Portsmouth	2 Sep 1939–29 Sep 1939
No.3 Initial Training Wing, Hastings, Sussex	29 Sep 1939–11 Dec 1939
No.12 Elementary Flying Training School, Prestwick	12 Dec 1939–27 Apr 1940
No.5 Flying Training School, Sealand, Clwyd	27 Apr 1940–26 Jul 1940
No.11 Operational Training Unit, Bassingbourne, Cambridgeshire	26 Jul 1940–23 Sep 1940
No.78 Squadron, Dishforth, Yorkshire	1 Oct 1940–12 Apr 1941
No.104 Squadron, Driffield, Yorkshire	12 Apr 1941–4 Jul 1941
No.22 Operational Training Unit, Wellesbourne	4 Jul 1941–14 Mar 1942
Central Flying School, Upavon, Wiltshire	14 Mar 1942–10 Apr 1942
No.22 Operational Training Unit, Wellesbourne	14 Apr 1942–23 May 1942
No.1501 Blind Approach Training School, Abingdon	24 May 1942–30 May 1942
No.22 Operational Training Unit, Wellesbourne	30 May 1942–11 Sep 1942
No.22 Operational Training Unit, Gaydon, Warwickshire	11 Sep 1942–27 Sep 1942
No.149 Conversion Unit, Mildenhall, Suffolk	27 Sep 1942–4 Oct 1942
No.1657 Stirling Operational Training Unit, Stradishall, Suffolk	4 Oct 1942–8 Nov 1942

No.15 Squadron, Bourn, Cambridgeshire	8 Nov 1942–18 Jan 1943
No.214 Squadron, Chedburgh, Suffolk	19 Jan 1942–2 May 1943
No.1665 Conversion Unit, Waterbeach, Cambridgeshire	2 May 1943–6 May 1943
No.1651 Conversion Unit, Waterbeach, Cambridgeshire	6 May 1943–10 Sep 1943
No.138 Squadron, Tempsford, Bedfordshire	10 Sep 1943–8 Feb 1944
Missing on Operations	
Personnel Holding Unit, Morecombe	5 May 1944–19 Jul 1944
ACAS (I)	19 Jul 1944–6 Aug 1944
Highgate	6 Aug 1944–24 Aug 1944
No.2 Personnel Dispatch Centre	22 Mar 1945–28 Mar 1945
HQ, Air Command South East Asia	28 Mar 1945–12 Aug 1945
(En route to Far East	19 Jul 1945–21 Jul 1945)
Air HQ, Burma	12 Aug 1945–19 Dec 1945
Release Centre, Worli	19 Dec 1945–19 Jan 1946
No.104 Personnel Dispersal Centre	19 Jan 1946–8 Feb 1946
Released	8 Feb 1946
Last Day of Service	15 Apr 1946
Supernumerary on Recall, HQ 46 Group	1 Jan 1949–10 Jan 1949
HQ, Transport Command	10 Jan 1949–10 Feb 1951
No.31 Squadron, Hendon, England	19 Feb 1951–12 Mar 1951
HQ, Transport Command	12 Mar 1951–7 May 1951
No.31 Squadron, Hendon	31 Mar 1951–14 Feb 1952
Voluntary retirement retaining Rank of squadron leader	19 Jul 1952

Promotions

Aircraftman Second Class	25 Aug 1939
Sergeant Pilot, Under Training	26 Aug 1939
Sergeant Pilot	31 Dec 1940
Temporary Pilot Officer	1 Aug 1941
Flying Officer	2 Aug 1942
Acting Flight Lieutenant	1 Dec 1942
Flight Lieutenant	18 Apr 1943
Acting Squadron Leader	22 Sep 1943

Permanent Commission as Flight Lieutenant	1 Jan 1949
Retired with the rank of Squadron Leader	19 Jul 1952

Aircraft Types Flown 1939–46

Type	Engine
De Havilland 82 Tiger Moth	DH Gypsy Major
Airspeed Oxford Mk I	A-Siddeley Cheetah X
Vickers Wellington	Bristol Pegasus XVIII
Armstrong Whitworth Whitley V	Rolls-Royce Merlin X
Vickers Wellington II	Rolls-Royce Merlin X
Miles Magister	DH Gypsy Major I
Miles Master	Rolls-Royce Kestrel XXX
Avro Anson	A-Siddeley Cheetah X
Short Stirling V	Bristol Hercules
Handley Page Halifax II	Rolls-Royce XV
Douglas Dakota	Pratt & Whitney Wasp
Beechcraft Expeditor	Pratt & Whitney Wasp Jr
Consolidated Catalina	Pratt & Whitney Wasp
De Havilland Mosquito	Rolls-Royce Merlin
Percival Proctor	DH Gipsy Queen II

War Medals

Squadron Leader T.C.S. Cooke was entitled to wear:

- Distinguished Flying Cross
- Air Force Cross
- Distinguished Flying Medal
- 1939–45 Star
- Air Crew Europe Star
- Burma Star
- Italy Star
- Defence Medal
- War Medal
- Air Efficiency Medal

Only five Royal Air Force officers received this combination of decorations and therefore Cooke's set of medals, with the Stars and AE, must be unique, combined with being an evader and a member of the Caterpillar Club.

TOM COOKE'S
OPERATIONAL FLIGHTS

78 Squadron					
1940	**Target**	**Aircraft**	**Serial No.**	**Operational Hours**	**Crew**
7/8 Oct	Berlin	Whitley V	P4958[1]	1000hrs	Sgt G Samson, Sgt T.C. Cooke, P/O G.W. Brown, Sgt W.G. Cording, Sgt J. Barker
11/12 Oct	Stettin (bombed Harburg)	Whitley V	P4958	0750hrs	Sgt. G. Samson, Sgt T.C. Cooke, P/O G.W. Brown, Sgt W.G. Cording, Sgt J. Barker
15/16 Oct	Leuna (bombed Duisburg Docks)	Whitley V	P4958	0900hrs	Sgt G. Samson, Sgt T.C. Cooke, P/O G.W. Brown, Sgt W.G. Cording, Sgt J. Barker
19/20 Oct	Aosta, Italy	Whitley V	P4958	1015hrs	Sgt G Samson, Sgt T.C. Cooke, P/O G.W. Brown, Sgt W.G. Cording, Sgt J. Barker
8/9 Nov	Milan, Italy	Whitley V	P4958	1105hrs	Sgt G Samson, Sgt T.C. Cooke, Sgt A.W. Steven, Sgt W.G. Cording, Sgt J. Barker
13/14 Nov	Leuna (bombed Osnabruck)	Whitley V	P4958	0525hrs	Sgt. G. Samson, Sgt T.C. Cooke, P/O D. Balmforth, Sgt W.G. Cording, Sgt K.B. Wears

15/16 Nov	Hamburg	Whitley V	T4236	0730hrs	Sgt G.W. Holden, Sgt T.C. Cooke, P/O D. Balmforth, Sgt W.G. Cording, Sgt E.C. Gurmin
17/18 Nov	Gelsenkirchen	Whitley V	T4236	0755hrs	Sgt G.W. Holden, Sgt T.C. Cooke, P/O D. Balmforth, Sgt W.G. Cording, Sgt E.C. Gurmin
19/20 Nov	Rhuland (bombed a train)	Whitley V	T4236	1105hrs	Sgt G.W. Holden, Sgt T.C. Cooke, Sgt A.W. Steven, Sgt W.G. Cording, Sgt K.S. Wears
22/23 Nov	Bordeaux, France	Whitley V	T4165[2]	0950hrs	Sgt G.W. Holden, Sgt T.C. Cooke, Sgt A.W. Steven, Sgt W.G. Cording, Sgt K.B. Wears
28/29 Nov	Stettin	Whitley V	T4203[3]	0950hrs	Sgt G.W. Holden, Sgt T.C. Cooke, Sgt A.W. Steven, Sgt K.B. Wears, Sgt W.G. Cording
8/9 Dec	Bordeaux	Whitley V	T4204[4]	0900hrs	Sgt G.W. Holden, Sgt T.C. Cooke, Sgt F.H. Unwin, Sgt K.B. Wears, Sgt W.G. Cording
13/14 Dec	Kiel	Whitley V	T4236	0635hrs	Sgt G.W. Holden, Sgt T.C. Cooke, Sgt A.W. Steven, Sgt K.B. Wears, Sgt W.G. Cording
1941					
3/4 Jan	Bremen	Whitley V	T4215	0620hrs	Sgt T.C. Cooke, Sgt L. Thorpe, Sgt A.W. Steven, Sgt E.C. Gurmin, Sgt W.G. Cording
9/10 Jan	Gelsenkirchen (bombed Hamburg)	Whitley V	T4263	0635hrs	Sgt T.C. Cooke, Sgt L. Thorpe, Sgt A.W. Steven, Sgt E.C. Gurmin, Sgt E.A. Grunsell
13/14 Jan	Dunkirk, France (no attack made)	Whitley V	P5105	0455hrs	Sgt T.C. Cooke, Sgt L. Thorpe, Sgt A.W. Steven, Sgt G.R. Armstrong, Sgt K.B. Wears
10 Mar	Boulogne, France	Whitley V	Z6490	0350hrs	Sgt T.C. Cooke, Sgt W.G. Rogers, Sgt J.W. Boggis, Sgt R. Smith, Sgt M. Chadwick
27/28 Mar	Düsseldorf	Whitley V	Z6508[5]	0500hrs	Sgt T.C. Cooke, Sgt W.G. Rogers, Sgt J.W. Boggis, Sgt R. Smith, Sgt G.A. Fraser

| 30/31 Mar | Brest, France | Whitley V | Z6483[6] | 0645hrs | Sgt T.C. Cooke, Sgt W.G. Rogers, Sgt J.W. Boggis, Sgt B. Ward, Sgt R. Smith |

104 Squadron

1941	Target	Aircraft	Serial No.	Operational Hours	Crew
8/9 May	Bremen	Wellington II	W5435 EP-F[7]	0520hrs	Sgt T.C. Cooke, Sgt Huggins, P/O Verver, Sgt Haynes, Sgt Simpkin, Sgt Stevenson
9/10 May	Ludwigshaven	Wellington II	W5435 EP-F	0730hrs	Sgt T.C. Cooke, Sgt Huggins, P/O Verver, Sgt Haynes, Sgt Simpkin, Sgt Stevenson
15/16 May	Hannover	Wellington II	W5435 EP-F	0625hrs	Sgt T.C. Cooke, Sgt Huggins, P/O Verver, Sgt Haynes, Sgt Simpkin, Sgt Stevenson
18/19 May	Kiel	Wellington II	W5435 EP-F	0540hrs	Sgt T.C. Cooke, Sgt Huggins, P/O Verver, Sgt Haynes, Sgt Simpkin, Sgt Stevenson
13/14 Jun	Schwerte (bombed Dortmund)	Wellington II	W5435 EP-F	0600hrs	Sgt T.C. Cooke, Sgt Huggins, P/O Verver, Sgt Haynes, Sgt Simpkin, Sgt Stevenson
16/17 Jun	Cologne	Wellington II	W5435 EP-F	0540hrs	Sgt T.C. Cooke, Sgt Huggins, P/O Verver, Sgt Haynes, Sgt Simpkin, Sgt Stevenson
18/19 Jun	Bremen	Wellington II	W5435 EP-F	0615hrs	Sgt T.C. Cooke, Sgt Huggins, P/O Verver, Sgt Haynes, Sgt Simpkin, Sgt Stevenson
25/26 Jun	Kiel	Wellington II	W5485[8]	0605hrs	Sgt T.C. Cooke, Sgt Hodge, P/O Verver, Sgt Simpkin, Sgt Davey, Sgt Stevenson

No.22 Operational Training Unit

1942	Target	Aircraft	Serial No.	Operational Hours	Crew
30/31 May	Cologne	Wellington II	R1522[9]	0530hrs	P/O T.C. Cooke, P/O F.T. Johnson, Sgt J.G. Cameron, F/Sgt A.J. Owens, F/Sgt G.W.A. Austen
1/2 Jun	Essen	Wellington IC	R1522	0445hrs	P/O T.C. Cooke, P/O F.T. Johnson, Sgt J.G. Cameron, F/Sgt A.J. Owens, F/Sgt G.W.A. Austen

| 10/11 Sep | Düsseldorf (abandoned at Dutch coast) | Wellington 1C | R1621 | 0315hrs | P/O T.C. Cooke, Sgt R.A. Williams, F/Sgt K.E. Crosby, Sgt R. Cuffey, Sgt P.S. Murphy |
| 13/14 Sep | Bremen | Wellington 1C | R1776 | 0615hrs | P/O T.C. Cooke, P/O F.T. Johnson, Sgt D. Heap, P/O J.A. Neville, Sgt R. Cuffey |

15 Squadron

1942	Target	Aircraft	Serial No.	Operational Hours	Crew
20/21 Nov	Turin, Italy	Stirling I	N3669 LS-H	0830hrs	F/O T.C. Cooke, Sgt R.W. Lewis, Sgt J.S. Reed, Sgt E. Bell, Sgt J.G. Harrison, Sgt R.L. Beattie, Sgt A. Collins
22/23 Nov	Stuttgart	Stirling I	W7518 LS-C[10]	0810hrs	F/O T.C. Cooke, Sgt Ripley, Sgt R.W. Lewis, Sgt J.S Reed, Sgt E. Bell, Sgt J.G. Harrison, Sgt R.L. Beattie, Sgt A. Collins
27/28 Nov	Stettin	Stirling I	W7518 LS-C	0130hrs	F/O T.C. Cooke, F/Lt O. Chave, Sgt R.W. Lewis, Sgt J.S. Reed, Sgt E. Bell, Sgt J.G. Harrison, Sgt R.L. Beattie, Sgt A. Collins
28/29 Nov	Turin, Italy (abandoned)	Stirling I	W7518 LS-C	0130hrs	F/O T.C. Cooke, Sgt G. Ware, Sgt R.W. Lewis, Sgt J.S. Reed, Sgt E. Bell, Sgt J.G. Harrison, Sgt R.L. Beattie, Sgt A. Collins
2/3 Dec	Frankfurt	Stirling I	R9168 LS-R[11]	0650hrs	F/O T.C. Cooke, F/O J. Welford, Sgt R.W. Lewis, Sgt J.S. Reed, Sgt E. Bell, Sgt J.G. Harrison, Sgt R.L. Beattie, Sgt A. Collins
16/17 Dec	Diepholtz Airfield	Stirling I	BF411 LS-A[12]	0440hrs	F/O T.C. Cooke, P/O W. Moffat, Sgt R.W. Lewis, Sgt J.S. Reed, Sgt E. Bell, Sgt J.G. Harrison, Sgt R.L. Beattie, Sgt A. Collins
1943					
14/15 Jan	Lorient, France	Stirling I	R9274 LS-B[13]	0530hrs	F/Lt T.C. Cooke, Sgt R.W. Lewis,

214 Squadron

1943	Target	Aircraft	Serial No.	Operational Hours	Crew
7/8 Feb	Lorient	Stirling I	R9258[14]	0510hrs	S/L T.C. Cooke, Sgt R.W. Lewis, Sgt J.S. Reed, Sgt E. Bell, Sgt J.G. Harrison, F/Sgt R.L. Beattie, Sgt A. Collins
13/14 Feb	Lorient	Stirling I	R9258	0550hrs	S/L T.C. Cooke, Sgt R.W. Lewis, Sgt J.S. Reed, Sgt E. Bell, Sgt J.G. Harrison, F/Sgt R.L. Beattie, Sgt A. Collins
16/17 Feb	Lorient	Stirling I	R9258	0515hrs	S/L T.C. Cooke, Sgt R.W. Lewis, Sgt J.S. Reed, Sgt E. Bell, Sgt J.G. Harrison, F/Sgt R.L. Beattie, Sgt A. Collins
17/18 Feb	Mining, Gironde	Stirling I	R9258	0715hrs	S/L T.C. Cooke, Sgt R.W. Lewis, Sgt J.S. Reed, Sgt E. Bell, F/Sgt R.L. Beattie, Sgt A. Collins
19/20 Feb	Wilhelmshaven	Stirling I	R9258	0510hrs	S/L T.C. Cooke, Sgt R.W. Lewis, Sgt J.S. Reed, Sgt E. Bell, Sgt J.G. Harrison, Sgt R.L. Beattie, Sgt A. Collins
25/26 Feb	Nürnberg	Stirling I	R9258	0715hrs	S/L T.C. Cooke, Sgt R.W. Lewis, Sgt J.S. Reed, Sgt E. Bell, Sgt J.G. Harrison, P/O D.B. Gaunt, Sgt R.L. Beattie
28 Feb/1 Mar	St-Nazaire, France	Stirling I	R9258	0520hrs	S/L T.C. Cooke, Sgt R.W. Lewis, Sgt J.S. Reed, Sgt E. Bell, Sgt J.G. Harrison, Sgt R.L. Beattie, Sgt A. Collins
1/2 Mar	Berlin	Stirling I	R9258	0820hrs	S/L T.C. Cooke, Sgt R.W. Lewis, Sgt J.S. Reed, Sgt E. Bell, Sgt J.G. Harrison, Sgt D.B. Gaunt, Sgt A. Collins
5/6 Mar	Essen	Stirling I	R9258	0410hrs	S/L T.C. Cooke, Sgt R.W. Lewis, Sgt J.S. Reed, Sgt E. Bell, Sgt J.G. Harrison, P/O D.B. Gaunt, Sgt A. Collins
8/9 Mar	Nürnberg	Stirling I	R9258	0730hrs	S/L T.C. Cooke, Sgt R.W. Lewis, Sgt J.S. Reed, Sgt E. Bell, Sgt J.G. Harrison, P/O D.B. Gaunt, Sgt A. Collins

10/11 Mar	Mining, Gironde	Stirling I	R9258	0615hrs	S/L T.C. Cooke, Sgt R.W. Lewis, Sgt J.S. Reed, Sgt E. Bell, Sgt J.G. Harrison, P/O E.K. Ward, Sgt A. Collins
22/23 Mar	St–Nazaire	Stirling I	BK653[15]	0330hrs	S/L T.C. Cooke, Sgt R.W. Lewis, Sgt J.S Reed, Sgt E. Bell, Sgt J.G. Harrison, P/O D.B. Gaunt, Sgt A. Collins
27/28 Mar	Berlin	Stirling I	BK653	0730hrs	S/L T.C. Cooke, Sgt R.W. Lewis, Sgt J.S. Reed, Sgt E. Bell, Sgt J.G. Harrison, P/O E.K. Ward, Sgt A. Collins

138 Squadron

Please note: crew not listed in 138 Squadron records but almost certainly the crew is the same each night as that listed below on 10/11 December 1943 and 7/8 February 1944

1943	Target	Aircraft	Serial No.	Operational Hours	Crew
4/5 Oct	France	Halifax II	LW275 NF-O	0640hrs	S/L T.C. Cooke and crew
8/9 Oct	Norway	Halifax II	LW276 NF-E	0845hrs	S/L T.C. Cooke and crew
11/12 Oct	Norway	Halifax II	LW284 NF-T[16]	0805hrs	S/L T.C. Cooke and crew
17/18 Oct	France	Halifax II	'S'	0300hrs	S/L T.C. Cooke and crew
5/6 Nov	Germany & Belgium	Halifax II	LW275 NF-O	0525hrs	S/L T.C. Cooke and crew
7/8 Nov	France	Halifax II	LW275 NF-O	0700hrs	S/L T.C. Cooke and crew
11/12 Nov	France	Halifax II	LW275 NF-O	0355hrs	S/L T.C. Cooke and crew
17/18 Nov	Norway	Halifax II	LW275 NF-O	0740hrs	S/L T.C. Cooke and crew
10/11 Dec	France/N. Africa	Halifax II	LW275 NF-O	0600hrs	S/L T.C. Cooke, F/O R.W. Lewis, F/O J.S. Reed, P/O E. Bell, F/O L.J. Gornall, F/O A.B. Withecombe, F/O R.L. Beattie
18/19 Dec	Poland	Halifax II	LW275 NF-O	0915hrs	S/L T.C. Cooke and crew
22/23 Dec	Italy to UK	Halifax II	LW275 NF-O	0620hrs	S/L T.C. Cooke and crew

1944					
4/5 Feb	France	Halifax II	LW275 NF-O	0725hrs	S/L T.C. Cooke and crew
7/8 Feb	France	Halifax II	LW275	missing	S/L T.C. Cooke, F/O R.W. Lewis, F/O J.S. Reed, P/O E. Bell, F/O L.J. Gornall, F/O A.B. Withecome, F/O R.L. Beattie

Notes

1 P4958 crashed on take-off 2 Dec 1940 and written off.

2 T4165 lost with No.1419 Flight, 11 April 1941.

3 T4203 missing 10 January 1941 raiding Gelsenkirchen.

4 T4204 abandoned after icing up near RAF Lindholme, 1 January 1941.

5 Z6508 missing Mannheim, 28 August 1941.

6 Z6483 abandoned over UK, out of fuel, 4 May 1941, returning from Cologne.

7 W5435 crashed Yorkshire, 3 September 1941.

8 W5485 missing Karlsruhe, 6 August 1941.

9 R1522 went to No.14 OTU, crashed at RAF Cottesmore, 6 December 1942.

10 W7518 missing Berlin, 2 March 1943.

11 R9168 shot down by night-fighter, Diepholz raid, 17 December 1942.

12 BF411 ditched returning from Wilhelmshaven, 20 February 1943.

13 R9274 shot down by night-fighter over Holland, 4 February 1943.

14 R9258 lost on Hannover raid, 23 September 1943.

15 BK653 missing Mannheim, 17 April 1943.

16 LW284 struck off charge with No.1586 Flight, 4 August 1944.

INDEX